Radical Animism

Environmental Cultures Series

Series Editors:
Greg Garrard, University of British Columbia, Canada
Richard Kerridge, Bath Spa University

Editorial Board:
Frances Bellarsi, Université Libre de Bruxelles, Belgium
Mandy Bloomfield, Plymouth University, UK
Lily Chen, Shanghai Normal University, China
Christa Grewe-Volpp, University of Mannheim, Germany
Stephanie LeMenager, University of Oregon, USA
Timothy Morton, Rice University, USA
Pablo Mukherjee, University of Warwick, UK

Bloomsbury's *Environmental Cultures* series makes available to students and scholars at all levels the latest cutting-edge research on the diverse ways in which culture has responded to the age of environmental crisis. Publishing ambitious and innovative literary ecocriticism that crosses disciplines, national boundaries, and media, books in the series explore and test the challenges of ecocriticism to conventional forms of cultural study.

Titles available:
Bodies of Water, Astrida Neimanis
Cities and Wetlands, Rod Giblett
Civil Rights and the Environment in African-American Literature, 1895–1941, John Claborn
Climate Change Scepticism, Greg Garrard, George B. Handley, Axel Goodbody and Stephanie Posthumus
Climate Crisis and the 21st-Century British Novel, Astrid Bracke
Colonialism, Culture, Whales, Graham Huggan
Ecocriticism and Italy, Serenella Iovino
Ecospectrality, Laura A. White
Fuel, Heidi C. M. Scott
Literature as Cultural Ecology, Hubert Zapf
Nerd Ecology, Anthony Lioi
The New Nature Writing, Jos Smith
The New Poetics of Climate Change, Matthew Griffiths
Reclaiming Romanticism, Kate Rigby
Teaching Environmental Writing, Isabel Galleymore
This Contentious Storm, Jennifer Mae Hamilton

Forthcoming Titles:
Cognitive Ecopoetics, Sharon Lattig
Ecocriticism and Turkey, Meliz Ergin
Eco-Digital Art, Lisa FitzGerald
Environmental Cultures in Soviet East Europe, Anna Barcz
Imagining the Plains of Latin America, Axel Pérez Trujillo Diniz
Weathering Shakespeare, Evelyn O'Malley

Radical Animism

Reading for the End of the World

Jemma Deer

BLOOMSBURY ACADEMIC
LONDON • NEW YORK • OXFORD • NEW DELHI • SYDNEY

BLOOMSBURY ACADEMIC
Bloomsbury Publishing Plc
50 Bedford Square, London, WC1B 3DP, UK
1385 Broadway, New York, NY 10018, USA
29 Earlsfort Terrace, Dublin 2, Ireland

BLOOMSBURY, BLOOMSBURY ACADEMIC and the Diana logo are trademarks of
Bloomsbury Publishing Plc

First published in Great Britain 2021
This paperback edition published 2022

Copyright © Jemma Deer, 2021

Jemma Deer has asserted her right under the Copyright, Designs and Patents Act,
1988, to be identified as Author of this work.

For legal purposes the Acknowledgements on p. viii constitute an extension
of this copyright page.

Cover design: Paul Burgess / Burge Agency
Cover image © Shutterstock

All rights reserved. No part of this publication may be reproduced or
transmitted in any form or by any means, electronic or mechanical,
including photocopying, recording, or any information storage or retrieval
system, without prior permission in writing from the publishers.

Bloomsbury Publishing Plc does not have any control over, or responsibility for, any
third-party websites referred to or in this book. All internet addresses given in this
book were correct at the time of going to press. The author and publisher regret any
inconvenience caused if addresses have changed or sites have ceased to exist, but can
accept no responsibility for any such changes.

A catalogue record for this book is available from the British Library.

A catalog record for this book is available from the Library of Congress.

ISBN: HB: 978-1-3501-1115-8
PB: 978-1-3502-4940-0
ePDF: 978-1-3501-1116-5
eBook: 978-1-3501-1117-2

Series: Environmental Cultures

Typeset by Newgen KnowledgeWorks Pvt. Ltd., Chennai, India

To find out more about our authors and books visit www.bloomsbury.com
and sign up for our newsletters.

How is't with you,
That you do bend your eye on vacancy,
And with th'incorporal air do hold discourse?
Shakespeare, *Hamlet*

Contents

Acknowledgements	viii
Note on the Text	ix
List of Abbreviations	x
Introduction: Reading for Life	1
1 Radical Animism: Climate Change and Other Transformations	7
2 Surviving the Anthropocene: Revolutionary Rhythms	55
3 Animals at the End of the World: The Evolution of Life and Language	99
4 Hatching: Psychoanalysis and the Textual Unconscious	143
Conclusion	185
Notes	187
Bibliography	215
Index	225

Acknowledgements

I owe much to Nicholas Royle, who has been an inspiration since I was an undergraduate and later became a mentor and friend. This book would not have been written without his continued support. I am grateful to all the friends and family who sustained me over the years I was writing, especially Alex Casey, Hannah Geller, Reuben Golden, Jessica McDiarmid and Rachael Sergeant, who helped me through. There are too many others to name here; you know who you are. I am thankful to the English department at the University of Sussex, where I completed the PhD that was the roots of this project, and to the Harvard University Center for the Environment, where it grew to maturity. Special thanks to Mareike Beck, Sara Crangle, Joe Luna, Michael Jonik, Liz Walker and Di Yang who supported me over the years at Sussex (academically and otherwise), and to Sarah Wood for writing the book that encouraged me to begin this project and for giving the guidance that got me here.

This is for life.

Note on the Text

Definitions and etymologies of words, unless otherwise stated, are taken from the *Oxford English Dictionary Online*.

Scripture quotations are from The Authorized (King James) Version. Rights in the Authorized Version in the United Kingdom are vested in the Crown. Reproduced by permission of the Crown's patentee, Cambridge University Press.

Abbreviations

A   Jacques Derrida, *The Animal That Therefore I Am*, ed. Marie-Louise Mallet, trans. David Wills (New York: Fordham University Press, 2008).
BPP   Sigmund Freud, 'Beyond the Pleasure Principle', *SE* XVIII.
GW   Sigmund Freud, *Gesammelte Werke*, vols I–XVIII (London: Imago, 1940–52).
OED   *Oxford English Dictionary Online* (Oxford: Oxford University Press, 2019).
SE   Sigmund Freud, *The Standard Edition of the Complete Psychological Works of Sigmund Freud*, vols I–XXIV, trans. and ed. James Strachey, in collaboration with Anna Freud, assisted by Alix Strachey and Alan Tyson (London: Hogarth Press, 1953–74).

Introduction: Reading for Life

The following pages are concerned with animism – or rather with *animisms* in the plural – with the myriad activities and agencies of entities both organic and inorganic. Non-human and non-living forces act, create, read, write and respond in ways that have often been assumed to be exclusively human. In this age of climate breakdown, the disavowal of such forces is becoming increasingly difficult to maintain, as long-held scientific, philosophical and psychological paradigms are challenged by agencies beyond the human. I elaborate a radical new animism for a planet in crisis, recognizing the non-human powers that assert themselves around us, in us and through us. This is not an anthropological study; rather, this book is concerned with sketching a generalized rethinking of animism that is neither mystical nor 'primitive' and that is attentive to forms of animism that are alive even in the most scientific or modern worldviews. I am also very much concerned with the *animism of literature*: the ways in which literary writing has a strange and active 'life' that has the power to disturb, startle and transform the contexts in which it is received, the futures into which it is born. The work of Jacques Derrida, effecting as it does a sustained deconstruction of anthropocentrism, is essential to my thinking throughout.

My subtitle, 'Reading for the End of the World', should be understood in two ways. First, it can be read in an apocalyptic vein, as referring to the kind of reading that might be appropriate to this time of catastrophic climate change, a reading for the end of the world. Second, however, it can also be read in an affirmative tone. If we take the etymological sense of the word 'world' as 'the age of man' (coming from the Old Danish *wær-æld*, meaning literally 'man-age') and the word 'for' in the sense of 'in defence or support of; in favour of, on the side of', this would be a mode of reading that is *in favour of* the end of the age of man – a reading that is *for* the end of the *wær-æld*. To be clear, I am not advocating for the extinction of the human. On the contrary, I am recognizing that the future of human life in fact depends upon the end of a world in which human beings narcissistically act as if they are separable from or independent of other living things. The end of the *wær-æld* would be the beginning of a less destructive or pathological relationship between humans and the other forms of life with which we share this planet.

The importance of *reading* should also be stated here. While, as this book will make clear, notions of reading, writing and text are all generalizable beyond the narrow human definition – we are not the only entities reading and writing the world – it is to the act of reading that I give special emphasis. To read is both receptive and creative. To read is to open oneself to alterity, to open oneself to the possibility of transformation. Reading is, as Sarah Wood recognizes, a *force* – and one among others.[1] It turns, by necessity, to the future.

As such, it should be an essential activity for a time of crisis. How should we read the Anthropocene? How should we read texts – literary and otherwise – in the Anthropocene? How is the Anthropocene reading us? These are some of the questions around which the following pages will turn.

Other recent studies have sought to explore the ways in which literature responds to the Anthropocene and climate change. Adam Trexler's *Anthropocene Fictions* provides a survey of 'climate novels', accounting for the ways in which the current ecological context 'make[s] new demands on the novel itself, forcing formal and narrative innovation'.[2] Meanwhile, Tom Bristow's *The Anthropocene Lyric* and Sam Solnick's *Poetry and the Anthropocene* both focus their attention on poetry and the ways it 'responds to the challenges of the Anthropocene epoch', as Solnick remarks.[3] These studies, that is to say, examine how literature written in the context of climate change recognizes and responds to that context. In contrast, the majority of literary texts discussed in this book predate the human recognition of the climate crisis, and so are certainly not 'about' climate change or the Anthropocene in any direct sense. Instead, the readings that I offer here show how literary texts might resonate differently in this age of environmental crisis, effectively transforming themselves and transforming the ways we read them, moving beyond authorial intention and crossing historical contexts. In an essay on Joseph Conrad's story 'Typhoon', Nicholas Royle writes of the '*futurological power*' of a text, 'its capacity to cast light on what comes later, on what ostensibly post-dates the work', so that it 'carries its own future in itself'.[4] Like a living organism, a text grows and changes over time, being constantly shaped by – and in turn shaping – its environment. This book attempts to recognize and reckon with this animistic potency of literature, and in so doing demonstrates how an animistic worldview is neither primitive nor naïve.

What follows is divided into four chapters. The first chapter, 'Radical Animism: Climate Change and Other Transformations', thinks through the geophysical and conceptual alterations of contemporary environmental crises, and suggests, via a reading of Franz Kafka's *Metamorphosis* (1915), why animism has renewed potency in such a context. I discuss the planetary transformations that have earned the designation of a new era – the Anthropocene – and consider how this works to decentre the human and trouble various assumptions about agency, animality and responsibility. I elaborate three ways in which the notion of 'Anthropocene reading' might be understood, describe how language can be thought of as radically metaphorical and show how 'life' is a concept that should be generalized beyond the organically living. I go on to discuss three 'blows to human narcissism' – the Copernican, Darwinian and Freudian paradigm shifts – and suggest that climate change is the fourth blow, which, unlike the others, animistically issues from non-human agency.[5] Global warming can be explicitly linked to the inherent contradictions of capitalism that Marx identified, and I indicate how socio-economic inequality and environmental catastrophe are intertwined. I then give an account of the historical use of the word 'animism' in the works of E. B. Tylor, James Frazer and Sigmund Freud – texts which have contributed to some of the enduring associations of the term. Noting how all three writers employ a more equivocal use of the word than is often assumed, I propose a generalized rethinking of animism for life and living in the Anthropocene, as non-human, non-living forces insist they be reckoned with.

The next three chapters take as their starting points the Copernican, Darwinian and Freudian paradigm shifts and trace their heightened significance in light of climate change. Chapter 2, 'Surviving the Anthropocene: Revolutionary Rhythms', looks at the decentring and rescaling force of the Copernican revolution, and the ways in which it not only disturbs the place and prominence of humans within the universe but also undermines the reality of human sense perceptions. I elaborate an animism of rhythm, a non-human force that voices itself in (but that is not reducible to) human language. I read Virginia Woolf's *To the Lighthouse* (1927) and *The Waves* (1931), two works that particularly exhibit her attunement to the wild force of rhythm and the animism of the non-human world more generally. Both novels, I argue, can be read as post-Copernican in their decentring movements and apprehension of non-human scales, animistically breaking down conventional notions of objectivity, interiority, identity and characterization. Woolf inscribes a universe that is dynamically animated by non-human and non-living forms of life, and that opens itself to scales of space and time both vast and minute – as was being revealed by the astronomy and quantum physics of her time. Both works also exhibit the modern preoccupation with entropic extinction – a thought that resounds today as we face the threats posed by climate change. Guided by Derrida's concept of 'survivance' or 'living on', I suggest how a generalized notion of text can be seen to oppose entropy. I go on to discuss (in relation to nuclear war) the anthropogenic mass extinction event that is currently occurring and the challenges to thinking it poses.

Chapter 3, 'Animals at the End of the World: The Evolution of Life and Language', deals with the blow to human narcissism struck by the work of Darwin: the revelation that there is no rigorous distinction between human beings and other animals, that all life is intimately related and radically interdependent, and that complexity can be produced without intentional agency. I discuss how the origin and evolution of language and organic life animate each other more than metaphorically, and, through a reading of Genesis, elaborate how human language and naming work to both assert and disrupt human identity. After illustrating the necessity of metaphor and fiction for any apprehension of non-human animals, I read Helen Macdonald's *H is for Hawk* (2014) and Nicholas Royle's *Quilt* (2010) – both of which are moved by encounters with non-human animals, problems of representation, the life of language and the experience of deep time. Such concerns are, as I discuss, revealing themselves to be increasingly important in the Anthropocene. I then look to the commodification and consumption of non-human animals in global capitalism, the environmental degradation this engenders and the dissimulations which make such bipartite violence possible. Finally, I turn to Lewis Carroll's *Alice's Adventures in Wonderland* and *Through the Looking Glass* (1872) – a work which incessantly complicates the distinction between human beings and other animals, troubling assumptions about who or what is meant for eating.

Chapter 4, 'Hatching: Psychoanalysis and the Textual Unconscious', concentrates on the blow struck to human narcissism by Freudian psychoanalysis. The revelation that there are unconscious forces at work in the mind undermines notions of human agency at individual, linguistic, social and global scales, an apprehension which is key to understanding the human responses – or lack thereof – to global warming. I examine the necessity of language, translation and literature to Freud's work, and the ways in which psychoanalysis deals with, or in, animism. To elaborate a 'textual unconscious' – both the unconscious operations of text and the textual operations of the unconscious – I read *Beyond the Pleasure Principle*

(1920) alongside Shakespeare's *Hamlet* (1600). I indicate some of the literary and theatrical debts of Freud's text, its narrativization of life and death, and the magical, animate play of language that voices itself throughout. I then turn to Clarice Lispector's 'The Egg and the Chicken' (1964), a text in which the acts of reading and writing are shown to be radically co-implicated, undermining notions of authorial intention and control. The text raises questions that are particularly resonant in light of climate change – questions about cause and effect, translation and futurity, agency and instrumentality. Returning to Freud, I illustrate how the literary debts of psychoanalysis run at a deeper level than allusions and examples, structuring the very mode of its operation, and I conclude by considering how the pathological forms of human narcissism that have shaped our history and engendered climate change might be recast in light of the arguments of this book.

1

Radical Animism: Climate Change and Other Transformations

Can such things be,
And overcome us like a summer's cloud,
Without our special wonder? You make me strange

Shakespeare, *Macbeth*[1]

Awakening

How to live with the strange radiance of this new dawn? All action reveals itself as interaction, *in terre* action, actions graved into the earth, interred but not put to rest, resurfacing, rupturing, interrupting the ground on which we stand – or fall.

Ear to the ground: beating heart of earth, under threat. Listen.

*

Radical animism has to do with life and living, with what living *is*, at root, or with what is living, even if it is not, in the strict sense, 'alive'. It entails a discovery or rediscovery of buried life and a careful or curious attention to the living breathing waking spirit of what is unearthed. It has to do with the experience of being alive, with others, here on planet earth. It involves thinking the pasts and the futures that cannot be separated from such an experience. It must reckon with the events happening now that are named under the heading 'climate change', the radical transformations of planetary environments and the multiplicitous implications – many unforeseeable – of these events for life on earth. It involves a careful thinking through the phrase 'life on earth' and the dependent relation it encapsulates: the relation between the *anima*, spirit or psyche, and the material, terrestrial ground. It recognizes that all that is vital, quick, beating with the fragile defiance of life must also come or succumb to death: vitality is mortality. But it also recognizes that the traits or characteristics of life are not restricted to what we usually think of as 'living things', that non-human and non-living entities are also animated, alive. It involves thinking through the terms 'environment', 'ecology', 'economics' and 'extinction'. It has to do with response and responsibility. It will need what lives in language.

The planet is in transformation. Everything is changing. Things are strange and becoming stranger. Humans are implicated. We are responsible, even as we fail to respond. The conditions in which civilization flourished are altering, becoming other. This epoch is being called the Anthropocene: an age in which the human species has become a geological force, incalculably transforming the earth's systems on every level – altering the hydrosphere, atmosphere, lithosphere and biosphere. You are becoming aware of the fact that the ground on which you stand is not stable, passive and unmoving, but that it too is a force, has agency, responds. The way things once were begins to feel like a dream.

> As Gregor Samsa woke one morning from uneasy dreams, he found himself transformed into some kind of monstrous vermin. He lay on his hard, armour-like back, and if he lifted his head a little, he could see his curved brown abdomen, divided by arch-shaped ridges, and domed so high that the bed cover, on the brink of slipping off, could hardly stay put. His many legs, miserably thin in comparison with his size otherwise, flickered helplessly before his eyes.
>
> 'What has happened to me?' he thought. It was not a dream. His room, a proper, human being's room, rather too small, lay peacefully between its four familiar walls.[2]

Franz Kafka's *Die Verwandlung*, translated as *The Metamorphosis* or *The Transformation*, is a story for the Anthropocene. The *-wandlung* ('change') of Kafka's title comes from the same root as the English verbs 'wander', 'wend' and 'wind': the Old Germanic *wend*, 'to turn'. This is a transformation in which something turns into something else, in which things are moving, tides and times are turning, perhaps taking a turn for the worse. The German prefix *ver-* has multiple different associations – one of which has to do with change: the transformation of the *ver-wandlung*. But it also often implies something going wrong, a misstep (*ich habe mich verlaufen*; I got lost) or a mistake (*eine Verwechslung* or *ein Versehen*). When Gregor awakes to find himself turned into a monstrous vermin, we can only assume that such a transformation is not a positive one. Another possible translation, then, might be *The Catastrophe* (from the Greek κατά, 'down', and στρέφειν, 'to turn') – given its sense of 'an event producing a subversion of the order or system of things' (*OED*).

Climate Change and Other Transformations

You are, right now, living that strange morning. Having woken to the reality of anthropogenic climate change, human beings find that they have become the 'monstrous vermin' or 'pests' of the world: animals that are destructive, noxious or troublesome and that, like parasites, live to the detriment of other animals or plants. For a long time, we got away with it. But our collective body is now so swollen that the cover, like Gregor's, is slipping off. It is not a dream. We look on, helplessly. Our home, the planet earth, familiar as the four walls of Gregor's room, has, without changing size at all, suddenly become 'too small'. The place, the technologies, the lifestyles which we have for so long assumed to be our property, or proper to us – just as Gregor sees 'his room, a *proper* human being's room' – become altogether inappropriate. 'What has happened to me?' he wonders. Or, as German grammar demands, 'What has happened *with* me?', '*Was ist* mit *mir geschehen?*' Gregor is somehow implicated. We all are. I am reminded of Heidegger's questions at the beginning of *The Fundamental Concepts of Metaphysics*. He asks, 'What is happening to us here? [*Was geschieht da mit uns?*] What is man, that such things happen to him in his very ground?'³ In this age of anthropogenic climate change, these questions acquire a strange new force, as the assumptions upon which our conception of being is based are called into question and redrawn within an entirely altered framework of responsibility.

Kafka's tale takes up similar questions: the transformation of its title is not limited to Gregor but also concerns a transformation of what it means to be a human being, what it means to be an animal and what it means to live and die together. 'What has happened to me?' asks Gregor. A transformation, a change, a *Verwandlung*. Above I noted that the '-*wand*' in this word is a 'turn', the old Germanic root of which has several incarnations in English. The verb 'wend' (as in 'to wend one's way') wanders through a plethora of senses: it means not only 'to turn' or 'change' but also 'to translate', 'to go', 'to proceed', 'to leave', 'to cease to exist', 'to die' – thereby shadowing or foretelling Gregor's whole tale. The related verb 'wonde', now obsolete, means to turn away, 'to shrink from, avoid, shun; to refuse', just as, perhaps, the rest of the Samsa family turn from their transformed son. In German, as well as the turning motions of *Wandlung* (transformation), *Wendung* (a turn, or a turn of phrase: a trope) and *wandern* (to wander) – all of which occur in the text – the etymologically distinct word *Wand* also means 'wall': the four walls of Gregor's confinement, the walling-in of his world. Whether or not Kafka was consciously playing on the rich history that turns in this word is not my concern; instead, as will become clear, one of the endeavours of this book will be to pay careful and curious attention to the radical animism of language, to the strange way it does things of its own accord.

I open with this text because it touches on so many of the strange events occurring today, in this age of anthropogenic climate change. Climate change is an animal problem – a problem for animals and a problem that is animate, monstrous, alive. *Die Verwandlung* brings human beings face to face with a non-human other, with a living thing that they do not recognize as a fellow – despite their once-intimate relation. It also concerns the becoming-monstrous of the human: the precipitous mutation through which our way of living is revealed to be no longer compatible with the planet. It is about the responsibility we bear to human and non-human others, as well as the capacity, or incapacity, to respond. It is about forms of expression and language beyond the limits of human comprehension. It is moved by the uncanny or the *Unheimliche* – the strange and unsettling disturbance of that most familiar and familial of places: the home.

The transformation

Everyone alive today is a creature of the Anthropocene, even if the word did not exist when they were born. Retroactively ascribed, it is a term that belongs to a time that is very much out of joint. The Holocene – the geological epoch in which, until not too long ago, humans thought they were still living – was brought to an end by the emergence of what Antonio Stoppani called, in 1873, a 'new telluric force': human beings.[4] The *OED* defines the Anthropocene as the 'era of geological time during which human activity is considered to be the dominant influence on the environment, climate, and ecology of the earth'. Paul Crutzen, credited with coining the word 'Anthropocene' in 2000, dates its advent to 1784, with the invention of the steam engine and the subsequent transformation of industry – and, indeed, this correlates with the increased concentration of greenhouse gases read from polar ice cores.[5] Humans have, however, left their mark on the planet in other ways too: by clearing forests and practising extensive agriculture, by cultivating and modifying certain plant crops and 'livestock', by directly or indirectly causing the extinction or endangerment of millions of species of plants and animals, by producing great swathes of non-degradable waste (some of it radioactive), by damming rivers and by spreading diseases and non-native species to new parts of the world. All of this accumulates force as the human population grows exponentially.

The denomination of the Anthropocene has been criticized for figuring human agency as a unified – or unifiable – force. T. J. Demos, in *Against the Anthropocene*, notes how the word 'tends to disavow differentiated responsibility (and the differently located effects) for the geological changes it designates, instead homogeneously allocating agency to the generic members of its "human activities"'.[6] While this is a crucially important point – and one to which we will be returning – I disagree with Demos's suggestion that we should avoid the term 'Anthropocene' altogether. This is for three reasons. First, as Adam Trexler recognizes, while notions of climate change or global warming are susceptible to being framed as mere 'prognostications that might yet be deferred' – however deluded such a stance may be – 'the Anthropocene names a world-historical phenomenon that has arrived'.[7] Or as Bruno Latour remarks in *Facing Gaia*, the designation of a new epoch serves to mark climate change not just as a transitory event, a 'passing crisis', but rather as *'a profound mutation in our relation to the world'*.[8] Second, the naming of a geological epoch massively broadens the frame through which we view human history, thereby effecting temporally what the 1968 'Earthrise' image did spatially, imaginatively providing a radical new perspective from which to understand the contemporary moment – *including* the unequal distribution of culpability and power by which it is characterized. Third, the term asks us to recognize that *all* human actions are now – and in fact always have been – inextricably embroiled within the bio-geo-chemistry of the planet. Eating, drinking, breathing, excreting, shopping, driving, farming, composting, hunting, mining – all of these activities, to a greater or lesser extent, are bound up with planetary systems that are beyond the scope of human sense perceptions.

Given the multitude of factors that have contributed to our increasing impact upon the planet, along with the relatively long timescales involved, it is hard to finally or precisely date the ascension of the *anthropos* to the level of a 'telluric force'. As Jeremy Davies discusses in *The Birth of the Anthropocene*, stratigraphic opinion as to the most appropriate start date for the new epoch remains divided.[9] What all the marks of human life that I have listed above have in common, however, is their potential endurance, their *legibility*. The designation of the Anthropocene as a new geological epoch transforms our thinking of the future as well as the past: it is the recognition that, in millions of years from now, whatever becomes of the human race and life on earth, the story of human civilizations will be told by the planetary records we are leaving behind. Sarah Wood calls the Anthropocene 'an age in which human agency has written itself, with radically destabilizing effect, into the geology, the chemistry, the plants on our planet'.[10] To speak of the Anthropocene in terms of writing and legibility is no mere metaphor. Rather, the writing of words and the writing of geological traces (and, as we will see in Chapter 3, the writing of life) reveal themselves to be but different species of the same genus. All of these species of writing possess a transformative force that extends far beyond the time and place of inscription. This book will be concerned with elaborating the shared – and animistic – traits of writing in a broad sense, and with showing how the kind of reading that we do when approaching a literary text is not fundamentally different from the kind of reading that geologists do.

The legibility of the Anthropocene brings with it a certain irony: these unintentional relics will far outlast any deliberate monument, any piece of art, any living language. As Davies notes, what will remain to be read in the far future is not our 'inward self-imagining' but rather the 'shape and intensity of [the human species'] material interactions with other beings and forces – coal, rice, coral, nitrogen, iron'.[11] That given, the recognition of the Anthropocene also demands a conception of agency that is decoupled from conscious intention. Human actions on the planet may be influential enough to warrant the designation of a new epoch, but this is hardly a matter of sovereign control. Timothy Clark writes,

> The newly recognized agent of humanity as a geological force is something indiscernible in any of the individuals or even large groups of which it is composed. It is a power that barely recognizes itself as such and which is not really capable of voluntary action or planning, as it arises from the often unforeseen consequences of the plans and acts of its constituents.[12]

The apex of human influence morphs into something above and beyond human power, and geological permanence is ironically tied to a threat to the conditions of lived existence. Even as geological agency is attributable to human actions, it is an agency so vast, so interconnected and so intractable that its force is more-than-human, uncannily invading or disrupting our sense of identity. As Bronislaw Szerszynski puts it, the 'becoming geological of the human is a "denouement" which is both our apotheosis and our eclipse'.[13] The naming of the Anthropocene – somewhat counterintuitively – actually marks the *limits* of human agency, acknowledging as it does the fact that we are, in a vertiginous and absolute sense, as individuals, as states and as a species, not in control. In Wood's phrase, we are 'without mastery'.[14] The Anthropocene is perhaps the name we have given to this realization.

So how are we to conceive of agency in the Anthropocene? As I have just said, it does not need intention and it does not need consciousness. It is also not simply the way that one thing might act upon or effect another, for this, as Jane Bennett writes, relies upon 'an atomistic rather than a congregational understanding'.¹⁵ Agency is something that happens *between* things, an emergent property of the dynamic inter-actions of all kinds of forces (human and non-human, conscious and unconscious, organic and inorganic) as they act upon and through each other. The point is not to newly identify or elevate non-human forms of agency – things have always acted upon other things. Rather, it is to recognize that what we think of as human agency is never purely human nor purely intentional, even or especially when it seems to be. To think animistically in the Anthropocene entails, as will be elaborated throughout this book, a recognition of and respect for these emergent, relational and unintentional forms of agency.

Clark writes that the Anthropocene is a time in which the 'environment' 'ceases being only a passive ground, context and resource for human society and becomes an imponderable agency that must somehow be taken into account, even if we are unsure how'.¹⁶ It has, of course, always been this way, but in the Holocene, it was still possible to disavow this reality, to act *as if* the environment were merely 'a passive ground' and *as if* agency were something proper to human beings. But now, as Clark points out, the 'environment' can no longer be conceived as a mere 'environment'. It does not environ – or revolve around – us; it is not even separable from us. It destabilizes the opposition between inside and outside. It can no longer be thought of as something at a material or philosophical distance from human beings but is instead revealed to be something within which we are inextricably embroiled. Consider, for example, how far human actions are swayed by something as simple as change in the weather. As David Wallace-Wells notes, increased heat measurably increases violent behaviours – including murder, rape, assault, theft and suicide.¹⁷ That the warming world will make humans more violent is just one of the ways in which climate change twists and transforms our sense of what agency is and who – or what – might be possessed of it. In such a time, animism takes on, as I will argue, a new and forceful significance.

Anthropocene reading: An autobiography in deconstruction

If the Anthropocene is a matter of marks or traces being *written* into the earth, it is also a matter of reading. The notion of *Anthropocene reading* can be understood in three interconnected ways – all of which are important to this book. First, it is the work of stratigraphers that I have been discussing above: the apprehension or reading of the nonlinguistic traces (such as atmospheric carbon dioxide or radionuclide fallout) that are being interpreted as markers of the Anthropocene.[18]

Second, it is a mode of reading texts – literary and otherwise – in the context of today's environmental mutations. Such reading is not only attentive to the non-human forces at work in texts (at the levels of character, narrative, form, 'meaning', etc.) but also aims to recognize the ways in which even a critical stance may be subject to transformation in the context of the Anthropocene. As Clark notes, 'received or mainstream modes of reading and criticism, even when socially "progressive" in some respects, are now, despite themselves, being changed into what are effectively implicit forms of denial as the world alters around them'.[19]

The third form of *Anthropocene reading* would involve reading the phrase another way: reading the Anthropocene not as the object being read but as *the thing doing the reading*. Not only, then, are humans reading the Anthropocene, but the Anthropocene is also reading *us*, revealing hidden meanings and strange unintentional ventriloquies, finding resonances and discrepancies that – until now – we have not noticed. Just as a new reading of a literary text can transform its meaning or significance without changing the words on the page, the Anthropocene works to radically transform long-established human self-conceptions. How might concepts like 'humanity', 'responsibility', 'rights' and 'agency' be recast in light of anthropogenic climate change and its effects?

We might think of the Anthropocene as a kind of autobiography of humankind – though its composition, heralding as it does the Sixth Mass Extinction Event, radically rethinks the phrase 'the death of the author'. David Wills suggests that autobiography can be understood 'as something other than the writing of one's life in the prospective of death – something other than simply what survives the end of a given life'; 'instead, it is something like a graphic automation or inanimation that precedes and even gives rise to life'.[20] As soon as one writes an autobiography, the life described therein is extended and transformed by that very description, demanding an endless supplementation: 'as I record my life, I add to the life that my autobiography will henceforth have to take account of, along a future vanishing point that only death can interrupt.'[21] If, as I just suggested, the Anthropocene can be understood as the autobiography of humankind, its fundamental unfinishability is also its inherent power of transformation. The auto-deictic nature of autobiography – its self-awareness – transforms the very 'I' it signifies, so that the Anthropocene marks itself not only stratigraphically into the planet but also into what it means to be human. Its threat is our chance. The Anthropocene is an autobiography that ruptures the self-conception by which it is named, revealing an *anthropos* that is more animal, more inanimate and more open to transformation than the writing of History – inscribed as it is under the delusion of an authorial intention – has ever before had cause to admit.

Anthropocene responsibility

Nicholas Royle writes of the phrase 'climate change' that there is 'something absurd' about it,

> as if the 'change' were something simply going on apart from – at a distance from – ourselves, as if our hallucinatory place at the centre of the world were left entirely intact and unaffected by what is going on outside, over there, somewhere else. There is something laughable also about the pacifying use of 'change' rather than, say, 'disintegration' or 'transformation', and about the calm insistence on this noun in the singular.[22]

Indeed, the 'business-as-usual' approach to climate change (with the emphasis perhaps on *business* here – and we will return to the force of capital later) has something slightly surreal, something comically Kafkaesque about it. After more than three decades of IPCC conferences,[23] the urgent need to transition away from carbon-based energy sources is beyond question. And yet fossil fuel companies scramble in the Arctic and under tar sands to keep their reserve replacement ratios at 100 per cent, deliriously and wilfully blind to the fact that infinite extraction on a finite planet is a blatant non sequitur. But who could retain logic or reason when everything that is happening undermines the very ground of such thinking? When everything appears so vastly out of our control?

Denizen of another kind of post-truth reality, Gregor Samsa finds that having become a 'monstrous vermin' of some kind, he is now unable to master his limbs – as if their motion is driven by a causality beyond his remit:

> He would have needed arms and hands to raise himself; but instead of those, he had only these many little legs, which were continually fluttering about, and which he could not control anyhow. If he tried to bend one of them, it was the first to stretch; and if he finally managed to get this leg to do what he wanted, all the others were flapping about meanwhile in the most intense and painful excitement, as if they had been let loose. (32)

Despite his rather significant incapacity, Gregor is determined to carry on as normal, to 'get up quietly without any disturbance, get dressed, and above all have his breakfast', and then go off to work (32). This is, however, a contradictory kind of morning: assertions, as soon as they are made, mutate into something different. Upon hearing that the chief clerk has come to the house to see why he is so late to work, we read that Gregor 'almost froze' – though this almost-but-not-quite stillness is undone by the fact that 'his little legs only danced all the faster' (34). He then, 'more as a consequence of [his] agitation … than as the consequence of a proper decision', swings himself out of the bed – landing with either a 'loud thump', or, perhaps it was only a 'not-so-very-noticeable dull thud', on the floor (34). He begins to assure the clerk, through the locked door, that it is merely a 'slight indisposition, an attack of giddiness', that has prevented him from getting up:

> I'm still lying in bed. But I'm quite fresh again now. I'm just getting out of bed! Just a little moment's patience! It's not yet going as well as I thought. But I'm fine now. Oh, the things that can come over a person! Yesterday evening I felt fine, my parents can tell you, or rather, yesterday evening I already had a little premonition. They must have noticed it. … In any case, I can still take the eight o'clock train and be off. (36–7)

'I'm still lying in bed,' he says. He is actually on his back on the floor, rocking his way across the room towards the wardrobe. But he is getting up, he assures the clerk, even if it's 'not yet going as well as [he] thought'. The important thing seems to be, whatever the actual state of affairs, to assure the clerk that he is 'fine now' and will shortly be going to work, even if such an undertaking remains, in truth, ludicrous. Perhaps it is the kind of 'fine' that he was 'yesterday evening', when he might, now he thinks of it, have 'had a little premonition': the kind of 'fine', that is to say, that is transformed by its relation to the future.

His protestations, however, are spoken in vain. The people he is addressing – his family and the clerk – cannot understand him. After the transformation, Gregor is 'startled' when he hears 'his own voice': 'merging into it as though from low down came an uncontrollable, painful squealing' (31). 'That was an animal's voice,' the clerk says (37). Even though he has always borne the responsibility for the whole family (as I shall go on to discuss), Gregor is now denied the possibility of response. His attempts at communication are missed or ignored, and so, 'as he couldn't be understood, no one, not even his sister, even dreamt that he was able to understand others' (47). This incapacity is precisely the designation by which human beings differentiate themselves from other animals. Jacques Derrida writes in *The Animal That Therefore I Am* that 'all the philosophers we will investigate (from Aristotle to Lacan, and including

Descartes, Kant, Heidegger, and Levinas), all of them say the same thing: the animal is deprived of language. Or, more precisely, of response, of a response that could be precisely and rigorously distinguished from a reaction.'[24] And yet, while human beings may assume that they have the power to respond, this is no guarantee that they will fulfil their responsibility, nor that they are immune from the kind of 'reaction' supposedly reserved for non-human animals. Indeed, as Wills writes, 'the whole ethico-ethological discourse of agency and responsibility ... presumes that only *respons*-ive humans can be *respons*-ible, but ... fails to acknowledge the residual structure of automaticity functioning not only in reaction but also in response'.[25] When confronted by Gregor, his father is reduced to 'hissing like a savage' (42), and his mother is left short of breath, 'with a wild look in her eyes' (68). Indeed, Frau Samsa's encounters with Gregor consistently result in loss of controlled motor function: collapsing, screaming, breathlessness, coughing or loss of consciousness (39, 42, 68, 56). The German word for 'unconsciousness' is '*Ohnmacht*', literally 'without-power' or 'impotence'; she is left powerless before the animal in an inversion of the usual relied-upon relation.

The reason that Gregor is so determined to go to work, despite the situation, is because of the burden he has taken on of his parents' 'debt' to the boss (30). The German word *Schuld*, translated here as 'debt', has several connotations and can also be 'blame', 'fault', 'guilt', 'due' or 'obligation'. As Joyce Crick recognizes, '"Schuld-as-debt" is one associated meaning to "Schuld-as-guilt" that lends itself to treatment in literal terms which are capable, in Kafka's hands, of elaborate narrative development'.[26] There is not only the parent's debt to Gregor's boss but also the blame Gregor might bear for his mother's ill health – it is 'perhaps through his fault [*Schuld*] she was close to death' (56/53), and the blame his father lays on him, assuming 'that he was guilty [*zuschulden*] of some violent act' (57/53). Later, in a fit of 'stubbornness', the father forgets 'the respect which, after all, he owed [*schuldete*] his tenants' (68/71). We might assume, given the fact that Gregor has taken on his parents' debt, that he too, transformed or not, is a tenant whose due respect has also been forgotten. Indeed, it seems that Gregor has taken on the *Schuld* of the entire family, rendering them totally 'innocent [*unschuldigen*]', their 'behaviour' 'excused [*entschuldigte*]' (34/16, 36/18). After Gregor's death, fully relieved of their burden, and having 'earned' a day off, they 'sat down at the table and wrote three notes of excuse [*Entschuldigungsbriefe*]' (73/80). An '*Entschuldigung*' could also be an 'apology' or 'exculpation' – the Samsas declare themselves free from guilt or blame. Crick comments on the way that Kafka 'takes the latent concrete meanings of words and phrases and daily sayings, and exploits their lost metaphorical meaning by representing them quite literally':

> '*Am eigenen Leib erfahren*', literally, 'to experience in one's own body', is a faded metaphor used mainly in the weak sense of 'to experience for oneself', but Kafka not only restores it to full strength in the officer's terrible apparatus [in 'In the Penal Colony'], but has already hidden it in Gregor's litany of his miseries as a travelling salesman, 'when it is only once he is at home that he can feel in his own flesh the serious consequences they entail'; the phrase itself suggests some of the causes for his literal transformation into something subhuman.[27]

Kafka's texts disturb the distinction between metaphorical and literal language. This animation of metaphor brings to light those turns of phrase that have become so normalized that you no longer notice them – like 'brings to light', for example, or 'turns of phrase'. Reading Kafka, we begin to realize that language is radically metaphorical, alive with an underground life that stirs of its own accord, whether or not this is the author's conscious intention. Such disturbance of normal, everyday language could be thought of as analogous to what is happening in the Anthropocene: just as metaphors that usually go unnoticed come to have fresh and startling significance in Kafka's writing, banal and seemingly innocuous activities like driving a car or using an internet search engine become monstrous planetary actions, contributing to the destabilization of the climate and the concomitant suffering or death of many millions of creatures – some of them human. As Clark notes, 'modes of thinking and practice that may once have seemed justified, internally coherent, self-evident or progressive now need to be reassessed in terms of hidden exclusions, disguised costs, or as offering a merely imaginary closure'.[28] Such modes of thinking and practice begin to carry, like Kafka's literalization of metaphor, new and strange significance. What is happening with us?

Animality of the letter

The word 'metaphor' comes from the Greek μετα (*meta*), meaning either 'beyond, above, at a higher level', or 'change, transformation, permutation, substitution', and φέρειν (*phérein*), to 'bear' or 'carry'. It has, then, to do with a certain bearing, where one thing bears another, or – because we are in the realm of the *meta*, in which normal rules of physics or logic do not apply – both things bear or carry each other. It also has to do with the transformative force of this relation. In neither thing, in neither bearer nor borne, but in the relation, in the act of bearing itself, something that we might call 'meaning' stirs. I suspend the word 'meaning' here to admit that I do not really know what it *means*, if we assume 'meaning' to be something separable from its verbal expression, something 'proper' or 'true', something that is not metaphorical. A banal enough assumption. But what if there is no 'meaning' without metaphor, no meaning that is not also metaphorical meaning? What if the meaning of 'meaning' can only be metaphorical too?

The problem with trying to say something *about* metaphor, is, as Derrida identifies, that you cannot say anything *without* metaphor – and so you will always find your words suspended impossibly from their own bootstraps. 'I cannot produce a *treatise* on metaphor that is not *treated with* metaphor, which suddenly appears intractable.'[29] *Intractable* – 'Of persons and animals: Not to be guided; not manageable or docile; uncontrollable; refractory, stubborn' (*OED*). Metaphor is a wild and wilful beast, then, one that cannot be tamed – nor, if that 'refractory' might also be refracted into 'refractive' (and it does this of its own accord), is it unified or identifiable but instead casts a polymorphous spectrum, a chimærical rainbow that recedes as soon as you attempt to approach. Derrida carries on as follows:

> What is going on *with* metaphor? Well, everything: there is nothing that does not go on with metaphor and through metaphor. Any statement concerning anything whatsoever that goes on, metaphor included, will have been produced *not without* metaphor. … And what gets along *without* metaphor? Nothing, therefore, and one ought to say instead that metaphor gets along without anything else, here without me, at the very moment when it appears to be going on by way of me. … [I]n its withdrawal, one should say in its withdrawals, metaphor perhaps retires, withdraws from the worldwide scene, and does so at the moment of its most invasive extension, at the instant it overflows every limit.[30]

Erinaceously pervasive, or pervasively erinaceous, metaphor haunts as it hides, at once curling itself up, invisibly nestling in the curve of a letter at the same time that it lays itself out: the vast ocean out of which life emerges, the blank page upon which a mark can be made. If, for a moment, or for most of the time, you forget about metaphor and carry on as if you could do without it, it will carry on with and without you – irrepressibly 'active and stirring', alive.[31] (And, I write, curled up for now in a parenthesis that will later expand itself through the fourth chapter of this book, the same might perhaps be said for the wild animal that

Freud called the unconscious, that withdraws from sight at the same time that it invisibly infects every move 'I' make.)

The phrase which heads this section, 'the animality of the letter', is taken from Derrida's *Writing and Difference*. Let us now turn to the passage in which it appears, with *Die Verwandlung* in mind. Derrida is writing on the poet Edmond Jabès, and his words perhaps take on or carry something of the spirit of the latter (and isn't Derrida's writing so often metaphorical in this way, bearing another's bearing, taking on other characteristics?):[32]

> The animality of the letter certainly appears, at first, as *one* metaphor among others. ... But, above all, it is metaphor *itself*. ... Metaphor, or the animality of the letter, is the primary and infinite equivocality of the signifier as Life. ... This overpowerfulness as the life of the signifier is produced within the anxiety and the wandering of the language always richer than knowledge, the language always capable of the movement which takes it further than peaceful and sedentary certitude.[33]

The life of metaphor, like an animal, moves through space and time. The 'anxiety' of language grows out of the uncertainty of its future, its 'wandering' neither entirely aimless nor absolutely determinable. As Wood notes in her commentary on *Writing and Difference*, 'the animality of the letter means that the letter does not speak to explain itself or its frame of reference; it is metaphor without end, equivocal and uncertain and, Derrida insists, *alive*'; this is a matter of 'an experience of difference as the origin of meaning'.[34] And this uncertainty or equivocality is not a privation but a plenitude: its wandering is 'always richer than knowledge', its openness to possibility always richer than the immobility and closure of 'sedentary certitude'.

'Metaphor, or the animality of the letter' is what allows Gregor to 'literally' turn into a monstrous vermin, but such a transformation is not reducible, as we have seen, to two states, one 'actual' and one 'metaphorical' – a fact demonstrated by the ever-expanding menagerie of interpretations that speculate upon the possible tenors of Gregor's transformation (Jewishness, disability, alienation, etc.). The metaphor of *Die Verwandlung* – if there is one – is not in the text itself, but rather is born out of (or borne by) our readings: readings which thereby transform the text in a manner not altogether different from the metamorphosis which inexplicably befalls Gregor. The transformation from human to vermin is no less thorough-going than the transformation from the text on the page to the 'meaning' we ascribe to it: in neither case is the latter state manifest in the former state. The 'life' of the signifier, the 'wandering of the language' (an errancy already announced in the Ver*wandlung* of the title) will always be on the move, multiplying its significance, abyssally polysemic – so there is no 'meaning' at bottom, no 'certitude' to be achieved, just the generative and intractable turns of metaphor.

If 'the animality of the letter' is 'metaphor *itself*', what becomes of 'animality' – or of *life itself* – in this relation? One would have to apprehend the animality of organic life not as the vehicle for the 'metaphorical' ascription of the 'life' of the signifier but just as one of its incarnations. One would have to apprehend, that is to say, not that life is a metaphor for metaphor, but that the *life of metaphor* is also a metaphor for life. The vitality or animatedness of every metaphor – its relationality, its agency, its affective power – can help us to think about or understand the vitality of organically living things. Or, as Wills puts it in *Inanimation*, there is not 'simply real, literal, organic life, on one hand, and a series of metaphorical extensions of that literality, loose figurative usages of the word, on the other'. Instead, as his book elaborates, life functions 'through a variety of forms that never reduce to organic examples, however dominant and numerous the organic examples be'.[35] The life of language is, therefore, non-metaphorical – or no more metaphorical than the life of life 'itself' (which, as I have just said, might be thought of in terms of various forms of non-organic life, including language and metaphor). I will return to the relation between these two distinct species of life in the third chapter.

Bearing others

Above, I discussed the blame, guilt or debt that Gregor bears for his family – and Kafka also literalizes the metaphors of bearing or carrying, and what cannot or will not be borne (metaphors *par excellence*, perhaps, given that they invoke the 'literal' meaning of 'meta-phor' as what carries). To bear the blame (*Schuld tragen*) can both be to *be* responsible, to be at fault or to *take on* the responsibility or blame, to carry it for someone else. Both meanings are strong in *Die Verwandlung*, and both are significant for thinking in the Anthropocene.

'*Die Welt ist fort, ich muß dich tragen.*' 'The world is gone, I must carry you.'[36] This is the last line of a poem by Paul Celan, to which Derrida often returns. This line, both constative and performative, imports 'necessity and duty, inflexible injunction' and inscribes the relation between self and other – the point, Derrida writes, 'where ethics begins':

The world is far, the world has gone, in the absence or distance of the world, I must, I owe it to you, I owe it to myself to carry you, without world, without the foundation or grounding of anything in the world, without any foundational or fundamental mediation, one on one, like wearing mourning or bearing a child.[37]

This is a duty before reason and logic – 'without any foundational or fundamental mediation' – that takes on, unconditionally, the past ('like wearing mourning'; remembering the dead) and the future ('bearing a child'). It is a duty to the other *as* other, to a 'you' that lives in a world that could be (as Gregor's has apparently become) 'different to the point of the monstrosity of the unrecognizable, of the un-similar, of the unbelievable, of the non-similar, the non-resembling or resemblable, the non-assimilable, the untransferable, the incomparable, the absolutely unshareable'.[38]

Before his transformation, it was Gregor who bore the rest of the family, having been, thanks to his hard work, 'in a position to take on [*zu tragen*] the expenditure of the whole family' (49/40). This involves getting up very early to send off his 'orders [*Aufträge*]', while others 'are only just having their breakfast' (30/9). After the transformation, it is the rest of the Samsa family that must bear the burden of responsibility, but they do not seem able or willing to bear it. While struggling to get out of bed, 'it occurred to him how simple it would all be if someone came to help him':

> Two strong people – he thought of his father and the maid – would have been entirely up to it; all they would have to do was put their arms under the dome of his back, unpeel him out of his bed in this way, stoop down with their load, and then merely wait patiently with him until he had managed to swing over on the floor, when, he hoped, his legs would do what they were intended to do. Well now, quite apart from the fact that the doors were locked, should he really have called for help? In spite of his distress, he couldn't suppress a smile at the thought. (33–4)

The idea of his family bearing him, instead of the other way around, is a source of amusement for Gregor, even in his current predicament. Later we find out that his parents 'wouldn't have been able to bear [*nicht ertragen können*] finding out more about his food than they were told' (47/37) and that the mere 'sight' of Gregor 'was still intolerable [*unerträglich*, unbearable]' to his sister Grete, 'and was bound to remain intolerable for the future' (51/44).

In the end, it is the Samsas' inability to bear the responsibility that brings things to a head:

> 'We must try to get rid of it,' his sister now said solely to their father, since their mother couldn't hear anything for coughing, 'it will be the death of you both, I can see it coming. If we all have to work already as hard as we do, we can't put up with [*ertragen*] this endless agony as well. I certainly can't go on any more.' And she broke into crying so vehemently that her tears fell on to her mother's face, which she wiped dry with mechanical movements of her hand. (69/73)

It is significant that just at the moment at which Grete proclaims that the three of them can no longer 'put up with' or bear Gregor any longer, she appears to lose her human quality, her movements becoming 'mechanical', as if there is a certain reactionality or automaticity underlying her response. This comes shortly after the point at which Gregor has undergone a further transformation: from 'he' to 'it'; from 'brother' to 'monster':

> 'Parents dear,' said his sister, striking the table with her hand by way of introduction, 'it can't go on like this. I will not utter my brother's name in front of this monster, so I will simply say: we must try to get rid of it. We have tried everything humanly possible, looking after it and putting up with it; I don't think anyone can reproach us in the slightest for that.' (68)

Grete contradicts herself here. The phrases translated as 'looking after it and putting up with it' are the German '*es zu pflegen und zu dulden*' (68/72). *Pflegen* comes from the same root as the English 'pledge' – to become a surety for, to make oneself responsible for. *Dulden* comes from the same root as the now-archaic English word 'thole' – to endure, suffer or tolerate. In this juxtaposition of two incompatible terms, Grete's words recall a passage earlier in which their 'family duty [*Familienpflicht* – from *pflegen*] towards him commanded that they should swallow their disgust, and put up with him [*zu dulden*], just put up with him' (59/57). Whereas a pledge is an oath or a promise, and therefore unconditional, tolerance is always bounded or limited, never unconditional. Something will only be tolerated up to a certain point, or under certain conditions. As Derrida remarks, 'tolerance is actually the opposite of hospitality. Or at least its limit. If I think I am being hospitable because I am tolerant, it is because I wish to limit my welcome, to retain power and maintain control over the limits of my "home", my sovereignty, my "I can".'[39]

Even though ostensibly it is Gregor that transforms into a monstrous animal, while the rest of his family remain human, the encounter also reverses these roles. When, as quoted above, Grete underlines Gregor's animality, referring to him as an 'it', she also attempts to reinscribe the rest of the family's humanity – 'We've done everything *humanly* possible,' she says. Yet by transforming him into an 'it', into a 'monster [*Untier*]', this is also the moment where she announces the limit of their tolerance, the point at which they are no longer willing to bear the burden of Gregor, and thus their very humanity, or compassion – their responsibility to the other – is called into question. Once Gregor is dead and disposed of, 'seen to' by the charwoman, the family watch as 'a butcher's boy' with a 'tray [*Trage*]' of meat 'came climbing proudly [up the stairs] towards them', so that the intolerable corpse of one animal is replaced by one altogether more palatable and, it seems, bearable (73/80).

Grete defends her renunciation of Gregor by proclaiming that 'it's not possible for human beings to live with such an animal [*Zusammenleben … nicht möglich ist*, coexistence, life together is not possible]' (69/74).[40] Such a statement now reads as a dark indictment of the human-animal relations that characterize twenty-first-century life. The ongoing Sixth Mass Extinction Event, for which human actions are singularly responsible,[41] represents a literalization or realization of Grete's assertion: that life together – at least in the current form – is not possible. Michael Wood, discussing Kafka's *The Trial*, writes of its narrative condition as 'neither literal nor metaphorical and not even virtual but something like a change of moral lighting, a stark alteration of an unaltered life'.[42] It is this quality, precisely, that makes Kafka's texts so resonant in the Anthropocene, as we ourselves begin to experience 'a stark alteration of an unaltered life'.

Ethics aside

The ethical implications of the Anthropocene also throw an unforgiving light upon human relations with each other, as levels of economic disparity interface catastrophically with the effects of climate change. If all human beings were to have equal rights to food, energy and technology, as would be just, the development needed to bring the universal living standards of a still-growing global population in line with those of Western Europe and North America would ensure environmental catastrophe – especially as it is becoming increasingly evident that most developed countries are not willing to reduce their consumption in significant ways. On the individual level, people in wealthy nations may be happy to switch the light off when not in use, but few are willing to forgo their car or air travel, and on a societal level, governments maintain their focus on economic growth over emissions reductions. This problem might lead us to questions of human population control and to what has been dubbed 'ecofascism'. Many find the notion of restricting people's right to reproduce distinctly uncomfortable, given its association with dictatorial regimes. But human and individual rights are pre-Anthropocene formulations that naturally place individual and social freedoms before the survival of the species (the latter not having previously emerged as an issue). Faced now with the reality of climate change, we are forced to ask ourselves: at which point do forms of social control that might correctly be deemed fascistic become acceptable or even necessary in the name of averting total ecological breakdown? Is it more 'just' to protect current ideals of personal and social freedom, which will almost certainly result in the suffering or death of many millions of humans, as well as the extinction or endangering of millions of other life forms, than it is to restrict the former in the name of the latter? The choice may not be in reality as stark as this, and perhaps it is possible to imagine new ideals of personal and social freedom that do not have such a destructive impact, but, either way, my point stands: any barometer of ethics, morality or justice is necessarily transformed by the new context of the Anthropocene.

The fourth blow

Early in the twentieth century, Freud described three blows or wounds (*Kränkungen*) to the '*naïve* self-love of men', three scientific revelations that worked to decentre and destabilize the concept of 'Man'. These are as follows:

1. the Copernican revolution, which revealed the earth to be 'only a tiny fragment of a cosmic system of scarcely imaginable vastness', thereby exploding the belief that Man is the centre of the universe;
2. the work of Charles Darwin, which, according to Freud, revealed humankind's 'ineradicable animal nature', thereby undermining any notion that Man is distinct from and superior to other animals; and finally,
3. the work of psychoanalysis itself – the 'most wounding' blow – which revealed that there are unconscious forces at work in the mind, thereby destroying the long-held conviction that humans are agents of an entirely conscious will. As Freud writes, the ego 'is not even master [*Herr*] in its own house'.[43]

This last formulation, which figures the blow of psychoanalysis as a loss of mastery, is, in a later text, more explicitly linked to all three of the blows – implying that Man's 'self-love' or narcissism is consistently founded upon the delusion of mastery. Freud writes that the 'cosmological' blow destroyed the illusion of the 'dominating part [*herrschende Rolle*]' Man saw himself occupying in the universe, thwarting his 'inclination to regard himself as lord [*Herrn*] of the world'; the 'biological' one revealed the fiction by which Man cast himself in a 'dominating position [*Herrn*] over his fellow-creatures'; and the 'psychological' one showed that he is not 'supreme [*souverän*] within his own mind', that part of the mind's activity 'has been withdrawn from your knowledge and from the command [*Herrschaft*] of your will'.[44] Ironically, then, the assertion of mastery over the external world attempted by scientific enquiry undermines itself at each of these significant breakthroughs.

In an essay that discusses these blows, Simon Glendinning notes how the concept of 'Man' – tied up as it is with a Graeco-European identity founded on reason and science – is traumatized by the very thing that was used to justify its centrality in the first place:

> Europeans will have been *vexed* by the very achievements that made them great, that made them so sure they were at the centre of the centre. The world constructed in the name of a certain Greco-European memory, a Greco-Romano-Christian memory, the world that gave itself 'Man' as the name of its own Being, that world is also the site of offences and injuries that have cumulatively chipped away at that *construction*, making of that world, at the same time, the site of its *deconstruction*. There where a certain conception of the humanity of man flourished there also began a movement of its decay.[45]

Scientific knowledge is the ground for Man's centrality, dominion and rationality, whilst simultaneously coming to demonstrate that such notions do not hold up to deep scrutiny. And yet, foundational though this ontological decay may be, a century has passed since Freud wrote of these blows, and it seems the 'naïve self-love of Man' has proved itself extremely resilient, demonstrating a capability for repression that allows it to go on functioning – not by denying the truth of the discoveries but by failing to take them into account. The construction of 'Man' (and I retain the gendered term, for the construction itself operated from and maintained that same gender bias) and the ideologies and actions it facilitates still stand strong and powerful in the worlds of politics, economics and law, if not quite so much in philosophy and science – and unfortunately it is not the latter two which shape the way the majority of the human race relates to the world. While we may accept the post-Copernican view that the earth is not the centre of the physical universe, 'Man' remains at the centre of a conceptual universe which forecloses or ignores the rights of non-human or non-living entities and revolves (*versus*) only around our one (*uni-*) 'human' way of being.

While many educated people intellectually accept the Darwinian realization that *Homo sapiens* evolved as part of a vast and incalculable evolutionary tree, the implications of this fundamental interconnectedness have not transformed humanity's relationship with the environment and other living species in the way that one might hope or expect. Indeed, there remains the fact that one of the most powerful countries in the world continues to permit schools to teach evolution as a 'controversial theory' alongside Creationism – the latter being a narrative which stands in stark contrast to both scientific and animistic worldviews, and which is propounded to the detriment of both. The work of psychoanalysis commands even less respect: most humans continue to live and act as if they are the agents of a purely conscious will, while popular culture dismisses or ridicules Freud's work through the reductive metonymy of the 'Oedipus complex' or 'penis envy' (though Freud might have seen this coming when he said that in 'emphasizing the unconscious in mental life we have conjured up the most evil spirits of criticism against psycho-analysis').[46] The truly post-Freudian ethical, juridical and political systems that Derrida called for in *Without Alibi* continue to remain a far cry from the reality of these institutions.[47] In short, the 'naïve self-love of Man' remains operationally intact and continues to define the dominant ideological structures of our political and economic systems.

Anthropogenic climate change, I argue, poses the fourth and final blow to pathological human narcissism: it is the destruction of ecology by the so-called economy, the societal dependence on monetary growth rendering impotent the reciprocally generative processes upon which life depends and thereby bringing the extinction of the human species – along with that of millions of other species – into the horizon of imminent possibility. It can also be read as a direct result of our failure to take into account the previous three blows. These were scientific discoveries that stood testament to humankind's power of reason whilst simultaneously decentring that reason. Climate change, however, whilst being inadvertently caused by the actions of human beings, is a blow that issues *from the earth itself*: it is the animism of a complex of living and non-living matter into an agency or force that works to both materially and philosophically destabilize the ground upon which we stand.

Readers of Derrida's *Specters of Marx* will remember that a fourth blow has already been named there: the trauma of the ideology and legacy of Marxism. I do not entirely discount this claim but rather aim to show that climate change is the inevitable reverberation of what Derrida describes as the fourth blow. This blow, he writes, is distinct from the previous three in its severity and its movement; it is the 'deepest wound' as it 'accumulates and gathers together the other three':

> It carries beyond them by carrying them out, just as it bears the name of Marx by exceeding it infinitely. The century of 'Marxism' will have been that of the techno-scientific and effective decentring of the earth, of geopolitics, of the *anthropos* in its onto-theological identity or its genetic properties, of the *ego cogito* – and of the very concept of narcissism.[48]

Yes, but … how is it that these movements of decentring happened but also, and in a very real sense, *did not happen*? While the scientific discoveries of the twentieth century could or should have been the end of the very possibility of anthropocentrism (at least in its most crude or destructive manifestations), it was nevertheless a century in which the centrality of the *anthropos* (that is to say, the Graeco-European, scientifically and rationally minded, Christian, neoliberal, capitalist, white, male *anthropos* – and all of these categories are of course allied) continued to determine and justify our relation to the earth, to other species and to each other – the century in which, perhaps, Man became a master of doublethink, where morality and (in)justice became ever more entangled with power relations and the economic imperative of capitalist expansion gained rather than lost force (as, indeed, its structure demands). The very possibility of this doublethink has to do, I suggest, with what Derrida calls the real trauma of the Marxist *coup*, which lies 'in the body of its history and in the history of its concept',[49] which is to say in the force of its oppositional yet inseparable aspects, both the messianic communist dream and the horrors of totalitarian reality, and how this inconsonant history continues to reverberate today. Glendinning writes,

> What happens when we attempt to realize the Marxist dream of creating an ideal form of social life for 'Man' (and of course that dream was never only a Marxist dream – it is *the* dream of 'the end of Man' in the discourse of Europe's modernity), what happens when we attempt to realize, through our own hands, conditions of actual equality in a classless society, what happens is: disaster, the horror of the history of the totalitarian world.[50]

It is this history that contributes to the ongoing repression of the previous traumas that otherwise should or could have decentred the concept of Man. The possibility of Man as the protagonist of a progressive history is swept away by the event that was proclaimed to be not just a milestone but also the very pinnacle of that progression. The trauma undoes not only the ideals of equality and emancipation it should have heralded but also their credibility: communism becomes a dirty word, and capitalism – the force that created the inequality and alienation which Marx saw as so unsustainable and only ending in inevitable revolution – becomes itself inevitable, ingrained in the common consciousness as the only possible system, lauded as the end of history. Reading the passage from Glendinning quoted above, I cannot help but note how up until the colon there seems to be a question mark on the horizon, the promise of a promise, an open hope for this ideal dream, but the question never comes because we all know the answer, and there is no use today in asking questions about socialist ideals.

To live in a world dominated by, as Glendinning remarks, 'those who would prefer to think that it is all over for emancipation and progress', makes it feel as though we are 'lost today in a way that can seem beyond any hope'.[51] Indeed, the thought of such a world inspires an immense sadness. Derrida reminds us that the *idea* of democracy – the 'emancipatory promise' of a messianic justice to come – remains intact, yet it stands ever more at odds with 'its current concept and from its determined predicates today'.[52] This has to do with the unforgiveable levels of inequality allowed to exist and increase worldwide. Calling for a 'new international', in a passage it is necessary to quote at length, Derrida writes of

> the limits of a discourse on human rights that will remain inadequate, sometimes hypocritical, and in any case formalistic and inconsistent with itself as long as the law of the market, the 'foreign debt,' the inequality of techno-scientific, military, and economic development maintain an effective inequality as monstrous as that which prevails today, to a greater extent than ever in the history of humanity. For it must be cried out, at a time when some have the audacity to neo-evangelize in the name of the ideal of a liberal democracy that has finally realized itself as the ideal of human history: never have violence, inequality, exclusion, famine, and thus economic oppression affected as many human beings in the history of the earth and humanity. Instead of singing the advent of the ideal of liberal democracy and of the capitalist market in the euphoria of the end of history, instead of celebrating the 'end of ideologies' and the end of the great emancipatory discourses, let us never neglect this obvious macroscopic fact, made up of innumerable singular sites of suffering: no degree of progress allows one to ignore that never before, in absolute figures, never have so many men, women, and children been subjugated, starved, or exterminated on the earth. (And provisionally, but with regret, we must leave aside here the nevertheless indissociable question of what is becoming of so-called 'animal'

life, the life and existence of 'animals' in this history. This question has always been a serious one, but it will become massively unavoidable.)[53]

Specters of Marx speaks to us from nearly three decades ago, but each point that Derrida makes continues to resonate in a world that, under the current economic system, can only continue to become more and more unequal. In fact, when we read this passage again in this time of catastrophic climate change, the terms take on new depths of meaning: violence, inequality, exclusion, famine, economic oppression, innumerable singular sites of suffering, subjugation, starvation, extermination – these are words fed and nurtured by neoliberal capitalism and grown monstrous in the age of climate change, as our governments and the corporations to which they answer consistently choose profit over the rights of humans and other living beings. Today, that parenthetical animal question can no longer be left aside.

It has been argued that to blame the climate crisis on capitalism is to oversimplify things. Clark notes how 'the processes culminating in the Anthropocene include events that predate the advent of capitalism, primarily the invention of agriculture, deforestation and the eradication over centuries of large mammals in all continents beyond Africa as humanity expanded across the globe', while Trexler comments that 'climate criticism's reflexive Marxism suffers from … grave shortcomings', 'obscur[ing] the fact that other economic structures – particularly Russian oligarchy, Chinese communism, and Middle Eastern monarchies – have had abysmal environmental records and produce tremendous quantities of greenhouse gases'.[54] Clark and Trexler both make points that are important to keep in mind but which do not exonerate capitalism in the way they imply. Clark is right to note that the geological markers of the human species predate capitalism, but it is only in the age of capitalism that human effects on the planet have accumulated enough force to change the entire climate. Meanwhile, Trexler's claim that there are 'other economic structures' that 'produce tremendous quantities of greenhouse gases' effaces the extent to which the 'abysmal environmental records' of these other structures are themselves implicated in global neoliberal capitalism. Post-Soviet Russia may not have had the most successful free market, but that does not mean that it should not now be considered a capitalist nation; much of China's manufacturing industry (and the emissions it produces) feeds the capitalism of the rest of the world; and Middle Eastern oil has accounted for a quarter of global oil supplies. None of these nations, that is to say, are entirely separable from the global capitalist economy. Capitalism is not a simple or easy culprit, but its role in the climate crisis should not be downplayed. Above all else, it is surely the idol of profit that has handicapped any attempts to reduce emissions, whether through corporate-sponsored misinformation programs (such as that produced by the Heartland Institute), through governmental interests or through the culture of consumerism which creates such an effective means of distracting citizens.

The catastrophe of anthropogenic climate change is the final and fullest reverberation, the ongoing apocalypse, of everything that is invoked under the name of Marxism and its history: the original injustice of the capitalist mechanism, the contradiction between a finite planet and the principle of infinite growth, the inequalities produced, maintained, exacerbated and justified, the dream of an equal world and the horror of its calamitous realization, and the consequential fortification of the capitalist system into a 'best possible world' – for the 1%. This fourth blow accumulates and gathers together the previous three in ways this book will elaborate, but for now let us recognize that its absolute trauma lies in the fact that it comes *at* the human from *beyond* the human, it comes *from the earth itself*. It is the Anthropocene reading us.

This is the uncanniness and the *unheimlichkeit* of climate change, where we learn all at once that, on the one hand, everything is interconnected in the profoundest of ways and that we are inextricably a part of the nature we have always tried to subjugate, and, on the other hand, that our home is not necessarily a home *for us*, and that it never has been. It is about knowing something that we should have known all along, about the undoing of all we thought we knew (the negation, so to say, of our putative 'canniness') and the becoming unhomely (*unheimlich*) of the home. It poses an absolute threat, yet one that cannot be pinned down, fenced off or eradicated.

The double apocalypse of climate change brings to the fore both the social injustices upon which our economy has been built and the absolute limitations of an extractive relationship with the planet (both revelations were, as I shall go on to explain, identified by Marx). To be clear, the former has to do with the notion of the 'monstrous' inequalities that Derrida invokes in the passage quoted above. It is the people who live in the poorest parts of the world, those with the least 'techno-scientific, military, and economic development' (which all boils down to a lack of accumulated capital), who are on the front lines of climate change. In a cruel irony, it is less economically developed parts of the world that tend to lie in regions that are currently being hit hardest by extreme weather (though, of course, the extreme weather has not been exclusively hitting these places). Not only are such nations less prepared for disasters (which means that the effects tend to be worse) but they also lack the money to look after their people or to repair the damage done. They cannot afford, when crops fail, to import food from elsewhere. Further, it has always been poor areas that have been the essential sacrifice zones, the out-of-sight sites of suffering so necessary to the economies of the developed world. As Naomi Klein notes, sacrifice zones are particular areas of land or water, and particular sections of humanity, that matter little enough to make 'poisoning in the name of progress somehow acceptable'.[55] These are the places that we raze and burn, mine and pollute: the human beings and other species that we poison, starve, kill and forget – all the while proclaiming that this neoliberal capitalist free market economy is creating a better world for all. Such violence is what Rob Nixon calls 'slow violence': a violence dispersed over space and time to such an extent that 'the casualties incurred typically pass untallied and unremembered', and the perpetrators escape all culpability.[56] Capitalism has always operated via such violence (in, for example, the delayed effects of poor working conditions and in unequal access to education and healthcare), but climate change multiplies its logic, causing widespread and long-term suffering devoid of clearly assignable blame. Derrida speaks of the '*sacrificial* structure' of Western philosophical discourses and culture that includes 'a place left open ... for a noncriminal putting to death'.[57] He is referring to the putting-to-death which is not classed as murder because it takes non-human life: namely, the meat industry (and we will return to this in the third chapter of this book). This sacrificial structure is also inherent to capitalism in its reliance on sacrifice zones – both spatially and temporally dispersed – to facilitate profit, as it multiplies the deaths (or, indeed, extinctions) of innumerable species of non-human life and sanctions the 'noncriminal putting-to-death' – direct or indirect – of humans.[58] As Wallace-Wells notes, the death toll of 'air pollution alone' is already 'at least seven million deaths' per year, equivalent to 'an annual Holocaust'.[59]

The existence of sacrifice zones brings me to the second revelation of the double apocalypse of climate change: that we live on a finite earth and we always have done. Now that conventional fossil fuel reserves are nearing depletion, the industry is forced (by the capitalist structure that demands infinite growth) to find new ways to get at fossil fuels in places previously untapped, notably in the fracking boom. Suddenly the dangerous side effects of extraction are happening where we ('we', the developed world, 'we' who owe that development to innumerable sacrifice zones past and present all over the world) can see and feel them. In the communities close to fracking sites in the United States, not only have water sources been poisoned (as has been widely reported), but there has also been greatly increased incidence of small earthquakes, and, perhaps more seriously, there has been an increase in miscarriages, hysterectomies and birth defects – an incursion on the future before it comes.[60] The furore around fracking has brought to light not only the horror of the lethal effects of an industry our governments are blindly expanding but also the horror of the fact that it is only when the toxic destruction of the extractive industries encroaches into places presumed sacrosanct that the majority of people in the developed world begin to question them at all ('not in *my* backyard'). What climate change reveals to us, then, is that the heretofore assumed and relied upon *distance* of sacrifice zones (rendering them both discreet and discrete) – morally reprehensible though this is – is a delusion: in fact, we have been treating the entire planet as a sacrifice zone all along. As Clark writes, our economy has long operated upon 'the false supposition of an infinite earth, an inexhaustible externality in both space and time', assuming that 'natural resources (air, water, soil, and tolerable weather) are free gifts' and that 'future time and the terrestrial space can act as bottomless repositories for waste or for issues that thinking wishes to avoid'.[61] Yet the by-products of the irresponsibility and greed of the developed world have been accumulating in the atmosphere faster than they can be absorbed, and global warming reveals how irrefutably this 'supposition of an infinite earth' is false: 'the distance is closing, and soon enough no one will be safe from the sorrow of ecocide', writes Klein.[62]

A century and a half ago, Marx recognized the fundamental contradiction between an economic system that demands constant expansion and the limited earthly resources upon which it draws. Writing at a time when, to most people, the planet would have still seemed infinite in its capacity to provide the raw materials for the magical dance of commodities, and infinite in its capacity to subsume the waste created in the process, Marx nevertheless perceived an 'irreparable rift' in the metabolic relation between man and his environment, which was based upon 'the exploitation and the squandering of the powers of the earth'.[63] Capitalism operates, as Marx identified, by 'simultaneously undermining the original sources of all wealth – the soil [*Erde*, earth] and the worker'.[64] For Marx, it was to be the worker who would inevitably take offence at this inequitable structure and revolt. Yet there are certain self-protective mechanisms of the capitalist system which have prevented things from playing out in the way Marx assumed they must. These mechanisms include:

(1) the literal and psychological distancing of producers from consumers;
(2) the ideological ties between wealth and status that render certain sections of humanity inhuman enough to be an effectively disposable labour force,

whilst other sections – those in the 'middle' that are duped into thinking they are better off, and those at the top that reap the benefits of such a system – either do not see or do not care;

(3) the increased availability of commodities that would once have been markers of high wealth (such as laptops, smartphones and fast fashion), which works to reduce some visible signs of inequality and thereby coerce those with least economic power into supporting the very system which does so little for them;

(4) the animistic thinking which endows 'corporations' with legal rights and status,[65] and the 'market' with freedom and agency;[66] and

(5) the inherent tendency of capital and its concomitant power to exponentially accumulate and thereby facilitate the reinforcement of the ideology which made such accumulation possible in the first place (for example, in the mutually supportive relationship – the so-called revolving door – between corporations and the media).

Marx's conviction that a workers' revolution would be inevitable was destined – in its fatal underestimation of the self-propagating power of capital – to prove false. I wonder if he ever dreamed that it would be the soil – *the earth itself* – that would revolt?

Such a question cannot be dismissed as hyperbole. As Wallace-Wells describes in *The Uninhabitable Earth*, it is no longer only the case that capitalism is one of the main drivers of the climate crisis; rather, capitalism is itself now 'endangered' by climate.[67] Not only does climate change inhibit the growth essential to the capitalist system, 'producing a global economic stagnation that will play, in some areas, like a breathtaking and permanent recession', but it will also make salient 'an increasingly stark income inequality' that will push the self-protective mechanisms I listed above into collapse.[68] And so, Wallace-Wells suggests, for 'the religion of free trade as a just and even perfect social system … a major reformation is coming'.[69]

Coming to life

It is time to engage with the vital and, now more than ever, 'massively unavoidable' question of the animal: the question of life itself. Derrida writes that 'of the three wounds to anthropic narcissism, the one Freud indicates with the name Darwin seems more intolerable than the one he has signed himself'.[70] This is because the 'essential opposition of man to animal – or rather to animality, to a univocal, homogeneous, obscurantist concept of animality', is the means by which Man defines himself.[71] When there is no longer any rigorous distinction between human beings and other animals, the very concept of 'Man' is called into question – for if we subtract the 'not-animal' from its definition, what is left? One cannot, as Darwin recognized, definitively demarcate between species: they are all part of the same vast and incalculable family tree.[72] Species distinctions do, of course, prevent interbreeding and are useful to humans in classification and conservation efforts. But it is worth remembering that no one generational difference – including that which became the difference between species – would have been any greater than that between you and your parents. And the implications go even further than that. If we were to follow evolution back far enough, at some point, that infinitesimal difference between generations would be the difference between life and what preceded it: non-living, 'inanimate' matter.

Wills notes that 'prior to knowing what living means ... there is an encounter with the nonliving, with what we might call, presuming to know what *animate* means, the in- or non-animate'.[73] If we recognize that at some time in the murk of the distant past, life emerged out of non-living matter – its 'chemically active, but inorganic, origin' – we must also recognize that the animate is persistently (and paradoxically) animated by the inanimate, and the concept of 'life' therefore, cannot be reduced to the organic.[74] Or as biologist Nick Lane puts it: 'Plainly there is a *continuum* between non-living and living, and it is pointless to try to draw a line across it.'[75] There is more to life, or more life, than the living. Such a realization – given violent force by the event of climate change – stretches that 'animal' question rather wider. Derrida writes,

> Beyond the edge of the *so-called* human, beyond it but by no means on a single opposing side, rather than 'The Animal' or 'Animal Life' there is already a heterogeneous multiplicity of the living, or more precisely (since to say 'the living' is already to say too much or not enough), a multiplicity of organizations of relations between living and dead, relations of organization or lack of organization among realms that are more and more difficult to dissociate by means of the figures of the organic and inorganic, of life and/or death. These relations are at once intertwined and abyssal, and they can never be totally objectified. They do not leave room for any simple exteriority of one term with respect to another.[76]

Given the 'intertwined and abyssal' relations between human and non-human, living and non-living, animate and inanimate – relations that are becoming all the more salient in the Anthropocene – an ontology that operates outside of or beyond such distinctions becomes increasingly necessary: a new theory, that is to say, of animism.

Rethinking animism

The word 'animism' has often been used to refer to primitive belief systems that ascribe life, soul or spirit to the inanimate, a designation which originates from nineteenth-century anthropologist E. B. Tylor. As the popular conception of his work has it, the animist ontology rests upon a fundamental misunderstanding of the world: an inability to discern distinctions between 'subjective and objective, between imagination and reality'.[77] Historically, then, animism has been posited as a worldview that is progressively superseded by the rationality and objectivity of modern science. As Caroline Rooney writes in *African Literature, Animism and Politics*, it has become 'a rather unfashionable term because of the ethnocentric, universalizing and ill-informed ways in which it has been used. It belongs to the repertoire of terms that have aimed to distinguish between primitive and modern thought'.[78] She goes on to suggest that the idea of animism within 'Western intellectual culture' entails 'a double disavowal: an anti-naturalism that seeks to deny that all human beings are a part of nature; and a certain hyper-materialism that seeks to deny the vitality or dynamism of matter. Simply, it is an insistence on the dualisms of spirit/body, mind/matter, energy/mass, man/nature, human/animal, and so on'.[79] We should also add the animate/inanimate dualism to this list.

Latour, in *Facing Gaia*, similarly figures the disavowal of animism as a 'movement of deanimation', born of a very precise agenda:

> Although the official philosophy of science takes the ... movement of deanimation as the only important and rational one, the opposite is true: animation is the essential phenomenon; and deanimation is the superficial, auxiliary, polemical, and often defensive phenomenon. One of the great enigmas of Western history is not that 'there are still people naïve enough to believe in animism,' but that many people still hold the rather naïve belief in a supposedly deanimated 'material world'. And this is the case at the very moment when scientists are multiplying the agencies in which they – and we – are more and more implicated every day.[80]

The deanimation of matter brought about by scientific knowledge enables and defends the (illusory) supposition that the earth is a passive ground and that agency is only attributable to humans. Ironically, it is this same scientific tradition that today – in light of global warming – reveals such deanimation to be the rather more 'naïve' belief. For who could continue to posit human beings as separate from 'nature' at a time when the extinction of our own species occupies a possible horizon? Who could continue to deny the vitality or dynamism of matter at a time when, in innumerable ways, the planet is not only responding to the way we live but is also demanding that we respond in turn, demanding, in short, a dialogue? It is in the face of this crisis that animism acquires a new significance, in the experience of a time in which the deconstruction of anthropocentrism issues from the planet itself. To understand the full implications of this fourth blow to human narcissism would also be to realize that it represents no less of an autoimmune movement than the previous three: there has just been an expansive generalization of the *auto*, from 'Man', 'humanity' or 'the human' to include all life (and non-life) on earth – another reason why the Darwinian blow might be the 'more intolerable' of the three Freud named.[81] As Tom Cohen writes, 'the swarming logics of climate change arrive to deconstruct the artefactual real of human modernity *as if* from without (though this arrival discloses that there was no "outside" as such)'.[82]

Radical animism: Animism of roots and the roots of animism

The two words that I am using to guide my thinking here – 'animism' and 'radical' – perhaps do not immediately convey to you all the associations that I now have in mind, so they will bear a little digging, in order to unearth some of the intricacies that may have been buried or forgotten. In what follows, I will trace their etymologies and cultural histories, before suggesting how a radical animism of literature might be thought in the context of contemporary environmental crises.

The word 'radical' (from the Latin *radix*, 'root') is today most often used to describe revolutionary (and especially left-wing) politics, or ideas that are progressive, unorthodox or innovative, that are characterized by 'independence of or departure from what is usual or traditional' (*OED*). This sense comes from the notion of changing things from the very root: deep changes rather than superficial or surface ones. I have no wish to distance myself from these associations, and, indeed, I believe the challenge of climate change calls for nothing less than such a radical – in the sense of revolutionary or innovative – response. However, the other meanings of the word are equally important to my thinking. According to the *OED*, 'radical' has also carried the following associations: 'fundamental to or inherent in the natural processes of life, vital'; 'inherent in the nature or essence of a person or thing'; 'relating to or forming the root, basis, or foundation of something; original, primary'; 'of, belonging to, or relating to the root of a word'; 'esp. of change or action: going to the root or origin; touching upon or affecting what is essential and fundamental; thorough, far-reaching.' Further, a root is that part of a plant that remains underground even if the top has been extirpated; it stays in the ground, stays grounded, an organic anchor against the elements. It is sustenance, nourishing both the plant that grows out of it and the animals that eat it. The radical animism that I am conceptualizing, then, would not only entail a revolution in political, economic and social thinking but also has very much to do with life and the living, with a concept of life that is not reducible to organic matter. It looks for what might be dormant underground, or under the grounds of reason. It entails a thinking of the connection to that which nourishes living beings, a 'literal' and 'metaphoric' – or material and conceptual – coming 'down to earth' (and an understanding that the two cannot be rigorously distinguished), as well as an appreciation of *growth* in ecological instead of economic terms. All of this also has to do with language, with the roots of words not only in the sense of etymological origins but also as what takes root and grows in the mind, and, finally, with the life – or animism – of letters.

The etymology of 'animism' is perhaps less deeply buried, though its historical usage has also diverged from its 'literal' meaning. It comes from the Latin root *anima*, meaning air, breath, life, soul, spirit – which is also, of course, the basis of the words 'animal', 'animate' and their derivatives. Etymologically, then, the physical actions of living and breathing are, at root, linked to what has often been thought of as the 'metaphysical' notions of soul and spirit. The latter, with its associations of what is incorporeal, immaterial or even supernatural comes from the Latin *spīritus*, 'breathing' or 'breath', thus folding the metaphysical back into the physical. These ties are not exclusive to Latin-derived languages but can be found all over the world: the Sanskrit *atman* ('soul', 'spirit', 'breath', 'sun', 'fire'); the Mohawk *atouritz* ('soul') and *atourion* ('to breathe'); the Chinese *ch'i* ('breath', the vital universal energy in the air); the Romani *dūk* ('breath', 'spirit', 'ghost'); the Aztec *ehekatl* ('wind', 'shadow', 'soul'); the Tibetan *lung* ('wind', 'animating principle'); the Javanese *ñawa* ('breath', 'life', 'soul'); the Hebrew *nephesh* ('breath', 'life', 'soul', 'mind', 'animal'); the Cree *orenda* ('wind', 'animating principle'); the Netela *piuts* ('life', 'breath', 'soul'); the Greek *psyche* ('breath', 'soul'); the Arabic *ruh* ('breath', 'spirit'); the Inuit *silla* ('air', 'wind', 'world', 'mind'); and the West

Australian *waug* ('breath', 'spirit', 'soul').[83] The widespread connection and interdependence of such concepts speaks of a bond that occurs underground, before or beyond its various linguistic emergences, as if what animates 'animism' is pre- or extralinguistic.

Above, I noted that the term 'anima' binds together the material and spiritual through its semantic linking of breath and soul. While some might baulk at any talk of 'spirituality' – a notion that is, after all, both rather vague and fatally subjective – there is also a way in which we can understand anima – in the sense of 'breath' – as the site of a concrete and empirically verifiable bond between living and non-living, between organisms and the so-called environment, and between the visible and invisible. As Elizabeth Povinelli notes in *Geontologies*, the apparently 'internal' membranes of human lungs in fact directly interface with a 'massive biotic assemblage ... including green plants, photosynthetic bacteria, nonsulfur purple bacteria, hydrogen, sulfur and iron bacteria, [other] animals, and microbes' – interactions which are responsible for 'the metabolism of the planetary carbon cycle'.[84] Breath, respiration or gaseous exchange constitutes the invisible – but nonetheless material and essential – relations between living and non-living things that make the planet what it is. As such, we might conceive of animism's privileging of the invisible and intangible as a way of recognizing the power and necessity of this planetary intra-activity in producing the biosphere in which we are enmeshed.

In the early eighteenth century, the word 'animism' was used in Latin by the German chemist and physician Georg Ernst Stahl to name the way that a living thing conserves itself against the dissolution and decay to which a dead body succumbs. It was, for him, a way of naming what was peculiar about organic living matter. His conception of *anima*, as Lester King writes, 'dealt not with the "soul" of religion but with properties, forces, or entities in the body', the 'directing force' that used the body as its 'instrument', and that was the cause of its motion.[85] This animism – or vitalism, as it was also known – swiftly found itself standing in opposition to a materialism that dismissed the notion that there is anything inherently different in organic matter, and instead argued that life and all its characteristics are merely the operations of the inherent properties of physical matter. Ironically, it is this materialist refusal of a fundamental distinction between living and non-living matter that aligns with what I am calling radical animism, where both living and nonliving things are animated or alive. Indeed, Tylor's 'primitive' forms of animism (as I discuss below) conceive of spirit as an 'ethereality, or vaporous materiality', and, he writes, 'the later metaphysical notion of immateriality could scarcely have conveyed any meaning to a savage'.[86]

Animism is, then, a kind of materialism – or, as Eduardo Viveiros de Castro comments, 'animism is the only *sensible* version of materialism'.[87]

A radical animism of literature extends this animistic materialism to the material body of texts. Just as there is something in the material arrangement of the organic body that gives it a living force greater than the sum of its parts, conserving itself against the decay to which it would otherwise yield, the animism of text turns the iterations of particular letters and words into a thing that gives rise to *meanings* – meanings that might be just as subject to birth, growth, reproduction, death and decay as their organic counterparts.

I will turn now to the cultural history of animism, to trace the movement from its etymological roots to the more derogatory associations it later inspired: its transformation from a word about *life*, to the ethnocentric and othering force of its later incarnations. Three key agents in this transformation were E. B. Tylor, James Frazer and Sigmund Freud, each of whom – as I will show – had a more nuanced and ambivalent conception of animism than the popular understanding of their work would have it. In what follows, I briefly sketch these discrepancies and show how a certain literary animism – the animism of text – might work to disturb the ways in which their work is understood today.

E. B. Tylor

In 1866, in an article on 'The Religion of Savages', Tylor adopted Stahl's word 'animism' to refer to the 'primitive thought' 'which endows the phenomena of nature with personal life' – thereby significantly transforming its sense.[88] (Ironically, given the widespread adoption of his sense of the word, this was not Tylor's first choice; he would have preferred 'spiritualism' but for its associations with 'a particular modern sect', as he explains in his later work, *Primitive Culture*.[89]) Tylor describes the 'early and savage opinion which sees both in waking and sleeping thought ... the impalpable forms, shades, souls, ghosts, or phantoms, not of men and beasts alone, but of trees and clouds, rocks and rivers, clothes and tools and weapons'.[90] Animism for Tylor is a generalized spirituality, which ascribes a soul or agency to both living and non-living things and treats them accordingly: 'what we call inanimate objects – rivers, stones, trees, weapons, and so forth – are treated as living intelligent beings, talked to, propitiated, punished for the harm they do'.[91] Tylor's 'we' here implicitly refers to a Western, enlightened, rational culture in distinct opposition to the 'primitive' cultures about which he writes. He concludes 'The Religion of Savages' as follows:

> Savages are exceedingly ignorant as regards both physical and moral knowledge; want of discipline makes their opinions crude and their action ineffective in a surprising degree; and the tyranny of tradition at every step imposes upon them thoughts and customs which have been inherited from a different stage of culture, and thus have lost a reasonableness which we may often see them to have possessed in their first origin. Judged by our ordinary modern standard of knowledge, which is at any rate a high one as compared with theirs, much of what they believe to be true, must be set down as false. But to be false, is not the same as to be motiveless. The tendency of research in this as yet little worked field is indeed to show more and more throughout the life of the lower races reasonable motives of opinion, and practical purposes of action, or at least the influence of ancestral tradition which once had itself a like intelligible basis.[92]

While the Victorian assumptions upon which this passage is based now read as patronizing and ethnocentric, Tylor is, as Martin Stringer notes, 'keen to emphasize that the human mind is the same throughout the world irrespective of the stage of social evolution reached by any one society' and sees the differences in progression to be a result of different levels of education.[93] Tylor's notion of progression, that is to say, is not genetic but *cultural* – and is based upon assumptions that continue to linger today in the language that still opposes the 'primal' (literally, 'first') to the 'civilized', and that still ranks certain forms of knowledge above others. Though the derogatory associations of the term 'animism' have often been attributed to Tylor, such all-out detraction was not, as Stringer shows, really his project.[94] While he does establish a firm divide between 'our ordinary modern standard of knowledge' and the 'ignorant' and 'crude' beliefs of 'savages', he also concedes the 'reasonable motives' and 'practical purposes' of their opinions. Indeed, Tylor's work demonstrates an appreciation for animistic worldviews that is often overlooked.

And, I ask, is it not the case that in this age of climate chaos, in which everything is in transformation, that some of Tylor's remarks could apply to current political practices? Despite the decades that we have been trying to 'do something' about global warming (the United Nations Framework Convention for Climate Change (UNFCCC) was formed in 1992), our action has been – to borrow Tylor's phrase – 'ineffective in a surprising degree'. As Klein notes, the UNFCCC has 'not only failed to make progress', 'it has overseen a process of virtually uninterrupted backsliding'.[95] Likewise, the capitalist model of infinite extraction and infinite expansion, shown to be untenable on a finite planet, could be read as 'thoughts and customs which have been inherited from a different stage of culture, and thus have lost a reasonableness' which they may 'have possessed in their first origin'. 'But,' as Tylor continues, 'to be false, is not the same as to be motiveless': and what stronger motivation is there today than the inhuman and unstoppable force of the market?

Indeed, the enduring power of 'free market capitalism' provides clear evidence for animistic thinking in the modern world. Yuval Noah Harari notes how entities such as the market – along with 'gods, nations and corporations' – do not exist as part of the real, sensuous world but are instead just 'imagined realities': and these imagined realities nevertheless wield an immense power dependent only upon our shared belief in them.[96] He notes how the very word 'corporation' is 'ironic, because the term derives from "corpus" ("body" in Latin) – the one thing these corporations lack. Despite their having no real bodies, the American legal system treats corporations as legal persons, as if they were flesh-and-blood human beings.'[97] They are less tangible than the 'trees and clouds, rocks and rivers' that Tylor's animists endow with personhood, and yet they are often more powerful. As Povinelli puts it, 'capitalists can be said to be the purest of the Animists' as 'nothing is inherently inert, everything is vital from the point of view of capitalization, and anything can become something more with the right innovative angle'.[98] Indeed, it is the animistic power of capitalism that accounts in a large part for the lack of political will behind meaningful response to climate change. As has often been noted, it is no longer a technological lack that is preventing the transition to a zero-carbon economy.[99]

Let us return to Tylor. In 1871, he went on to publish his research in a two-volume book, *Primitive Culture*, in which he describes, using a plethora of examples from around the world, the progressive evolution of 'philosophical speculation from savage to cultured thought' and concludes that 'the conception of the human soul is, as to its most essential nature, continuous from the philosophy of the savage thinker to that of the modern professor of theology'.[100] While firmly establishing a hierarchical framework between the 'lower', 'crude' beliefs of savages and the 'higher', refined beliefs of civilization, the notion of an evolution of thought also recognizes a *continuity* between the two. Tylor suggests that the 'failure' of rationality ascribed to animistic belief systems continues to form the basis of modern religion in civilized society:

> The animism of savages stands for and by itself; it explains its own origin. The animism of civilized men, while more appropriate to advanced knowledge, is in great measure only explicable as a developed product of the older and ruder system. It is the doctrines and rites of the lower races which are, according to their philosophy, results of point-blank natural evidence and acts of straightforward

practical purpose. It is the doctrines and rites of the higher races which show survival of the old in the midst of the new. ... Among races within the limits of savagery, the general doctrine of souls is found worked out with remarkable breadth and consistency. ... Thenceforth, as we explore human thought onward from savage into barbarian and civilized life, we find a state of theory more conformed to positive science, but in itself less complete and consistent. Far on into civilization, men still act as though in some half-meant way they believed in souls or ghosts of objects, while nevertheless their knowledge of physical science is beyond so crude a philosophy.[101]

In the light of modern science, Tylor argues, an animistic system is revealed to be, while both consistent and practical, categorically false: 'the savage or barbarian has never learnt to make that rigid distinction between subjective and objective, between imagination and reality,' which results from 'scientific education'.[102] But modern religion, as he makes clear in the passage above, remains guilty of the same category error, clinging to the idea of a human soul or an incorporeal spirit (God, for example) within a civilization that has (or at least *should* have) abandoned such notions. Animistic beliefs persist, that is to say, throughout human culture, even if they do not go by that name.

James Frazer

The next significant thinker to have used and shaped the term 'animism' was James Frazer in *The Golden Bough*. First published in 1890, this work follows Tylor in assuming an evolutionary progression of human thought, which Frazer divides into three stages: magic, religion and science. Robin Horton, in *Patterns of Thought in Africa and the West*, notes how Frazer's 'three-stage scheme of intellectual evolution' is defective in the following ways (and these criticisms could also be levelled at Tylor): first, 'there is no evidence for an initial phase of human thought dominated by magic and devoid of religion'; second, the supposed 'evolution' does not really progress with any regularity (religion is actually more logically inconsistent than magic, so the 'progression' appears to take a step backwards at the second stage); and third, it relies on an implicit 'racial/biological determinism' to justify why different groups are at different stages in the system.[103] However, as with Tylor, there seems to be beneath the ethnocentric veneer an undercurrent which recognizes the ingeniousness and utility of the systems of thought under discussion, which, Frazer concedes, cannot be fully differentiated from modern science, 'if under science we may include those simple truths, drawn from observation of nature, of which men in all ages have possessed a store'.[104] As Rooney writes, 'Frazer's explicit evolutionary ethnocentrism may be deconstructed by the openmindedness implicit in what he says'.[105]

Frazer's conclusion demonstrates a hesitation to accept modern science as an absolute or final truth, while also making frequent recourse to metaphor (that is, employing a linguistic animism even as he suggests that such magic has been supplanted). When he suggests that 'after groping about in the dark for countless ages, man has hit upon a clue to the labyrinth, a golden key that opens many locks in the treasury of nature', he retains the rather problematic assumption that 'nature' is a treasury to be unlocked by human beings and that science is the key – but he *also* recognizes that if there is such thing as an evolution of thought, it can, by definition, never be 'finished':

> The history of thought should warn us against concluding that because the scientific theory of the world is the best that has yet been formulated, it is necessarily complete and final. We must remember that at bottom the generalizations of science or, in common parlance, the laws of nature are merely hypotheses devised to explain that ever-shifting phantasmagoria of thought which we dignify with the high-sounding names of the world and the universe. In the last analysis magic, religion, and science are nothing but theories of thought; and as science has supplanted its predecessors, so it may hereafter be itself superseded by some more perfect hypothesis, perhaps by some totally different way of looking at the phenomena – of registering the shadows on the screen – of which we in this generation can form no idea. The advance of knowledge is an infinite progression towards a goal that for ever recedes. (932)

The future of thought cannot be foretold, but Frazer remains open to 'some totally different way of looking at the phenomena', which will once again redefine humanity's relation to the world. He goes on to suggest that 'the dreams of magic may one day be the waking realities of science' (933), and, indeed, the technological advances of the century following his publications (such as moving images, mechanized warfare, mobile communication, the internet, artificial intelligence and virtual reality – to name but a few innovations that would have seemed like a certain kind of magic when he was writing) surely fulfil this prediction. But, read another way, this sentence also unwittingly ascribes a cyclical possibility to his evolutionary progression of thought. What if, as I am suggesting, the age of anthropogenic climate change shows us how far the 'dreams of magic' that Frazer dismisses as 'error and folly' (930) – that is, the belief in and respect for nonhuman agencies – *are* now the waking realities of science?

Frazer opens a chapter entitled 'The Worship of Trees' by noting how in 'the religious history of the Aryan race in Europe the worship of trees has played an important part': 'Nothing could be more natural. For at the dawn of history Europe was covered with immense primaeval forests, in which the scattered clearings must have appeared like islets in an ocean of green' (144). He goes on to describe many examples of the ways in which people throughout the world worship trees – from the ubiquity of sacred groves, to the offerings, sacrifices or ceremonies made to trees, and the respect and reverence generally accorded to them. (It is not by coincidence that the word 'savage' comes from the Latin *silvāticus*, 'woodland', 'wild'.) 'To the savage the world in general is animate, and trees and plants are no exception to the rule. He thinks that they have souls like his own, and he treats them accordingly' (146). They are also seen to have beneficent powers: 'trees or tree-spirits are believed to give rain and sunshine', they 'make the crops to grow' and they cause 'flocks and herds to multiply, and women to bring forth easily' (155–6). Trees are, that is to say, treated with reverence because they are believed to create or maintain the conditions upon which humans rely to prosper. Writing of the indigenous people of North America, and their relationship with the giant cottonwood trees – that are 'supposed to possess an intelligence which, if properly approached, may help the Indians in certain undertakings' – Frazer remarks how the people 'considered it wrong to fell one of these giants' and that even in recent times 'some of the more credulous old men declared that many of the misfortunes of their people were caused by this modern disregard for the rights of the living cottonwood' (147).

Post-Enlightenment cultures, however, know that trees are just trees and that it would be foolish to grant them rights. And yet it is impossible to deny that a lack of respect for trees has played its part in exacerbating today's climate catastrophe. The brutal and ongoing extirpation of the Amazon (aside from being a tragic loss of beauty and biodiversity) is the destruction of what is currently our most effective carbon capture and storage plant – given that, at the time of writing, technological versions remain unviable at the necessary scale.[106] Further, the warmer and drier conditions caused by extant climate change have increased the incidence of forest fires that destroy even more trees, thereby releasing more carbon into the atmosphere, making the cleared area again hotter and drier. As Wallace-Wells writes, 'more burning only means more warming only means more burning. In California, a single wildfire can entirely eliminate the emissions gains made that year by all of the state's aggressive environmental policies.'[107] The feedback loops have taken on a life of their own, and the destruction that we initiated – like the Sorcerer's Apprentice in Goethe's poem of that name – we are now powerless to stop. '*Die ich rief, die Geister, / Werd ich nun nicht los.*' 'The spirits I have summoned / I cannot now dispel.'[108]

Bill McKibben describes how the continued decimation of the Amazon is disrupting weather patterns across America by interfering with the rainforest's function as a giant pump that moves water inland and circulates warm air out of the Amazon basin to higher latitudes. The effects are not just spatially but also temporally dispersed, as the rainfall over the Amazon 'is paralleled, four months later, by spring and summer rain across the U.S. corn belt'.[109] As McKibben remarks, the processes and relationships involved are 'wildly complicated'.[110] But perhaps one of the simplest ways to understand them would be to recognize that the planet's forests play an essential part in maintaining the weather systems around which our civilizations have been built, as well as naturally sequestering carbon, fixing soil and perpetuating the fertility of the land – or, to put it another way, the trees make 'the rain to fall' and 'the crops to grow', just as the animistic worldviews which Frazer describes had it (155–6).

Sigmund Freud

Freud adopted the term 'animism' in his essays 'Animism, Magic and the Omnipotence of Thoughts' (1913) and 'The Uncanny' (1919). In the former, following Tylor and Frazer, Freud attributes animism to 'primitive races' who 'people the world with innumerable spiritual beings both benevolent and malignant; and these spirits and demons they regard as the causes of natural phenomena and they believe that not only animals and plants but all the inanimate objects in the world are animated by them'.[111] He takes Tylor's and Frazer's evolutionary frameworks one step further, however, by aligning the 'phases in the development of men's view of the universe' with 'the stages of an individual's libidinal development': the 'primitive' races, that is to say, are like children.[112] Freud also discerns the practical motives of animism and notes that 'the mental life and cultural level of savages have not hitherto had all the recognition they deserve'.[113] He concludes with the following carefully worded concession, which, while retaining the analogy between 'savages' and children, goes quite far in refuting the assumption that their mental activities are of an altogether lower or cruder class:

> I am under no illusion that in putting forward these attempted explanations I am laying myself open to the charge of endowing modern savages with a subtlety in their mental activities which exceeds all probability. It seems to me

quite possible, however, that the same may be true of our attitude towards the psychology of those races that have remained at the animistic level as is true of our attitude towards the mental life of children, which we adults no longer understand and whose fullness and delicacy of feeling we have in consequence so greatly underestimated.[114]

There are more things in heaven and earth than are dreamt of in our philosophy, as Freud was so fond of reminding us.[115] Something that 'exceeds all probability' is not impossible, merely improbable. It is scientists who open their minds to such possibilities who have, as Freud was well aware, initiated some of the great paradigm shifts of intellectual history (including, of course, the three blows to human narcissism that he identified, and that form the framework of the rest of this book).

By recognizing the transformational force of these three blows, Freud, like Frazer, must also recognize that the 'realities' of science are subject to unforeseeable revolutions, a fact which perhaps accounts for his interest in and open-mindedness to things that his contemporaries deemed decidedly 'unscientific'. As Freud's friend, psychoanalytic colleague and biographer Ernest Jones tells us, the realm of the occult was a site of acute internal conflict for the father of psychoanalysis, who was subject to an 'exquisite oscillation between scepticism and credulity'.[116] He had a discriminating critical mind that refused to take things without evidence, yet at the same time he could not shake the feeling that there might be more to certain 'superstitious' beliefs than science currently allowed. While Freud was careful to keep these suppositions private, knowing they could damage the burgeoning field of psychoanalysis (which was already seen as 'unscientific' by many), Jones describes how his friend certainly did not dismiss such beliefs altogether. He remembers Freud engaging in 'apotropaeic acts' – such as smashing a valuable possession as a sacrifice to ensure the safety of a family member – and entertaining the idea of telepathy.[117] So while in his published work Freud was careful to distance himself from such beliefs, as readers, we would do well to remember that his thoughts were in fact rather more ambivalent.

Like his predecessors, Freud concedes that the animistic conceptions of spirits are continuous with modern monotheistic conceptions of human souls and that such views *should* be – but are not quite – surmounted by science. He puts it as follows:

> Animism is a system of thought. It does not merely give an explanation of a particular phenomenon, but allows us to grasp the whole universe as a single

> unity from a single point of view. The human race, if we are to follow the authorities, have in the course of ages developed three such systems of thought – three great pictures of the universe: animistic (or mythological), religious and scientific. Of these, animism, the first to be created, is perhaps the one which is most consistent and exhaustive and which gives a truly complete explanation of the nature of the universe. This first human *Weltanschauung* is a *psychological* theory. It would go beyond our present purpose to show how much of it still persists in modern life, either in the debased form of superstition or as the living basis of our speech, our beliefs and our philosophies.[118]

It appears I am not the first to propose a radical animism. Not only does Freud describe animism as the 'most consistent and exhaustive' system of thought, he says it gives a 'truly complete explanation of the nature of the universe', allowing us to understand it 'as a single unity [*Zusammenhang*, 'coherence'] from a single point of view'.[119] He then explicitly aligns animism to his own work, by recognizing that it is 'a *psychological* theory'. What he means by this is, I think, in accord with what de Castro has to say about animism, which is, he writes, 'not the *native's* mental condition, but a "theory of the mind" applied *by* the native. Indeed, it is a manner of resolving – or better, dissolving – the eminently philosophical problem of "other minds".'[120] Animism, that is to say, assumes that the qualities of agency, subjective experience and interaction with others by which we determine our own mind are generalizable beyond the human and even beyond the living. Whether that generalization consists in elevating non-human and non-living entities to the level of the human (as traditional animist ontologies do), or lowering human mental faculties to the level of the non-human (as psychoanalysis does in its revelation of unconscious, irrational drives), or in a complication between the two (as this book proposes), it has the effect of deconstructing human exceptionalism and placing human life within a broader agentic field.

In one of his characteristically perceptive though offhand remarks, Freud admits that animism does persist '*as the living basis of our speech*, our beliefs and our philosophies' – although, he says, it 'would go beyond our present purpose' to explain how.[121] By calling animism the 'living basis' of language, belief and philosophy, Freud recognizes the strange power of language that moves through human relations with the world and each other (perhaps another expression for what Derrida calls 'the animality of the letter').[122] He goes on to suggest that the belief in the 'omnipotence of thoughts' so characteristic of animistic worldviews is also retained 'in the field of art'.[123] Freud's appreciation of the animistic potency of language and art (as well as his regular inclusion of literary or theatrical examples in his arguments) is suggestive of a recognition that the animate workings of language cannot be rigorously distinguished or separated from what we think of as 'reality'. Thinking through such a recognition will be one of the central concerns of this book, and, in the fourth chapter, I will be more fully exploring the living potency – beyond any conscious control – that Freud here ascribes to language.

In 'The Uncanny', he writes further about the animistic belief in the 'omnipotence of thoughts' and how such beliefs persist in modern societies:

> We – or our primitive forefathers – once believed that these possibilities were realities, and were convinced that they actually happened. Nowadays we no longer believe in them, we have *surmounted* these modes of thought; but we do not feel quite sure of our new beliefs, and the old ones still exist within us ready to seize upon any confirmation. As soon as something *actually happens* in our lives which seems to confirm the old, discarded beliefs we get a feeling of the uncanny; it is as though we were making a judgement something like this: 'So, after all, it is *true* that one can kill a person by the mere wish!' or, 'So the dead *do* live on and appear on the scene of their former activities!' and so on. Conversely, anyone who has completely and finally rid himself of animistic beliefs will be insensible to this type of the uncanny. The most remarkable coincidences of wish and fulfilment, the most mysterious repetition of similar experiences in a particular place or on a particular date, the most deceptive sights and suspicious noises – none of these things will disconcert him or raise the kind of fear which can be described as 'a fear of something uncanny'.[124]

This passage seems to mime the 'exquisite oscillation' that Jones attributes to Freud's position on the subject. 'We' humans used to believe in the omnipotence of thoughts – that is, before we surmounted these primitive beliefs – although they *do* still lie in wait, ready to spring back into existence at certain provocations – *unless* of course one (presumably 'one' such as the thoroughly objective and scientific author of the essay at hand) has 'completely and finally rid himself of animistic beliefs' – or at least likes to act *as if* he had. We know from Jones's account that the remarkable coincidences, mysterious repetitions, deceptive sights and suspicious noises did in fact disconcert and fascinate Freud, despite his proclaimed insensibility to these phenomena. In someone with such a penetrating understanding of the human mind, these ambivalences are highly significant.

And so, while it is true that the word 'animism' has been connected with the history of ethnocentric othering that helped Western, scientific, 'enlightened' cultures to define their sense of progress and supremacy, we can see how each of the writers I have discussed had a more subtle appreciation of animism than is often attributed to them. The general denigration of animism in favour of 'enlightened', scientific civilization is far more simplistic than the accounts given by any of these writers and appears to be based on a selective reading that had such denigration as its motive.

Animism for now

To rethink animism today entails a double gesture: First, it is to redress the cultural violence and disrespect that has characterized Western understandings of and relations to animistic cultures, by approaching them with a new sensitivity and openness. This is being done in the work of David Abram, Nurit Bird-David, Philippe Descola, Tim Ingold, Bruno Latour, Elizabeth Povinelli, Isabelle Stengers, Eduardo Viveiros de Castro and others. The more accommodating and respectful notion of animism that grows out of such projects certainly informs my work here, but given that this book is not itself an anthropological study, I am not concerned with directly documenting or analysing cultures or practices that are animistic in the more narrow ethnographic sense. Rather – and this is the second point – the rethinking of animism I am undertaking looks to elaborate how the insights of animistic world views can be radically generalized, thereby transforming the ways in which we understand the infinitely complex and inextricably interrelated play of forces which make up what we call reality: from the quantum to the astronomical, from the non-living to the living, from 'fact' to 'fiction', from reaction to response – and everything in between. Such a generalization is particularly pertinent in the context of climate change, when, out of earth's systems emerges a scenario in which even the most 'naïve' forms of animism appear more rational than the world view which currently informs global politics and economics: the worldview, that is to say, that enables or forces us to continuing doing precisely the things that are threatening our existence.

To be clear, I am certainly not advocating some kind of neoprimitivism, or a return to a more 'natural' relation with the earth (as Timothy Morton and others have recognized, the very notions of 'Nature' or the 'natural' are highly problematic in the context of the Anthropocene).[125] Instead, a radical animism for today would involve an attempt to come to terms with the non-living and non-human forms of life and agency that are demanding to be reckoned with – even as they resist our apprehension and control. Latour's retrieval of James

Lovelock's Gaia theory does something similar. The figure of Gaia, as Latour elaborates, is a complex, dynamic and enclosed entity that is neither organism nor machine – and that therefore resists any such metaphorical ascriptions: there is, Latour writes, 'no precedent nor comparison possible'.[126] Gaia, that is to say, does not fit within our reckoning of what life or agency is or should be. Before the crisis of global warming, it might have still been possible to conclude that the figure of Gaia is 'merely' a myth, a story of something that is not 'really' alive, or that does not 'really' have agency. But today, such a dismissal becomes harder to maintain, and instead we might be forced to entirely rethink its terms. It is not, that is to say, that Gaia is not alive, but rather that the very concept of life demands to be rethought.

Indeed, there has been a more general move to recognize and respect life and agency beyond the human – even when the term 'animism' is not invoked or is shunned. Jane Bennett's new materialism is exemplary here. In *Vibrant Matter*, she highlights 'the material agency or effectivity of nonhuman or not-quitehuman things' and seeks to ask 'how analyses of political events might change if we gave the force of things more due'.[127] Bennett recognizes that her vital materialism 'has affinities with several nonmodern (and often discredited) modes of thought – including animism, the Romantic quest for Nature, and vitalism'.[128] She thereby distances her project from the narrow and often derogatory traditional concept of animism, while at the same time acknowledging that 'affinities' are there. But, if we take the broader conception of animism that I am proposing in the context of the Anthropocene, Bennett's stated aims – '(1) to paint a positive ontology of vibrant matter, which stretches received concepts of agency, action, and freedom sometimes to the breaking point; (2) to dissipate the onto-theological binaries of life/matter, human/animal, will/determination, and organic/inorganic …; and (3) to sketch a style of political analysis that can better account for the contributions of nonhuman actants' – clearly align with this wider definition.[129]

So why use the word 'animism', when, as Bennett and other new materialists prefer to do, we might think about non-living and non-human forms of life perfectly well without it? The advantage of reclaiming the term from its narrow and ethnocentric origin is that in so doing we can (as I suggested at the opening of this section) actively call into question the stance from which the animist worldview is denigrated as 'nonmodern' or 'discredited'. It is precisely such a stance that has led to the hubristic and myopic errors of 'modern' post-Enlightenment culture and the destructive force of its neoliberal, capitalist economies.

Contemporary accounts which do not shy away from the term 'animism' tend to share the following recognitions: that the animist perception of agency outside the human is not a delusion but is instead logically undeniable; that the dichotomies upon which 'enlightened' cultures are based (subject/object, nature/culture, art/science, body/mind, animal/human, etc.) are untenable; and that the notion of a pure scientific objectivity is fallacious.[130] This is not to invalidate or discount scientific knowledge but merely to call into question the position of absolute objectivity from which it purports to observe things. There is no 'viewpoint' that can be rigorously separated from what is being viewed. As Alf Hornborg writes, 'rather than viewing knowledge as *either* representation *or* construction, animism suggests the intermediate view that knowledge is a relation that shapes both the knower and the known'.[131] Or, as Ingold puts it, animism is not merely 'a way of believing about the world' but rather 'a condition of being in it'. He goes on:

> This could be described as a condition of being alive to the world, characterized by a heightened sensitivity and responsiveness, in perception and action, to an environment that is always in flux. ... Animacy, then, is not a property of persons imaginatively projected onto the things with which they perceive themselves to be surrounded. Rather ... it is the dynamic, transformative potential of the entire field of relations within which beings of all kinds, more or less person-like or thing-like, continually and reciprocally bring one another into existence. The animacy of the lifeworld, in short, is not the result of an infusion of spirit into substance, or of agency into materiality, but is rather ontologically prior to their differentiation.[132]

The radical reciprocity of which Ingold writes recognizes that there are not 'selves' or 'things' *within* a 'world' but rather that they *are* that world: a world composed of a complexly intertwined and dynamic 'field of relations'. Such dynamism is necessarily a temporal event, stretching into the past and future. This can be, as indeed Ingold frames it here, a very positive image. There is, however, a darker side to animism. Take Ingold's description of the 'dynamic, transformative potential of the entire field of relations' made up of 'beings of all kinds, more or less person-like or thing-like', and read it alongside Cohen's description of the 'fractal' interaction of events we so calmly call 'climate change':

> One can fill in a myriad of macro and micro threads, intersecting active backloops and different proleptic narratives from polar ice to microbials, medical toxins to oil, hyperindustrial psychotropies to species extinctions, geopolitical corporate plundering and regime maintenance to food riots, the credit collapse

and scientific prospects of synthetic biology and geo-engineering, resource wars and, yes, 'weather' militarization and 'population culling.' All these correspond to different *combinatoires* as the calculations of time-scales are adjusted.[133]

Apprehended like that, the animistic conception of the 'lifeworld' becomes rather more daunting, and the reciprocal 'bringing-into-existence' of person-like or thing-like entities is revealed to be a creativity that does not exclude destructiveness and cruelty from its rubric. The agency of human beings within this field of relations shrinks vertiginously, and we find ourselves at sea in the most violent of storms. Animism acknowledges powers beyond humans and recognizes the limits of our own powers. Animism, that is to say, provides no haven for what Freud calls the 'naïve self-love of Man'.

Ingold's conception of contemporary animism also informs what I am calling the animism of literature. As I will elaborate in the next chapter, writers, readers and texts are not rigorously separable entities but 'continually and reciprocally bring one another into existence' through the transformative force of writing that moves across space and time. In language, you are inhabited by, or find yourself inhabiting, something alien, something non-human, something alive, where alterity laps upon the shoreline of what you think is your identity. Can you read the letters on the page, inanimate little marks, apparently so silent and so still, without hearing the ghost whispers of language singing through your head, not my voice, and not quite yours, but a spirit summoned between us – us reader-writers who conspire to meet outside of space and time in a here and now that is never quite here or now? Whether I am inventing you, or you me, I cannot say. But such invention always entails a certain animism, the inspired or spirited life of language that moves beyond and before the lives of the humans that speak and write it.

2

Surviving the Anthropocene: Revolutionary Rhythms

'For it might end, you know,' said Alice to herself, 'in my going out altogether, like a candle. I wonder what I should be like then?' And she tried to fancy what the flame of a candle is like after the candle is blown out, for she could not remember ever having seen such a thing.
Lewis Carroll, Alice's Adventures in Wonderland[1]

The Copernican earthquake

Though the Polish astronomer and mathematician Nicolaus Copernicus had been entertaining the notion of a heliocentric system as early as 1514, his seminal work was not published until shortly before his death in 1543 – a delay at least partly attributable to the fact that *De revolutionibus orbium coelestium* would undermine the religious and philosophical assumptions of centuries. Of the three 'blows' to human narcissism identified by Freud, this was the '*cosmological one*' – repudiating the presumed 'central position of the earth', which had been, for Man, a 'guarantee' of his 'dominating role ... in the universe and appeared to fit in very well with his inclination to regard himself as lord of the world'.[2] Copernicus' work shook both the material and intellectual grounds of human self-conception, revealing a universe in which the very concept of 'cosmos' (Greek κόσμος, 'order') no longer had human beings as its origin and axis.

Copernicus demonstrated, as Freud writes, 'that our earth was not the centre of the universe but only a tiny fragment of a cosmic system of scarcely imaginable vastness'.[3] As this description recognizes, there were two distinct effects of this blow, which will also direct my thinking here: *decentring* – the shift (or elimination) of the centre point of the universe; and *rescaling* – the disclosure of previously unimagined scales, within which human existence shrinks towards imperceptibility, becoming 'a tiny fragment' within 'scarcely imaginable vastness'. The notion of a centre was shown to be a mere symptom of perception, and, as our understanding of the size of the universe grew, the earth's relative place within it necessarily shrunk, in a vertiginous dolly-zoom of astronomical proportions. This would also undermine the assumed veracity of human sense-perceptions, as Freud recognized:

> In the early stages of his researches, man believed at first that his dwelling-place, the earth, was the stationary centre of the universe, with the sun, moon and planets circling round it. In this he was naïvely following the dictates of his sense-perceptions, for he felt no movement of the earth, and wherever he had an unimpeded view he found himself in the centre of a circle that enclosed the external world.[4]

The horizon is shown to be merely a trick of the light: a *trompe l'œil*, that deceives the eye, or deceives the 'I', and sense-perceptions are destined to remain naïvely incommensurate to cosmological realities such as the movement of the earth. There will always be a beyond of the horizon of experience: if we are environed by anything, it is not the 'environment' but rather the inescapable limitations of our own perception – which, let us not forget, is always interrupted by the rather pervasive blind spot we call the 'unconscious'. Reality, as it is perceived, is structured by *fiction*, by a fictional centre and a fictional horizon, that are subjectively brought into being from moment to moment.

With regards to this cosmological *Kränkung*, the translation as 'blow' – in its sense of a striking movement (as opposed to 'wound', 'insult' or 'mortification') – is particularly appropriate. The revelation – that the earth is not the stable centre of a known or knowable universe but is instead an insignificant spinning speck within a fundamentally unknowable expanse – is one of *movement*: an earth-quake after which *terra firma* and firmament are firm and fixed no longer (and the new vastness of the post-Copernican universe was in fact an effect of acknowledging the earth's movement: as Timothy Ferris notes, 'geocentric, immobile earth cosmologies tended to inhibit appreciation of the true dimensions of space', and to 'set the earth in motion' necessitated a radical expansion of the size of the universe'[5]). Movement is the action or play of forces that is not restricted to human beings or even to the living. In the pre-Copernican universe, things moved, or revolved, around us. Struck by the blow of Copernicus' revelation, humankind is dislodged from its axial position and flung, dizzily spinning, to an inconsequential outpost of a dynamically animated and unfathomably vast universe. Things move, and they move us. The ground we stand on is tropically – in the 'literal' and 'figurative' senses – set in motion ('trope' is from Greek τρέπειν, 'to turn' – and much in the following pages will be concerned with what turns or re-turns): the earth or ground is literally turning, trop-ically spinning in the sky, *and* the philosophical figure of the 'grounds' of human centrality and dominion is unsettled. These two earthquakes reverberate through each other, undermining the possibility of a rigid distinction between the literal and the figurative. Derrida writes in 'White Mythology' that 'what is fundamental [in philosophy] corresponds to the desire for firm and ultimate ground, a terrain to build on, the earth as the support of an artificial structure'.⁶ When the earth quakes, so does the *ground* of reason, the *basis* of any logic: the imperceptible but *fundamental* movement of the earth disclosed by the Copernican revolution not only reveals the limited nature of our sense-perceptions but also shakes the very foundations of the rational discourse from which it originates. It is in this sense, too, that the work of deconstruction can be aligned with animism. As Derrida remarks, 'deconstruction moves. ... It is a sort of great earthquake, a general tremor, which nothing can calm.'⁷

Ellipsis: Revolutions without centre

The word 'revolution' has three distinct, and somewhat contradictory, meanings – all of which pre-date Copernicus.⁸ From the classical Latin *re-volvere*, a revolution is literally a re-turn or roll back. The first sense, then, is that of circular movement, of things that go round and around: celestial objects, for example, or bicycle wheels. This kind of revolution is predictable, regular, rhythmic. The second sense is that of change or upheaval, often dramatic or violent, and involves a reversal or disruption of the established order: revolutions in politics or belief systems. The third sense – now obsolete – is that of consideration or reflection: revolution as the meditation upon, or turning over in the mind of, an idea. The text that marks the turning point for the Copernican paradigm shift, *De revolutionibus orbium coelestium*, took as its explicit subject revolutions of the cyclical kind – though it animates all three senses of the word. Observation of the revolutions (first sense) of celestial objects in the sky formed the basis both of the old earth-centred conception of the universe *and* of Copernicus' challenging of it. The visible phenomena remained the same, while the interpretation shifted – making this a revolution (second sense) in *reading*, as well as thought. If a light in the sky always re-turns to trace the same arc, it must be, the ancients adduced, revolving around us. The Ptolemaic system thereby assumed earth to be the fixed point around which the sun, planets and stars circled. Yet some of these revolutions re-turned somewhat strangely. The planets were so named because they seemed to 'wander' in the sky ('planet' comes from the ancient Greek πλανᾶν, 'to lead astray', 'to wander'): their revolutions (first sense) seemed revolutionary (second sense), reversing their course for a time, changing direction. It was this errant behaviour that convinced Copernicus – and his Alexandrian precursors[9] – that a geocentric system did not make sense. As Jean Laplanche notes, 'the movements of these wandering, straying stars in the end defy all straightforward explanation in a system where the earth remains the centre of reference'.[10] It was whilst holding in revolution (third sense) the wandering and revolutionary (second sense) revolutions (first sense) of the planets that Copernicus came to his revolutionary (second sense) theory: thinking upon revolutions led to a revolution in thinking.[11] *On the Revolutions of the Heavenly Spheres* is a title already multiply divided, holding both regularity and upheaval within its turns.

While his name has come to signify the end of common belief in an earth-centred universe, Copernicus' system was far from perfect. Just as the Ptolemaic system had relied on epicycles to account for the irregularities of the observed revolutions, Copernicus too – because he retained the principle of perfectly circular orbits – was, as Hubert Krivine explains, 'forced to reintroduce, however marginally in his case, a system of epicycles, the only function of which was to better reproduce the actual trajectories (which in fact were ellipses, as we know thanks to Kepler)'.[12] 'Ellipse', the term used to describe the slightly oval shape of planetary orbits, derives from the ancient Greek ἐλλείπειν, 'to come short', and, of course, also describes the omission of words in an ellipsis. In another linguistic irony, it was Copernicus' refusal to entertain the possibility of elliptical orbits that led to the ellipse (or falling short) of his own theory, and to the ellipsis (or empty space) at its centre. As Krivine writes, 'since Earth's trajectory is elliptical, Copernicus could not account for it by a circle exactly centred on the Sun. He had to introduce a neighbouring *fictional* point as centre, the "average Sun"'.[13] This strange elliptical conclusion – that there was nothing at the centre of the solar system – actually serves to better describe the paradigm shift that his work would go on to effect. As Laplanche describes, 'the Copernican revolution, to some extent, opened up the possibility of the absence of a centre. In a world of quasi-infinite distances it becomes absurd to persist in trying to preserve one star among others – the sun or solar system – as centre.'[14] Today, the observable universe is estimated to contain trillions of galaxies, with one hundred billion stars per galaxy, disclosing a scale at which the planet we inhabit is not just insignificant but also invisible, and at which the notion of a centre is entirely untenable.

Rhythmic returns

There can be no thinking of revolutions without a thinking or reckoning of rhythm. (And one always *reckons* rhythm, counts its repetitions – the word 'rhythm' comes from the Old High German *rīm*: series, sequence, number.) Cyclic revolutions, in their repeated re-turns, beat a regular rhythm that anticipates its own continuation. Disruptive or subversive revolutions can only be recognized as such in their breaking with the established rhythm of history. Rhythm divides the present through its invocation of the past and future. Rhythm is universal – or, perhaps, *poly*versal, but, at any rate, versal – beating time in heart, breath or step, in the 'vacillating rhythm' of Freud's description of the instincts,[15] in music and song and dance, in days and years (the revolutions of this here heavenly sphere), in seasons' change and the ticking of clocks, in wavelengths or frequencies of light and sound, in rates of radioactive decay, in the (etymologically distinct) reckoning of algorithms that now automate so much of our world[16] and, indeed, in the pattering or pacing of language. Syncopated staccatos or sombre stomps – rhythm is in/cessant: it comes; it goes. Rhythm is in us and outside us, before and beyond us. It can be intoxicating; you might get 'rhythm-drunk'.[17] As Kirsty Martin writes, rhythm 'can create sympathy' by 'draw[ing] us into synchronicity with each other, connecting our energies to those outside us'.[18] It transgresses the bounds of the individual without recourse to verbal language and allows for sym-pathies, or shared feelings, that traverse and complicate the human/nonhuman divide. Rhythm facilitates sympathy via telepathy.

The word 'rhythm' comes from 'rhyme'. There was a time when the two words rhymed – back when the 'th' of 'rhy*th*m' was unvoiced or, as the *OED* puts it, 'voiceless'. But then the voiceless little non-sound, un-voiceable alone (how do you say 'th'?), insinuated itself, like a virus or parasite, into common pronunciation and split the word in two, leaving rhyme to rhyme and adding rhythm to rhythm (to the disyllabic voicing of 'rhy-thm', turning it trochee), even as it put an end to its rhyming – because there's nothing that rhymes with rhythm. *But*, of course, there's also nothing that rhymes *without* rhythm, no rhyming without instigating a rhythm: if words happen to rhyme, your prose will start to chime. As David Wills writes,

> Every time we read or hear a repetition in language, beginning with an alliteration, assonance, or rhyme, and going all the way to rhetorical emphases and thematic motifs, we receive them as the text's responding to itself and so animating or livening itself, calling and responding to itself as though it were conversing with, singing, or orating to itself. What iterability adds to that idea, transforming it in the process, is the insistence that there is harboured within such repeatability [an] irreducible automatism ... rewriting language's self-*response* as an auto*spontan*eity – language functioning *sponte sua*, of its own accord – which is a mode of the automotricity or autokinesis that we understand to be at work in every life-form.[19]

Even the 'linguistic universe', that is to say, does not have humans at its origin or centre, no matter how much one insists – as Western philosophy has long presumed it can – that verbal language is 'proper to man'. It determines our speech, putting words in our mouths as if it were alive. Language, as Wills writes, 'generates and self-generates as a privileged form, perhaps *the* privileged form, of inanimate life'.[20]

Virginia Woolf, a writer keenly aware of the non-human force of rhythm in language, felt that the 'rhythm' of writing is 'very profound' and 'goes far deeper than words'.[21] Rhythm is, she suggests, 'the most profound and primitive of instincts'.[22] She writes that music – of which rhythm is the 'winged creature' or 'soul' – 'incites within us something that is wild and inhuman like itself', and has 'the strange and illimitable power of a natural force'.[23] Woolf's apprehension of the wild and inhuman force of rhythm coalesces with her attunement to the animism of the non-human world more generally – so that she can be read as a remarkably post-Copernican thinker, inscribing a universe that does not have humans at its centre.[24] She writes a world dynamically animated by non-human and non-living forms of life: one that opens itself to scales of space and time both vast and minute, as revealed by astronomy and quantum physics, respectively. As she urges at the end of 'A Room of One's Own', the future of writing must attempt to 'escape a little from the common sitting-room and see human beings not always in their relation to each other but in relation to reality; and the sky, too, and the trees'.[25]

Woolf's Copernican revolution: 'The central shadow'

To the Lighthouse and *The Waves* can be read, as I will elaborate, as particularly post-Copernican in their radical decentring of the human and their preoccupation with non-human scales. They are concerned with the limits of seeing and knowing, with thoughts of death and survival, and are moved by the non-human, non-living life of rhythm and language. The apprehension of vast scales of space and time, and the sense of obliteration they engender, gives rise to thoughts of extinction – the fate predicted by the ineluctably entropic nature of the universe being disclosed in Woolf's time, and that is now presenting itself with renewed force and proximity in the age of catastrophic climate change. Extinction, while inevitable, structurally resists thinking. As I have elaborated elsewhere, the thought of extinction as the extinction of thought is a thought that cannot get going, that annihilates itself before it has even begun.[26] Both novels attempt this apparently impossible undertaking, offering to the reader glimpses of worlds devoid of human presence as well as being preoccupied with experiences of mourning and being-haunted, through the deaths of their 'central' characters (although, as I will show, notions of both 'centrality' and conventional 'characterization' are undone by Woolf). *To the Lighthouse*, which is set in a family's summer home in the Hebrides, has at its centre a depiction of the house left empty for ten years. This section, called 'Time Passes', describes the appropriation of the house by non-human, animistic forces; it is, as Woolf notes in her diary, 'all eyeless & featureless with nothing to cling to', and yet, she feels, 'spirited'.[27] Mrs Ramsay, who, in the first section of the novel, is a centre that compels the disparate party to come together – 'the whole of the effort of merging and flowing and creating rested on her' – is, after her death, felt as an emptiness: when Mr Ramsay stretches his arms out for her in the night, 'They remained empty', and Lily describes her absence as 'a centre of complete emptiness'.[28]

The Waves tells the stories of six friends' lives, from childhood to old age – but, as Woolf herself said, the 'characters' are not entirely distinct.[29] The novel (or 'playpoem', as Woolf called it) is framed and divided by 'interludes' – and the term recognizes the rhythmic, musical quality of the work – which describe the passing of a day or a year (from dawn to dusk, from spring to winter) full of the life of birds and trees and the breaking of waves on a beach.[30] The chapters are written entirely in the characters' voices; eschewing any traditional 'narration', *The Waves* refuses the singular, unified or objective reality conventionally drawn by fiction. The figure of Percival (like Mrs Ramsay in *To the Lighthouse*) is a centre around which the others gather – as Louis says, 'Look now, how everybody follows Percival. He is heavy'; he is figured as 'monolithic', 'giant', as having 'satellites', which orbit and imitate him.[31] Significantly, however, in a novel entirely made up of the speech of its characters, he has no words of his own. He is silent in a world made of voice, not present but only re-presented by others. He too dies at the (nearly exact) midpoint of the novel and leaves a centre of emptiness. Bernard remarks of Percival: 'About him my feeling was: he sat there in the centre. Now I go to that spot no longer. The place is empty' (131). Towards the end of the novel, Bernard is left with an intractable uncertainty as to what, if anything, constitutes the centre: 'What does the central shadow hold?' he asks. 'Something? Nothing?' (251).

Through the window

Through the open window the voice of the beauty of the world came murmuring.
Woolf, *To the Lighthouse*, 154

The 'Time Passes' section of *To the Lighthouse* inscribes, as I suggested above, an explicitly animistic – and non-human – universe.[32] It is *anima*, in the forms of air, breath and non-human life, that appropriates the empty house in the family's absence: 'certain airs' that 'crept round corners and ventured indoors', 'little airs' that 'mounted the staircase and nosed round bedroom doors' (138). The 'stray airs' have the character of some small and curious animal, its 'clammy breaths' 'nosing', 'rubbing', 'snuffling', 'prying' and 'nibbling' about the house (140, 138, 141, 150). It is the 'soft nose of the clammy sea airs' that asks 'Will you fade? Will you perish?' Such questioning invokes the anxiety about human transience that troubles Mr Ramsay throughout the novel and thereby subverts the assumed roles of humans as the sole questioners of, or answerers in, the universe – for it is 'Loveliness and stillness' that 'answer: We remain' (140). It is the 'triumph' of the 'trifling airs' that heralds the ascendancy of the non-human, in a passage in which sound clamours with sense:

> Idly, aimlessly, the swaying shawl swung to and fro. A thistle thrust itself between the tiles in the larder. The swallows nested in the drawing-room; the floor was strewn with straw; the plaster fell in shovelfuls; … Tortoise-shell butterflies burst from the chrysalis and pattered their life out on the window-pane. Poppies sowed themselves among the dahlias; the lawn waved with long grass; giant artichokes towered among roses; a fringed carnation flowered among the cabbages; while the gentle tapping of a weed at the window had become, on winters' nights, a drumming from sturdy trees and thorned briars which made the whole room green in summer. (150)

The initial sibilance of this passage is softened with the willowing of 'W's, which linger as the 'S's fade out – swaying, shawl, swung, swallows, strewn, straw, window, sowed, lawn, waved, towered, flowered, while, weed, window, winters – as if the wind is whistling through chinks in the prose. Meanwhile, repeated 'st'-sounds start to strike a gentle rhythm (thistle, thrust, nested, strewn, straw, plaster, burst, sturdy), the subtle insistence of the sound miming the background 'patter[ing]' and 'tapping' at the windowpane. Finally, the gentle rhythm resolves itself into 'drumming' – the onomatopoeia of which is underlined by the paragraph ending with the word 'summer'.

Most of the sentences are divided not by the halting closure of full stops but by the fenestral porousness of semi-colons – the kind of punctuation that lets sentences talk to each other, influence each other, like open windows. The coherence of sounds through the passage brings the variousness of life into a kind of harmony, as if the 'thrust' of the 'thistle' is in concord with the 'burst' of the 'butterflies', the 'towering' of artichokes with the 'flowering' of the carnation. Given Woolf's conviction that the rhythm of language 'goes far deeper than words',[33] we can assume that the symphonic aspects of this passage carry as much force as the literal 'sense'. Just as the empty house is taken over by various forms of non-human life, Woolf's writing is inhabited by the automatic machinations of the materiality of words. The repeated pairings of verbs with nouns (the sway of the shawl, the thrust of the thistle, the fall of the plaster, etc.) – along with the relative dearth of adjectives – not only inscribe an ubiquitous dynamism but also work to transform the adjective of the final line into a verb: when you read that the trees and briars 'made the whole room green in summer', you are transported to a room not passively but actively green, a room *greening*, as alive as all the things in and around it.

Indeed, Woolf's evident intention with both 'Time Passes' in *To the Lighthouse* and the interludes of *The Waves* is to affirm that the non-human world is *vital* – both full of life, lively; and necessary, essential, indispensable. Its life is as 'wild and inhuman' as the rhythm which infects and disturbs human language – and as irresistible. Such affirmation counters the subject/object dualism that posits the non-human world as devoid of subjectivity and at a tractable distance from human beings. Woolf's father Leslie Stephen, upon whom Mr Ramsay is based, writes that 'the whole history of philosophical thought is but a history of attempts to separate the object and the subject, and each new attempt implies that the previous line of separation was erroneously drawn or partly "fictitious".'[34] Woolf's writing does not redraw the line of separation, nor erase it entirely, but affirms the necessity and inevitability of its fictionality. When Lily attempts to understand Mr Ramsay's work on 'Subject and object and the nature of reality', Andrew tells her to 'think of a kitchen table … when you're not there':

> So now she always saw, when she thought of Mr Ramsay's work, a scrubbed kitchen table. It lodged now in the fork of a pear tree, for they had reached the orchard. And with a painful effort of concentration, she focused her mind, not upon the silver-bossed bark of the tree, or upon its fish-shaped leaves, but upon a phantom kitchen table, one of those scrubbed board tables, grained and knotted, … which stuck there, its four legs in air. (28)

What Lily is actually doing – instead of thinking of an object without a subject (the table 'when you're not there') – is projecting a 'phantom' object onto the scene in which she, the subject, *is*. The world she attempts to overwrite reasserts itself, as the 'silver-bossed bark of the tree' and 'its fish-shaped leaves' appear, by their mention, to resist her 'painful effort of concentration'. The table floating so incongruously in the pear tree is not evidence of Lily's inadequately philosophical mind but rather evidence of the irreducible fictionality of the subject/object separation. The notion of a pure objectivity – upon which classical science rests – presupposes that such separation is possible, that the observing subjectivity can be effectively erased from the equation (quantum physics empirically disproves this, as I will discuss later), as if you could view the world beyond the horizon of, or without the centre of, your experience. This is why, as David Krell writes, the charge of 'anthropocentrism is essentially duplicitous, for it always presupposes that a thinking could, if only it were rigorous enough, liberate itself from its human nexus'.[35] Or, in other words, it presupposes that thinking could see beyond its horizon, beyond its observable universe, that you could 'think of a kitchen table when you're not there'. 'Time Passes' and the interludes of *The Waves*, are, in a sense, like Lily's phantom kitchen table: the erasure of human subjectivity can only ever be partial and incomplete – or fictional – in works that are written and read by humans.

This is not, however, a failure on Woolf's part – she knows very well the strangeness of what she is attempting. As Bernard asks, towards the end of *The Waves*, 'how describe the world seen without a self?' (247). The answer is: through fiction. Given that the Copernican decentring of the universe has shown the fictionality – and inescapability – of every centre point and horizon, the challenge for thinking is to take this into account, to remain sensitive to its own limitations and to the possibilities of what lies and lives beyond every 'observable universe'. Erich Auerbach's seminal essay on Woolf shows how she eschews narratorial objectivity and omniscience.³⁶ This eschewal demonstrates, I suggest, an acute awareness of the inherent limitations of any unitary or 'objective' perspective. As Laura Marcus writes, Woolf 'demolishes the view held by the realist or naturalist novel that character is knowable and representable':

> As in a cubist painting, multiple perspectives recompose the outer shapes of objects into new 'inner' visual rhymes and associations. The 'enveloping' and interpenetrating effects of multiple consciousnesses are achieved through Woolf's radical uses of 'indirect speech' ... and of 'indirect interior monologue', in which the narrative consciousness speaks in and through the mental language of its characters, without becoming wholly identified with it. She also represents thoughts and images which are not clearly attributable to either a fictional subject or to a narrative voice, and effects transitions between one consciousness and another, often within the same sentence or paragraph, and between characters as objects and subjects of perception.³⁷

To the Lighthouse cannot be reduced to a linear sequence of 'events' (a 'storyline') or to the interactions of clearly definable 'characters'. The idea that, as Marcus puts it, 'the narrative consciousness speaks in and through the mental language of its characters, without becoming wholly identified with it' can be read as a more generalized complication of inner and outer at work in Woolf – just as, as I suggested above, rhythm speaks in and through human language without being reducible to it. Individuals are precisely not in-dividual but are multiplied by and entangled with their relations to human and non-human others. Distance and distinction between bodies and the 'external' world is collapsed or complicated. Windows are left, or blown, open. The terms 'indirect speech' and 'indirect interior monologue' downplay the strange and insistent shifting of the narrative between selves and the places they inhabit – and that inhabit them. *To the Lighthouse* is composed of, as Marcus continues, 'an extraordinarily complex interplay of eye lines and sight lines'.³⁸ Not all of them are human. The eponymous lighthouse, that flashes its rhythm all through the text, also has 'a yellow eye, that open[s] suddenly, and softly in the evening' (202). Its gaze searches you out, throws light on things, meets with that of Mrs Ramsay. It enters the house, needing no invitation, through the windows, and sends 'its sudden stare over bed and wall in the darkness of winter' (150).

Indeed, many of the cross-contaminations of inside and outside, internal and external that make up *To the Lighthouse* happen through windows. The first section of the novel is called 'The Window', and Mrs Ramsay is almost constantly said to be sitting or standing at one.³⁹ She would often, we are told, 'say they must keep the windows open and the doors shut' (18), and her ghostly return in the final section of the novel also appears in a window (211–12). The lighthouse itself, when seen for the first time at close range, is noticed by James to have windows: 'he could see that it was barred with black and white; he could see windows in it' (202). When Mr Ramsay 'does homage to the beauty of the world', allowing the sight of his family to assuage his anxieties, he too 'halts by the window' (42). Charles Tansley, however, who has just rather obnoxiously thought 'What damned rot they talk' about the rest of the people at dinner, has 'his back to the window precisely in the middle of the view' – as if his closed-mindedness is underwritten by his relation to the window (93). Françoise Defromont writes that, in Woolf's writing, 'to go to the window is like the sign of an opening onto the soul and onto the profound thoughts of him or her who dreams, and whose interiority thus communicates with what is exterior'.[40]

The word 'window' comes from the Old Norse *vindauga*: *vindr*, meaning 'wind', and *auga*, 'eye'. The window, then, is the meeting place of two of the main forces of the book: the non-human, non-living flows and currents of air or wind, animating the world through setting it in motion, as depicted by 'Time Passes'; and the creative force of perception – the reading eye. Windows are the place where the eye, or 'I', comes into contact with alterity. The relation, as figured by the transparent aperture of the window, is a reciprocal one based on openness: 'windows should be open', as Mrs Ramsay affirms (33). At dinner, when she feels the moment partakes 'of eternity', the room has 'uncurtained windows', the sight of which punctuates her rhapsody:

> There is a coherence in things, a stability; something, she meant, is immune from change, and shines out (she glanced at the window with its ripple of reflected lights) in the face of the flowing, the fleeting, the spectral, like a ruby; so that again tonight she had the feeling she had had once to-day, already, of peace, of rest. Of such moments, she thought, the thing is made that endures. (114)

In 'such moments', inner and outer worlds coalesce – have a 'coherence' – so that the window, usually an opening to the outside world, momentarily reflects the inner scene. Rather than excluding or obscuring externality, this further complicates the distinction between interior and exterior, revealing how far the inner world contaminates (literally 'touches together', from the Latin '*con-*', together, and '*tangĕre*', 'to touch') the outer, as well as being, from the outset, contaminated by it.

In *The Waves* too, the outside world invades through windows. In one of the interludes, for example, a breeze makes the curtains flap '*against the edge of the window*', letting in a light that '*browned a cabinet*', '*reddened a chair*' and '*made the window waver in the side of the green jar*' (157).[41] The interior is altered ('*browned*' and '*reddened*') by what comes in at the window, and, instead of the window reflecting the inside scene – as in the passage from *To the Lighthouse* discussed above – here the inside reflects the window, as it appears '*in the side of the green jar*': '*All for a moment wavered and bent in uncertainty and ambiguity, as if a great moth sailing through the room had shadowed the immense solidity of chairs and tables with floating wings*' (157). Certainty, solidity, interiority: all are disrupted by what comes through the window. Later, when Bernard loses or transcends his sense of individual identity – 'he is dead, the man I called "Bernard"', he says – his 'being seems' 'immeasurably receptive' as 'fine gusts of melody, waves of incense' come into his head, 'and the dark airs of midnight shake trees outside the open windows' (250).

Windows are the portal between inner and outer worlds, affording a view of what is outside, as well as giving ventilation, allowing the passage of air. The magical experiences of reading a novel – of time and space travel, of telepathic opening onto other consciousness – can be thought of in terms of the opening of such a window or portal, as Nicholas Royle writes.[42] We could think of the paradigm shifts set in motion by the Copernican revolution as the opening of a window: the disclosure of another world, not necessarily inhabitable as such, but now visible, tangible, for the first time, its breeze ruffling the world within, disrupting its cosy stability. In Woolf's writing, windows figure visually what rhythm gives aurally: an opening onto the otherness of the nonhuman world – even to its more threatening or destructive aspects, its 'wild and inhuman' nature. The life that drums at the window in 'Time Passes' demands to be thought beyond human life, and even beyond organic life, beating a rhythm akin to 'the monotonous fall of the waves on the beach' that Mrs Ramsay hears,

> which for the most part beat a measured and soothing tattoo to her thoughts and seemed consolingly to repeat over and over again ... the words of some old cradle song, murmured by nature, 'I am guarding you – I am your support,' but at other times suddenly and unexpectedly ... had no such kindly meaning, but like a ghostly roll of drums remorselessly beat the measure of life, made one think of the destruction of the island and its engulfment in the sea, and warned her whose day had slipped past in one quick doing after another that it was all ephemeral as a rainbow – this sound which had been obscured and concealed under the other sounds suddenly thundered hollow in her ears and made her look up with an impulse of terror. (20)

Scale effects: 'Things are huge and very small'

The terror felt by Mrs Ramsay above anticipates the opening of James Jeans's *The Mysterious Universe* (published in 1930, three years after *To the Lighthouse*), a book on twentieth-century advances in physics that Woolf would go on to read and find fascinating. Jeans writes,

> Standing on our microscopic fragment of a grain of sand, we attempt to discover the nature and purpose of the universe which surrounds our home in space and time. Our first impression is something akin to terror. We find the universe terrifying because of its vast meaningless distances, terrifying because of its inconceivably long vistas of time which dwarf human history to the twinkling of an eye, terrifying because of our extreme loneliness, and because of the material insignificance of our home in space – a millionth part of a grain of sand out of all the sea-sand in the world. But above all else, we find the universe terrifying because it appears to be indifferent to life like our own; emotion, ambition and achievement, art and religion all seem equally foreign to its plan.[43]

To the Lighthouse and *The Waves* both offer glimpses of the vast scales at which, as Jeans describes, human life is rendered insignificant. As Mr Ramsay asks in *To the Lighthouse*, 'what are two thousand years? … What, indeed, if you look from a mountain top down the long wastes of the ages?' (41). Lily, while contemplating the bay, muses that 'distant views seem to outlast by a million years … the gazer and to be communing already with a sky which beholds an earth entirely at rest' (25). Packed into these lines are the implications of living in a universe much vaster and much older than humans can even truly comprehend, as well as a recognition that to gaze out at the cosmos is to gaze into the past. Lily finds herself obliterated by the thought of deep time, as she envisions that 'already' the sky 'beholds an earth entirely at rest'. There is the sense, then, that the earth will continue to exist when life dies out (or, rather, '*an* earth' as she puts it – earth before or after life is by implication a very different place).

Likewise, in *The Waves*, there are moments when the apprehension of non-human vastness threatens to obliterate human significance – as, for instance, when the entire earth is figured as 'only a pebble flicked off accidentally from the face of the sun' (193). At such a scale, the King becomes ridiculous and the whole of English history becomes negligible: 'how strange it seems to set against the whirling abysses of infinite space a little figure with a golden teapot on his head,' as Bernard remarks; 'Our English past' is reduced to 'one inch of light' (194–5):

> It is a trick of the mind – to put Kings on their thrones, one following another, with crowns on their heads. And we ourselves ... what do we oppose, with this random flicker of light in us that we call brain and feeling, how can we do battle against this flood; what has permanence? Our lives too stream away, down the unlighted avenues, past the strip of time, unidentified. (195)

To see the pinnacle of human power structures (the sovereign) as merely 'a trick of the mind' is to recognize that power and importance are just concepts created by humans, not objective facts – even or especially when these concepts have very real and material effects. Earlier I figured the Copernican paradigm shift as a 'dolly-zoom' of the human place within the universe, and I believe it a fitting metaphor for thinking the effects of climate change consciousness. The cinematic dolly-zoom technique – pioneered in Alfred Hitchcock's *Vertigo*, and used to great effect in Steven Spielberg's *Jaws* – is achieved by simultaneously zooming in on an object whilst moving the camera further away, or zooming out whilst moving in. The effect is nauseating: the object stays roughly the same size, but the background shifts vertiginously. Gustavo Mercado notes that the effect is typically employed 'to underline a character's sudden realization that something is wrong', making it particularly apt for figuring the disturbing power of scale effects in the Anthropocene.[44] Woolf employs a similar technique when she introduces non-human scales into her characters' mundane experience. Take the following passage from *The Waves*:

> half-way through dinner, we felt enlarge itself round us the huge blackness of what is outside us, of what we are not. The wind, the rush of wheels became the roar of time, and we rushed – where? And who were we? We were extinguished for a moment, went out like sparks in burnt paper and the blackness roared. Past time, past history we went. (238)

The characters are 'half-way through dinner' when they are suddenly beset with a sense of the non-human universe getting larger, and of hurtling through 'blackness'. At the human scale, this contradicts the information relayed by sense perceptions (the cosy and stable restaurant and the other customers), but at the astronomical scale, it describes the reality of living on a ball of rock travelling at tremendous speeds through space. The earth moves at 67,000 miles per hour in its orbit around the sun (which is itself moving at 490,000 miles per hour within the Milky Way – which, in turn, is moving at 37,000 miles per minute through the cosmos).[45] These extreme and dizzying movements are imperceptible – but an awareness of them invites the uncanny realization that the world of direct experience is just one reality among many. The non-human in the above passage, while it can only be negatively defined – it is 'what is outside us', 'what we are not' – takes on agency (it 'enlarge[s] *itself*) and motive force, while diminishing senses of identity and control: 'we rushed – where? And who were we?'

Such vertiginous rescaling was first set in motion by the Copernican revolution, but, as Timothy Clark writes, it is in the Anthropocene that human beings find their daily lives irrevocably intertwined with such vastness: 'the Anthropocene enacts the demand to think of human life at much broader scales of space and time, something which alters significantly the way that many once familiar issues appear. Perhaps too big to see or even to think straight … the Anthropocene challenges us to think counter-intuitive relations of scale, effect, perception, knowledge, representation and calculability.'[46] The Anthropocene, that is to say, subverts the primacy and even validity of the scale at which we normally perceive things, demonstrating that human perception is in no way the measure of absolute reality, as Woolf was clearly aware. What is true locally, at a human scale (a weather event such as snow, for example), might contradict the larger reality (global warming). We cannot, however, just 'switch' to the global scale and leave human reality behind. Clark continues, 'We inhabit distance, height and breadth in terms of the given dimensionality of our embodied, earthly existence. The particular scale is inherent to the intelligibility of things around us, imbued with an obviousness and authority which it takes an effort to override.' We are forced, therefore, to comprehend and live both scales at once, which is why these scalar 'disjunctions', as Clark calls them, are so disorienting.[47]

In *To the Lighthouse*, while pondering over a rock pool, Nancy is also beset with the unsettling apprehension of more than one scale:

> Brooding, she changed the pool into the sea, and made the minnows into sharks and whales, and cast vast clouds over this tiny world by holding her hand against the sun, and so brought darkness and desolation, like God himself, to millions of ignorant and innocent creatures, and then took her hand away suddenly and let the sun stream down. Out on the pale criss-crossed sand, high-stepping, fringed, gauntleted, stalked some fantastic leviathan (she was still enlarging the pool), and slipped into the vast fissures of the mountain side. And then, letting her eyes slide imperceptibly above the pool and rest on that wavering line of sea and sky, on the tree trunks which the smoke of steamers made waver on the horizon, she became with all that power sweeping savagely in and inevitably withdrawing, hypnotized, and the two senses of that vastness and this tininess (the pool had diminished again) flowering within it made her feel that she was bound hand and foot and unable to move by the intensity of feelings which

reduced her own body, her own life, and the lives of all the people in the world, for ever, to nothingness. (83)

The first part of this passage, where Nancy enlarges the pool, has affinities with Bernard's game towards the beginning of *The Waves*, when a 'worm' becomes a 'hooded cobra' and 'stalks of flowers are thick as oak trees', their petals 'like purple windows'; 'We are giants, lying here, who can make forests quiver' (18–19). 'Everything is strange,' he says, 'Things are huge and very small', in a childlike diction that belies the important realization that hugeness and smallness are neither fixed properties nor mutually exclusive but instead are anthropomorphic designations and can, therefore, beyond human apprehensions of scale, both be true at once (18).

Susan Stewart writes that 'there are no miniatures in nature; the miniature is ... the product of an eye performing certain operations, manipulating, and attending in certain ways to, the physical world.'[48] In Nancy's fantasy, we see more fully the bidirectional action of scale effects, as her eye shifts its 'operations'. First, Nancy plays God, altering the climate of the little world she presides over (and the desolation she brings to creatures 'ignorant and innocent' seems to ironically posit humans in the former category – recalling as it does the 'dark of human ignorance' felt by Mr Ramsay previously (50) – in opposition to the 'innocence' of non-human animals). What is a fantasy for Nancy is now being realized (both acknowledged and made real) by human beings in the Anthropocene, as the cumulative force of individual action becomes as huge and potent as that of Nancy's 'leviathan'. Actions that seem insignificant to individuals compose the destructive global force of humankind. As Clark writes, 'the emergent force of scale effects is confusing because they take the easy, daily equations of moral and political accounting and multiply them both by zero and by infinity'.[49] This means, paradoxically, the more that individual potency and responsibility is diluted – by more people engaging in that action – the greater the cumulative impact. The carbon imprint of a flight you take is both significant *and* insignificant only in relation to the global aviation industry, and to the billions of other carbon-dioxide-producing activities that human beings partake in every day – a fact that renders your individual choice *both* important and meaningless on the planetary scale. The image of the leviathan in Woolf's passage, which recalls Hobbes's metaphor for the organism created by political society, today takes on a new significance, as seemingly harmless individual actions become engorged and monstrous in light of climate change. Nancy's leviathan slips 'into the vast fissures of the mountain side', just as humankind finds itself inadvertently becoming-geological in the Anthropocene.

When Nancy gazes upwards, her eyes find a 'wavering line of sea and sky,' as if the boundary between the two is starting to break down. Likewise, the 'tree trunks' are 'made [to] waver' by the 'smoke of steamers'. To 'waver' can be to 'flicker' or 'quiver', to move like a wave, but it can also be to 'falter', to 'show signs of giving way'. The wavering of the tree trunks, then, could be read both as the optical interference of the smoke and as figuring the relationship between human and non-human worlds – in which industry puts unprecedented pressure on life forms that have not evolved to deal with an Anthropocene planet. Such wavering could result in the sense of the word 'waver' as a noun: a 'tree left standing when the surrounding wood is felled' (*OED*), as the nebulous fumes of the steamer take on, through scale effects, a destructive power of extirpation.

The image of 'this tininess' 'flowering' within vastness, simultaneously has, as Nancy realizes, 'two senses': 'this tininess' is both her little rock pool world, flowering in the relative vastness of the beach, and also the entire planet, flowering in the vastness of the cosmos. The disturbance of scale that Nancy experiences is re-enacted by the sentence, as 'that vastness and this tininess' signifies on two incommensurably different scales at once. The two explanatory parentheses in the passage – '(she was still enlarging the pool)' and '(the pool had diminished again)' – seem conspicuous in such a lyrical passage, and a departure from Woolf's usual omission of such pointers.[50] What they do show, however, is Nancy's movement from an active to a passive force in the scene. Initially, *she* is enlarging the pool; she is godlike, omnipotent, in control. But then, as her 'eyes slide' upwards (an action mimed by the irresistible sliding into each other of the words 'eyes' and 'slide'), the pool diminishes *by itself* – and she has diminished with it. Much as Lily did earlier when contemplating the distant views, Nancy finds herself, and 'all the people in the world', reduced 'to nothingness'.

'Everything is strange': The quantum world

Early twentieth-century physics effected a kind of inverse Copernican shift through its revelation of the previously unimagined subatomic scale of the quantum world – a scale at which logics of cause and effect, subject and object not only do not apply but are also radically undone. This strange new reality defied the assumptions of classical science and again exposed the limits of human perception though its divulgence of the relativity of space and time; of a universe made entirely of waves; of particles that exist in two states at once and that register whether or not they are being watched; of vast empty spaces within every atom; and of what Einstein called 'spooky action at a distance': quantum entanglement. As Caroline Rooney notes, such discoveries – in their disclosure of a radically interrelated world in which absolute 'objectivity' is impossible, and in which there is a kind of subatomic agency or awareness – strike closer to the realities described by animistic philosophies than those of classical science.[51] Subatomic particles were shown to be able to express themselves differently depending on whether or not they were being observed – thereby disqualifying the notion of pure objectivity.[52] The rigorous subject/object dichotomy, upon which classical science is based, is shown, by the reality of the quantum world, to be entirely constructed or fictional.

The counter-intuitive and seemingly 'irrational' nature of the quantum world may appear to be irrelevant to, or at least to have no correlation with, the human-sized reality we know and live. However, as physicists Brian Cox and Jeff Forshaw state, human-sized reality is also defined by these strange facts, even if we do not perceive it to be so: 'The laws of quantum theory replace Newton's laws and furnish a more accurate description of the world. Newton's physics emerges out of the quantum description, and it is important to realize that the situation is not "Newton for big things and quantum for small": it is *quantum all the way*.'[53] Those 'big things' of course include living organisms, which, until recently, were assumed to be too 'hot, wet and messy' for 'quantum weirdness' to survive in.[54] However, the growing field of quantum biology is beginning to speculate about some of the ways in which living organisms might maintain and utilize quantum phenomena in processes such as avian navigation, smell and even – perhaps – consciousness. As Jim Al-Khalili and Johnjoe McFadden write in *Life on the Edge: The Coming of Age of Quantum Biology*, there are a growing number of scientists suggesting that 'aspects of quantum mechanics do indeed play a nontrivial, indeed crucial, role in the phenomenon of life'.[55] Al-Khalili and McFadden go on to elaborate how 'living organisms have roots that penetrate right down to the quantum bedrock of reality', thereby harnessing the quantum effects of 'coherence, superposition, tunneling or entanglement'.[56] Whether or not quantum effects seem 'rational' to humans is not what matters here; what matters here is their utility to living things.

Indeed, that the quantum world seems 'irrational' says more about the concept of 'rationality' being used to make such a judgement than about its object. This is not to state that human rationality is 'false' or without 'value' (because, of course, we have learnt that such concepts are also relative qualities as opposed to objective realities), but merely to recognize its limitations and the particular assumptions upon which it rests. The failure to make such a recognition, is, as Tim Ingold remarks, the 'impossible foundation' upon which classical science rests: 'it has to place itself above and beyond the very world it claims to understand.' To maintain the delusion of objectivity, he continues, science must pretend that it is not 'in' the world, as if observation did not depend upon 'participation ... between the observer and those aspects of the world that are the focus of attention'.[57] The end of objectivity heralded by quantum physics accords with Ingold's description of an animistic conception of the universe that I quoted in the previous chapter; both open 'the dynamic, transformative potential of the entire field of relations within which beings of all kinds, more or less person-like or thing-like, continually and reciprocally bring one another into existence'.[58] As Bernard admits in *The Waves*, he is 'made and remade continually' by others, who 'bring me into existence as certainly as you do' (114). The 'you' here apostrophizes the reader, thereby highlighting the textual nature of what we might call 'quantum animism': the reciprocal relation between subject and object, observer and observed is a *reading effect* – and one that, therefore, disturbs the boundaries of the text from the outset. I will be returning to this idea in the next section.

Perhaps what captivated Woolf most markedly within the world of quantum physics was Jeans's description of 'the tendency of modern physics ... to resolve the whole material universe into waves, and nothing but waves': 'bottled-up waves, which we call matter, and unbottled waves, which we call radiation or light'[59] – a revelation which clearly influenced the title and imagery of Woolf's novel. However, as Gillian Beer writes, 'physicists did not simply introduce ideas' to Woolf; 'rather, their insights and their language coalesced with hers. She saw realist fiction as an impoverishment of the real and in her own writing sought at once to condense and (as she put it) "insubstantise".'[60] The coalescence of Woolf's ideas with those of quantum physics can also be felt in her refusal of any definable opposition between 'fiction' and 'reality'. Jeans admits that 'the waves which form the universe ... are in all probability fictitious', which, he says, 'is not to say that they have no existence at all: they exist in our minds', and it is to this existence that 'we may temporarily assign the name "reality"'.[61] And twentieth-century physicists were certainly not the first scientists to use fiction and metaphor to describe reality. As Frédérique Aït-Touati describes in *Fictions of the Cosmos*, the reliance of science upon fiction might be traced to the seventeenth century, when, in order to convey Copernicus' heliocentric universe, scientists had to appeal to their audience's imagination rather than to the evidence of their senses (which told them that the sun moved and the earth was fixed): 'visual and fictional figuration played a central role, substituting a new mental image of the cosmos for the old one.'[62]

Even according to science, then, 'reality' is fundamentally fictitious, corroborating Woolf's earlier suspicion that 'reality' is not a stable and objective entity but is rather 'something very erratic, very undependable', that appears in flashes.[63] She makes the following rather cryptic entry in her diary regarding *The Mysterious Universe*: 'Talk about the riddle of the universe (Jeans' book) whether it will be known; not by us; found out suddenly: about rhythm in prose.'[64] What has 'rhythm in prose' got to do with 'the riddle of the universe'? Could it be that, for Woolf, the 'wild' and 'inhuman' force of rhythm animates both the enigmatic workings of the universe described in Jeans's book and the strange life of language in or by which she was so well versed? Or was it that the unelucidated discovery she has made 'about rhythm in prose' was a 'finding out' about a force as mysterious and inhuman as 'the riddle of the universe'? Woolf's diary entry is too elliptical for us to ascertain the exact nature of the tie between the mysteries of the cosmos and the rhythms of language – perhaps it eludes verbalization – but clearly, for her, a link is there. Woolf felt something in writing that moves beyond the limits of human language.

Waves – the newly revealed, albeit 'fictitious', essence of the universe – inundate both the novels I have been discussing, in the form of both light and water, tying the kind of waves that are not directly perceived as such by the naked eye (that is, paradoxically, light; for, while we can see light, we do not apprehend it as waves) to the more familiar visibly undulating waves of the ocean. In *To the Lighthouse*, alongside the background rhythm provided by 'the monotonous fall of the waves on the beach' (20), there are also the waters of sadness, which 'swayed this way and that' (33); the 'beam' and 'ray' of perception (55); the 'eddy', 'merging and flowing', of experience at the dinner party (91); the rippling and 'fluidity' of the outside world 'in which things waved and vanished, waterily' (106); the 'rhythm' and 'current' that bears Lily along whilst painting (174); the 'eternal passing and flowing' of life (176); and words which, like waves, 'broke and broke again' in Cam's mind (182). In *The Waves*, 'the concussion of the waves breaking' (24), '*drum[ming] on the shore*' (64), beats a '*thud[ding]*' rhythm in the interludes (92) that is riffed upon by the pervasive wave-imagery of the text's world – in which images of light and water are often conflated to underline their kinetic identity: 'flowers swim like fish made of light upon the dark, green waters' (9); desire 'must waver, like the light in and out of the beech leaves' (12); Rhoda cannot pull herself 'out of these waters' – she is 'turned' and 'tumbled', 'among these long lights, these long waves' (23); later she speaks of 'some check in the flow of my being; a deep stream presses on some obstacle' (48); Bernard feels 'a roll of heavy waters … dragging me open, laying bare the pebbles on the shore of my soul' (75); Jinny flutters, ripples and streams, 'like a plant in the river, flowing this way, flowing that way' (88); and, like 'the eternal renewal, the incessant rise and fall and fall and rise again', which Bernard says characterizes the world (the palindromic formation here miming the cyclical reality promised by the phrase 'eternal renewal'), he notes that 'in [himself] too the wave rises. It swells; it arches its back' (255). In this line, the metaphors double back on themselves, as the wave that Bernard ascribes to his being (thereby likening himself to a wave) is then described in terms of an animal 'arch[ing]' its back: animal is wave is animal; rise and fall and fall and rise again. As Beer recognizes, 'assonance, overlap between words, iteration and internal rhyme' – as in the passage from 'Time Passes' that I discussed towards the beginning of this chapter – 'express the wave-like fluidity of a newly imagined universe'.[65] The confluence of external and internal environments in both novels, aside from countersigning the wave-constitution of the universe, also serves to sweep away the classical dichotomies of self/world and subject/object, leaving in their place a reality more participatory, entangled and mutable. As Martin writes, Woolf's 'sense of sympathy between the energy of individuals and of the world leads to a re-shaping of the idea of individuality'.[66] The notions of 'character' and 'individual' find themselves unanchored, adrift on the currents and tides that move in and through Woolf's writing.

Essential drift

Experiences of reading and writing (in both their narrow and generalized senses) can also be thought on the basis of this animistic, quantum reality – a reality in which not only is 'identity' or 'meaning' shown to be irreducibly entangled with that which observes or reads it but also the causal logic of linear temporality is disrupted, so that texts can come to mean something other as they meet with the future – just as a quantum entity's wave/particle status can retrospectively alter itself. Karen Barad describes how when the double-slit experiment is modified so that the record of observation can be erased afterwards, the results change accordingly; an entity's wave/particle status can be determined 'after it has already gone through as either a wave (through both slits at once) or a particle (through one slit or the other)', thereby altering not only the past behaviour of a given entity but also its 'very identity': 'Its past identity, its ontology, is never fixed, it is always open to future reworkings'.[67] Similarly, as J. Hillis Miller writes in an essay on 'Anachronistic Reading', 'literary works program or encode their future readings, though in an unpredictable way' – so that the work can seem to know or mean things beyond the context of the time and place of writing.[68] A text does not come at a reader as a fully determined object, no matter how much the static solidity of the letters on the page may make it seem that way. While it is commonly taken for granted that writing and reading comprise a one-way passage from consciousness to consciousness via the vehicle of a text (which would correspond to the presumed 'objectivity' of classical science), such a conception, as Derrida describes in 'Signature Event Context', fails to apprehend the force of writing:

> A written sign carries with it a force that breaks with its context, that is, with the collectivity of presences organizing the moment of its inscription. This breaking force is not an accidental predicate but the very structure of the written text. … [The] allegedly real context includes a certain 'present' of the inscription, the presence of the writer to what he has written, the entire environment and the horizon of his experience, and above all the intention, the wanting-to-say-what-he-means, which animates his inscription at a given moment. But the sign possesses the characteristic of being readable even if the moment of its production is irrevocably lost and even if I do not know what its alleged author-scriptor consciously intended to say at the moment he wrote it, i.e. abandoned it to its essential drift.[69]

Even in the absence of the writer, in the absence of 'the entire environment and the horizon of [their] experience', the written sign still carries its force. It continues to be *animated*, that is to say, not by 'the intention, the wanting-to-say-what-[they]-mean' of the writer, but by something that operates with or without them. The text carries, therefore, the necessary possibility of the writer's absence in its essence – as well as the capacity for transformation or corruption: its 'essential drift'. What I mean to say might remain unread or unreadable, it might never come across. However, the essential possibility of going astray – of breaking with the context of inscription – is also what *enables* meaning to come across, to traverse the horizon of my experience and find its way into yours, for example. As Derrida writes, traces 'are constituted by the double force of repetition and erasure, legibility and illegibility'.[70] These characteristics are not limited 'strictly to "written" communication in the narrow sense of this word': 'the traits that can be recognized in the classical, narrowly defined concept of writing, are generalizable. They are valid not only for all orders of "signs" and for all languages in general but moreover, beyond semio-linguistic communication, for the entire field of what philosophy would call experience, even the experience of being.'[71] Derrida goes on to identify three essential traits of writing: its capacity for survival, its breaking force and its spatio-temporal spacing, or 'differance'.[72] The apprehension that these traits are generalizable to traces beyond or prior to human language might help us to think about the forces at work in the world, human and non-human, living and non-living: 'the experience of being', as Derrida remarks, is one of writing and reading, and one in which classical objectivity gives way to quantum play. What traces of twenty-first-century life will remain in fifty millennia? How will they be read? We may be the 'authors' of the Anthropocene, but its meaning remains to be determined by others.

Writing might be thought of as a surge of active creativity, the ejaculation into the world of word-shaped thought, while reading would be the passive receptacle, into which writing comes and means. Yet, in writing and reading as in sexual reproduction, the relation is far more reciprocal than this description would have it. As Rooney remarks, in the practice of writing, there is 'no conception without reception. And this reception is not the supposed empty passivity of the feminine but something active. It has to be, for a passive reception would be no reception at all.'[73] As you read these words, you animate them within the singular context of your life at this moment, a context that is forever beyond my control or jurisdiction – even at those moments when I seem to be right there with you, in your head. The reader is, as David Wills remarks, 'at least … the joint author of the book'.[74] So while the act of writing chronologically precedes the act of reading, the two are, at bottom, mutually constitutive, and in that sense, writing does not precede reading; there is, as Derrida says, a 'passageway of deferred reciprocity between reading and writing'.[75] Each time anew, the reader creates – but never fully determines – the 'meaning' of a text, becoming its 'joint author', its co-writer or ghostwriter. The writer, meanwhile, may find themselves in a more suggestive or receptive role than the term 'author' would imply. As Rooney notes, 'it could be said that at each moment of being produced the writing is that which is responding to itself, so that writing is also a reading process. … The "death of the author" could be reconfigured to mean reader-as-writer and writer-as-reader.'[76] The writer and reader are written by the text, and the text, in turn, is written by both writer and reader. As such, none of these elements can be rigorously determined in advance or in isolation. As I will explore in Chapter 4, one's 'self' or 'identity' (which is always a matter of writing and reading) is not a stable entity but is continually being-written and being-read, perpetually open to transformation through or by alterity.

Roots to the depths of the world: The radical animism of material identity

In his essay 'Far Out', Leo Bersani writes of the fundamental unity of all matter, of 'the material inscriptions in our body of a universe to which we belong, which we *are* before being born into it'.[77] The universe is *materially identical* insofar as all matter has the same origin, the same atomic makeup, the same physical laws governing it. The chemical elements of your body were formed in the hearts of stars and have gone through countless reincarnations before coming to participate in a human form. As Bersani puts it, the 'correspondences that most profoundly situate us outside ourselves are, perceived or unperceived, material correspondences. Living bodies do not unaccountably inhabit an alien space; they carry the memory of the origin they share with all material being.'[78] Life emerges out of matter, out of the universe, in the way that an apple emerges from a tree. It is not the creation of 'new' matter but rather the rearrangement or reincarnation of pre-existing matter – or energy – into new forms. That given, what could sound like 'mysticism' becomes a matter-of-fact description of the fact of matter, of its material reality: 'The human contains the inorganic nonhuman from which it has evolved. These cosmic correspondences are active in what we should recognize as the oneness of all being.'[79] Material 'oneness' has important implications for how we might conceive of human thought and its place or even 'role' within the universe, without recourse to religious moralism. Bersani continues:

> The body is the mind's most intimate world. It extends, both physically and ontologically, into the world that surrounds it, and into the universe inhabited by that world. The difficult and exhilarating demand made on the mind by all those worlds – the call they make to us – is not that we think about or against them, but rather that our thought be the passionately energetic delegate of the cosmic explosions, upheavals, movements, and settlings that, very late in their still unfinished history, at last gave birth to the human and nonhuman bodies in and among which we live, as well as to thought and its work.[80]

Human thought, that is to say, is a 'delegate' of the universe and cannot, in any rigorous or absolute way, be separated from anything else that exists. Consciousness arises from life, just as life arises from non-living matter. What we think of as 'individuality', then, while often defined by the spatio-temporal locus of a particular living body, is always interrupted by its material identity with, or reincarnation of, other spatially or temporally 'distinct' bodies (as well as the genetically distinct bodies of the microbiome with which it shares a locus).

In *The Waves*, Louis evinces a profound sense of material identity or 'oneness' – particularly in relation to the planet – throughout his life. As a child, he says, 'I hold a stalk in my hand. I am the stalk. My roots go down to the depths of the world' (9). Holding the stalk in his hand, Louis feels an intuitive sense of rootedness that binds him to the earth. In many of Louis's passages, there is a conflation of time and space, as his identity is enlarged beyond his body in both of these dimensions: deep into the earth, and into the distant past. He recognizes a need to think his lived experience within a greater history, to 'realize the meeting-place of past and present' (56). Sitting in an 'eating-shop', he sees it 'against the packed and fluttering birds' wings, many feathered, folded, of the past' (82), an image which depicts the past not as a static and immutable entity but as something alive, moving, beating itself into the present scene – like, perhaps, the 'impulses wilder than the wildest birds' that 'strike from [his] wild heart' (49):

> My roots go down through veins of lead and silver, through damp, marshy places that exhale odours, to a knot made of oak roots bound together in the centre. Sealed and blind, with earth stopping my ears, I have yet heard rumours of wars; and the nightingale; have felt the hurrying of many troops of men flocking hither and thither in quest of civilization like flocks of birds migrating seeking the summer; I have seen women carrying red pitchers to the banks of the Nile. (81–2)

Roots bring both nourishment and stability. They can survive even if the part of a plant that is above ground is destroyed. They are, quite literally, a *radical* (from the Latin *radix*, 'root') animism. For Louis, who often feels an outsider among his contemporaries, a sense of rootedness in the earth and history counters his anxiety.

The image of 'roots' that 'go down through veins of lead and silver' works in multiple ways, its layers of metaphor complicating the distinction between the organic and inorganic. Veins run through both animal and plant life forms, and, as the earth itself is here veined, it too is figured as a living organism, generalizing life beyond the organically living. Meanwhile, 'lead and silver' evoke the chemical elements out of which all matter is composed, rooting life in its pre-organic, chemical origins, as well as opening the earth's history out onto a wider, cosmic history.[81] The 'damp, marshy places that exhale odours' recalls the primeval swamp out of which Darwin suggested life originated – the action of exhaling or respiring being one common to all life forms. In a later passage, which again invokes his rootedness in the past, Louis remarks that he is 'now a full-grown man; now upright standing in sun or rain' (143). This linking of adulthood to standing erect alludes to Darwin's linking of ontogenesis to phylogenesis, as primates grew ever more upright in their evolution towards human form. Louis's roots, then, travel down both through the evolution of life and life's non-living mineral forbears (the silver and lead), to 'a knot made of oak roots bound together in the centre'. The stalwart anchorage offered by 'oak roots' – already a symbol of strength and endurance – is further reinforced by being 'bound' into a 'knot'.

Underground, Louis is 'sealed and blind, with earth stopping [his] ears', and yet still hears the nightingale and the troops, and sees the women carrying pitchers. His perceptions come from beyond his sense organs, implying a bodily memory not restricted to his individual life, a bodily memory that has 'lived a thousand lives already' (109). Identity, character and psychological unity are invaded from the outset by this material (and therefore unavoidable) externality, so that even when Louis later signs his name 'twenty times' – 'I, and again I, and again I' – asserting it is 'clear, firm, unequivocal', such unequivocality (if not already undermined by the repetitions of the 'I') is undone by the 'vast inheritance of experience' packed within it (142).

While Louis's rootedness is particularly earthbound, in the 'Time Passes' section of *To the Lighthouse*, a material oneness is evoked that stretches to a more astronomical scale, to what Bersani calls our 'memories of cosmic origins':[82]

> As summer neared, as the evenings lengthened, there came to the wakeful, the hopeful, walking the beach, stirring the pool, imaginations of the strangest kind – of flesh turned to atoms which drove before the wind, of stars flashing in their hearts, of cliff, sea, cloud, and sky brought purposely together to assemble outwardly the scattered parts of the vision within. (144)

Just as in *The Waves* the development of the lives of the characters is figured by the passing of a day or of the seasons in the interludes (so that morning and spring are youth, and evening and winter are old age, etc.), here we find that the nearing of summer brings wakefulness and hopefulness to those who walk the beach: the time of year reflects itself in the psyche. Indeed, earlier in the novel, as winter was closing in, this passage is counterposed by one in which a 'sleeper' walking on the sand finds no answer to 'his doubts' (140). The image of 'stirring the pool' recalls Nancy's earlier fantasy over the rock pool and the scale effects it heralded, which now shadow the 'imaginations of the strangest kind' that overcome the anonymous walkers. The notion of 'stars flashing in their hearts' invokes the fact that every atom in our bodies was once in the heart of a star, the ancient light of its explosion still 'flashing' in the living pulse of a heart (the 'flash' also recalling the 'flesh' of the previous clause, further tying the two images together). The 'flesh turned to atoms' driving before the wind works in the opposite way to Louis's deep-set roots, as bodily materiality is sent into the future, to be reincarnated in some as yet unknown formation, again extending being beyond the span of a single lifetime. The image of 'cliff, sea, cloud, and sky' being 'brought purposely together' recalls four of the Aristotelian elements – earth, water, air and ether – of which the universe is composed, renaming them with a verbal harmony, monosyllabic and doubly alliterative with the 'cl-' and 's-' sounds. The 'vision within' which these elements outwardly assemble seems to refer both to the vision of the human walkers on the beach – who feel their minds reflected in the world around them – and also to some kind of beneficent cosmological intention: 'it was impossible to resist', the passage continues, 'the strange intimation which every gull, flower, tree, man and woman, and the white earth itself seemed to declare … that good triumphs, happiness prevails, order rules' (144). To 'intimate' something is 'to make known', 'to communicate', but it is also of course 'to make intimate, to make familiar', and so the phrase 'strange intimation' brings together the intimate material ties of 'every gull, flower, tree, man and woman' and the strangeness of such an apprehension, the uncanny reality of a 'self' inhabiting, and inhabited by, a world not materially separable from it.

Living on: The flowers in the urn

Both of Woolf's novels express a concern about the transience of life and the entropic progress of what she called 'this scratching, clawing, and colding universe' towards extinction.[83] In the secular world of a post-Copernican cosmos, there is no promise of a divine afterlife to temper the thoughts of death. As Jeans explains in *The Mysterious Universe*,

> The science of thermodynamics explains how everything in nature passes to its final state by a process which is designated the 'increase of entropy.' Entropy must for ever increase: it cannot stand still until it has increased so far that it can increase no further. When this stage is reached, further progress will be impossible, and the universe will be dead.[84]

As Beer writes in *Darwin's Plots*, life and entropy constitute oppositional forces: evolution is a process of 'more and more complex *ordering*, while the second law of thermodynamics emphasizes the tendency of energy systems towards disorder'.[85] The word 'extinction' comes from the Latin *ex-stinguĕre*, to 'put out, quench (fire, light, anything burning or shining)' (*OED*): the heat death of the universe is the extinction to end all extinctions, the inevitable deaths of individuals and species being but precursors to a more final subsumption into darkness and timelessness. So while not all extinctions are a product of entropy, entropy will eventually see to those that escape the asteroid impacts, hunters' guns or changes in climate. Given that the extinction of a species or individual is a destruction of difference – one less species, one less individual – these 'premature' extinctions are entropic in their effects if not in their causes. A maximum entropy state would be the advent to end all advents, the arrival of a universal and static sameness, the extinction of all stars and galaxies, of all heat and light, of all movement: the extinction, fundamentally, of difference.

In *The Waves*, Bernard says, 'Our flame, the will-o'-the-wisp that dances in a few eyes, is soon to be blown out and all will fade' (236). By 'our flame', does he refer to the six friends of the narrative or to humanity in general? Or is 'our flame' the sun, and the fading of all life on earth implied by its inevitable extinction? The future perfect 'all will fade', the inevitability of what *will* happen, doubles itself into the present tense, the extinction of all will or volition: living will ('Our flame') is reduced to a will-o'-the-wisp, an *ignis fatuus*, or 'foolish fire'.[86] Later, a solar eclipse seems to foreshadow the entropic extinction of the earth and solar system:

> The woods had vanished; the earth was a waste of shadow. No sound broke the silence of the wintry landscape. No cock crowed; no smoke rose; no train moved. A man without a self, I said. A heavy body leaning on a gate. A dead man. With dispassionate despair, with entire disillusionment, I surveyed the dust dance; my life, my friends' lives, and those fabulous presences, men with brooms, women writing, the willow tree by the river – clouds and phantoms made of dust too, of dust that changed, as clouds lose and gain and take gold or red and lose their summits and billow this way and that, mutable, vain. (245)

Silent, still, dark and cold: identity is obliterated, selfhood disappears. Lives are reduced to a 'dust dance'. The allusion to the Bible ('for dust thou art, and unto dust shalt thou return', Gen. 3.19) emphasizes human mortality but without the promise of salvation or an afterlife: the 'loss' and 'gain' and 'chang[ing]' of the dust is, in the end, 'vain'. Even though the eclipse is only temporary, it foretells the earth's certain – and permanent – fate.

In *To the Lighthouse*, Lily says of the autumnal evening air that 'it suddenly gets cold. The sun seems to give less heat' – but her words also voice the anxiety of an age beset by the obliterative implications of entropy (24). Such implications are, for Mr Ramsay, tied to thoughts of human transience: 'The very stone one kicks with one's boot will outlast Shakespeare,' he thinks (41). There are scale effects at work again, as the name that represents a pinnacle of literary achievement is reduced to insignificance by deep time scales, 'the waste of the years and the perishing of stars' (41). Mr Ramsay's meditations on this matter take place on the terrace of the house and are punctuated by the repeated appearance of the 'stone urns' that sit there – their stoniness a sign that they too will 'outlast' the living things around them. He stops 'for one moment by the stone urn which held the geraniums'; he empties his pipe 'with two or three resonant taps on the handle of the urn'; later, 'the geranium in the urn became startlingly visible'; he stands 'stock-still, by the urn, with the geranium flowing over it'; and, finally, squaring 'his shoulders', he stands 'very upright by the urn' (39–41). The word 'urn' comes from the Latin *ūrĕre*, 'to burn', being traditionally a receptacle for the ashes of the dead. The urn holds the promise of Mr Ramsay's fear: the annihilation of identity, the anonymity of ashes, the impending extinction of 'his own little light' (41). Likewise, in *The Waves*, there are instances in which the appearance of an urn heralds thoughts of mortality, figured as subsumption into darkness. We find the light of spring – 'daffodils in March' – counterposed by the darkness of 'one urn in winter' (180); Louis and Rhoda 'stop for a moment by this stone urn' and find that the others 'vanish, towards the lake. … The dark has closed over their bodies' (196–7); a crisis of identity descends ('Who are you? Who am I?' asks Louis) as the 'southern sun flickers over this urn; we push off in to the tide of the violent and cruel sea' (199). There is also a passage in which, as remarked by Beer, 'the word "tea-urn" generates "eternity" a few lines down': 'I see the gleaming tea-urn; the glass cases full of pale-yellow sandwiches; the men in round coats perched on stools at the counter; and also behind them, eternity' (82). Beer suggests that Woolf here plays with the 'auditory likeness' of 'the most improbable concepts'.[87] Yet such a link is perhaps less 'improbable' when we take into account the symbolic significance Woolf gives to urns elsewhere in both these novels – where they often, as I have described, inspire thoughts of mortality.[88] Conceptual coherence and 'auditory likeness' thus go hand in hand.

But let us return now to the urns that Mr Ramsay unconsciously contemplates, and note that they also hold *life*: they are full of geraniums, which, significantly, seem to grow as his thoughts develop. In the instances that I have given above, they are at first 'held' by the urn, suggesting a kind of encapsulation or entrapment; in their next appearance, they become 'startlingly visible', as if beginning to break free of their confine, before, finally, 'flowing over it'. Some pages later, the geraniums are seen 'trailing' over the urns, suggesting they have grown even longer and reached the ground (48). Living things (such as geraniums, or language – because 'life' is not reducible to the organically living, as we have seen), have the essential capacity to move and change, to overflow their context (the urn), escape, translate or transport themselves elsewhere: not excluding the future. Beyond the limits of individual lifespans, living things send themselves into the future via reproduction. If we were to read the urns and the geraniums as symbolically representing the battle between 'death' and 'life', between entropy and différance, between extinction and survival – a battle that is waged in a certain way in both the novels I have been discussing – the geraniums would represent not just organic life but also the kind of life that survives, that lives on: like that of the trace or writing. I said that life sends itself to the future via reproduction. Reproduction of what? DNA: the 'non-living' code which voices itself through living organisms (and we can see here how 'living', even at the most basic level, is a reading practice). The survival of DNA is the survival of text – re-read or re-produced by each generation, sometimes altered slightly (evolution), sometimes interpreted differently (epigenetics).[89] Living on, sur-vival, operates before and beyond organic life.

Mr Ramsay sees 'again the urns with the trailing of red geraniums which had so often decorated processes of thought, and bore, written up among their leaves, as if they were scraps of paper on which one scribbles notes in the rush of reading – ' (48). The aposiopesis here means that we do not hear exactly what the geraniums 'bore, written up among their leaves', but presumably it is the very thought processes that they have just been said to decorate: the relation is a reciprocal one. The fact that the urns are seen '*again*' signals their potential iterability (and, as I discussed above, Mr Ramsay's reading changes slightly each time: the geraniums are first held, then visible, then overflowing, then trailing). The 'trailing' (from the Latin *trahĕre*, 'to draw') of the geraniums foreshadows the writing and scribbling of Mr Ramsay, their overflowing of the urns like the 'scraps of paper' (as opposed to the contained neatness of a notebook) scribbled upon in the 'rush of reading'.[90] These scraps of geranium/paper also find their way into *The Waves*, this time decorating a book that Neville reads, the page 'corrupt and mud-stained, and torn and stuck together with faded leaves, with scraps of verbena or geranium' (170). The 'faded leaves' here repeat themselves antanaclastically, transforming, mid-sentence, from leaves of a book to the leaves of 'verbena or geranium'.

Whether in scraps or trails, scribbles or traces, what is *written* – in the general sense, including, as I have been saying, the experience of being – is structured by a possibility of survival or 'living on' that extends the concept of life beyond the organically living, disrupting any stable opposition between the living and the dead. In *The Beast and the Sovereign*, Derrida writes of a sense of survival, or 'survivance' (using the middle voice not possible in English), 'that is neither life nor death pure and simple, a sense that is not thinkable on the basis of the opposition between life and death, a survival that is … not more alive, nor indeed less alive, than life, or more or less dead than death':

> a survivance … whose 'sur-' is without superiority, without height, altitude or highness, and thus without supremacy or sovereignty. It does not add something extra to life, any more than it cuts something from it, any more than it cuts anything from inevitable death or attenuates its rigor and its necessity. … And that is where there is some other that has me at its disposal; that is where any self is defenseless. That is what the self is, that is what I am, what the *I* is, whether I am there or not. The other, the others, that is the very thing that survives me … the survivor of me, the *there* beyond my life.
>
> Like every trace, a book, the survivance of a book, from its first moment on, is a living-dead machine, sur-viving, the body of a thing buried in a library, a bookstore, in cellars, urns [like those, perhaps, that hold Woolf's geraniums?] … but a dead thing that resuscitates each time a breath of living reading, each time the breath of the other or the other breath, each time an intentionality intends it and makes it live again by animating it, like … a body, a spiritual corporeality … animated, activated, traversed, shot through with intentional spirituality.[91]

Beyond what is organically living, there is a structure of survival that undoes the opposition of life and death, and that undoes the pure identity of the self in its relation to what necessarily survives it (starting with the 'I'). Survival is structured by its relation to the other, depending upon 'each time the breath of the other' to animate it again with 'intentional spirituality'. No survival without animism; no animism without others.

This is, I am arguing, precisely the affirmation of *To the Lighthouse* and *The Waves*. While many of the characters are troubled by anxieties about human transience and extinction, there remains or re-turns the survival of traces: the spectral apparition of Mrs Ramsay, the rhythmic returns of the lighthouse beam and the sea's waves, the returns of scraps of phrases in the mouths and minds of different characters. Such survivals are each time made possible by an openness to alterity, the leaving open of a wind-ow, the realization of an I, or eye (the '-ow' or '*auga*' of 'window') always subject to animation by the alterity of what Derrida calls the 'other breath' (the 'wind-'). Nothing, however, is guaranteed in advance. Non-survival, extinction, is the necessary condition of possibility of a survival that always depends upon others.

Let's look at how this moves in *The Waves*. The interludes are often read as framing the rest of the text: 'the majestic march of day across the sky' (233) shadows the linear progression towards death within which all life forms, including the human characters, are caught, as well as subsuming such linearity within the greater cyclical rhythm of renewal figured by the seasons, as Susan Dick points out.[92] The 'day' or 'year' of the interludes represents a larger cosmic story within which human beings, and the six friends of the narrative, are only a tiny fragment. The effect, however, is more complex than this: the passing of the day does not only 'tell' the story of the characters, but the characters also 'tell' its story. Certain images from the interludes are reiterated or anticipated by the characters, thereby subsuming the former within their own narratives, complicating the structure so that we can no longer rigorously define 'inner' and 'outer' or determine which 'narrative' frames the other. To give a few examples: in the interludes, the waves are twice likened to men with '*assegais*' drumming on the shore, an image which is recalled by Rhoda when she speaks of 'the drumming of naked men with assegais' (64, 92, 120). Louis's description of a train as a 'very powerful, bottle-green engine without a neck, all back and thighs' foreshadows the image of the waves drawing '*in and out with the energy, the muscularity, of an engine*' (25, 92). The 'stamping' of a 'beast' that Louis hears throughout his life (49, 57, 109) becomes the sound of the waves, which fall '*like the thud of a great beast stamping*' (128). In his final speech, Bernard 'leaps out of bed, throws up the window' (another window) and exclaims 'with what a whirr the birds rise!':

> You know that sudden rush of wings, that exclamation, carol, and confusion; the riot and babble of voices; and all the drops are sparkling, trembling, as if the garden were a splintered mosaic, vanishing, twinkling; not yet formed into one whole; and a bird sings close to the window. I heard those songs. … And from among them rise one or two distinct figures, birds who sang with the rapt egotism of youth by the window; broke their snails on stones, dipped their beaks in sticky, viscous matter; hard, avid, remorseless; Jinny, Susan, Rhoda. (212)

The fact that this passage so strongly recalls the interludes – the riot of birdsong in a garden that is described in nearly all of them; the *'sparkling'* of the water (6); the *'trembling'* sea-holly (155); the *'splinters'* of the day (177); the *'mosaic of single sparks not yet formed into one whole'* (23); the birds that *'plunged the tips of their beaks savagely into the sticky mixture'* (63) – gives the impression that Bernard, the novelist, writes the interludes, that they too are just a part of his final 'sum[ming] up' (204). The text itself is a 'splintered mosaic' that it is not possible, finally, to form into 'one whole'.

The co-implication of the interludes and the rest of the text presents what Derrida calls (in 'Living On') a 'double invagination': 'For all these quotations, quotations of requotations with no original performance, there is no speech act not already the iteration of another, no circle and no quotation marks to reassure us about the identity, opposition, or distinction of speech events.'[93] Derrida is here referring to Maurice Blanchot's 'The Madness of the Day', but his remarks are equally apt when applied to the structure of *The Waves*, within which we are no more able to determine the 'identity, opposition, or distinction of speech events'. As he goes on, 'it is impossible to say which one quotes the other. … Each includes the other, comprehends the other, which is to say that neither comprehends the other.'[94] Are the interludes and the other characters a part of Bernard – who does not 'know' if he is 'man or woman, Bernard or Neville, Louis, Susan, Jinny, or Rhoda' (242) – or are the human characters subsumed into the larger cosmic narrative presented by the interludes? Laura Marcus writes of *The Waves* that Woolf was not attempting to produce 'characters', but rather her concern was 'with the *experience* of identity and with its articulation through a discourse that, for the most part, cannot be named either as speech or as thought'.[95] An experience of identity, that is to say, beyond its locution, always chiasmatically invaginated through its contaminations with alterity. When Bernard begins to 'sum up', his attempt at providing a linear account of everything undoes itself: he can only 'pretend' to 'make out a plain and logical story' (215). While on one level *The Waves* does follow a highly linear narrative structure, albeit on two scales (the passing of the day, and of the human lives), its linearity is further complicated in two ways. First, as I said above, because the 'day' described by the interludes can be read to represent the larger cyclical rhythms of nature, it at once fits within *and* transcends the human lives. And second, the invaginations of the interludes and the other chapters work to generate the complex and untraceable movement of a chiasmic *mise-en-abyme*: 'the structure of a narrative in deconstruction'.[96]

Such a structure can 'come about in any text, whether it is narrative in form or not ... whether it speaks of it or not'.[97] It is, that is to say, the structural possibility of writing's essential capacity for survival. It opposes the extinction of entropy. Where the latter promises a decrease of difference until time itself can no longer be distinguished, the survival and repetition – or iterability – of writing operates through the multiplications of differences. In Michel Serres's reading of *To the Lighthouse*, he suggests that 'perception' (generalizing perception by suggesting that it is what 'receives, sends, processes, and stores information'; it is, that is to say, what reads and writes) 'reverses the entropy of the world'.[98] It is the textual nature of the universe – the sur-vival of matter, chemical compounds, DNA and so on – that opposes entropy. The conclusion we must draw from this is not, from our anthropocentric perspective, a comforting one. What survives, what lives on, is not 'life' itself – at least not in the sense of organic life, but rather the life of text (which is revealed, in DNA, to be the condition of the former). Beer suggests that *The Waves* is Woolf's attempt 'to think what a story can be, how it can begin and end and produce the consolation of containment in a world of ebbing tides, increasing entropy, and dissipating energy'.[99] If, however, as I have suggested above, the 'containment' of *The Waves* is no such thing, but is rather an uncontainable and chiasmatic series of iterations and invaginations which do not permit closure, could we read the work not as a mere 'consolation' but as an active opposition to the increase of entropy?

Thinking extinction: Climate change and the Cold War

Facing the threats posed by anthropogenic climate change, the possibility of a post-life earth makes itself felt aeons too early. Standing on the crumbling ground of such a precipice, we might well find ourselves disturbed by the motion of another Copernican paradigm shift. Elizabeth Kolbert, in her book *The Sixth Extinction*, writes how the mass extinction event that appears to be underway – the sixth in the history of life on earth, but the first to be directly attributable to the actions of a single dominant species – is likely to be humankind's 'most enduring legacy'.[100] Because of the radical interdependence of life, our destruction of other life forms threatens to undermine the conditions necessary for our own continued existence:

> Having freed ourselves from the constraints of evolution, humans nevertheless remain dependent on the earth's biological and geochemical systems. By

disrupting these systems – cutting down tropical rainforests, altering the composition of the atmosphere, acidifying the oceans – we're putting our own survival in danger. Among the many lessons that emerge from the geologic record, perhaps the most sobering is that in life ... past performance is no guarantee of future results. When a mass extinction occurs, it takes out the weak and also lays low the strong.[101]

What all mass extinction events have in common is, as Kolbert shows, a high speed of change – one that far outpaces that of evolution: 'Conditions change so drastically or so suddenly (or so drastically *and* so suddenly) that evolutionary history counts for little.'[102] Life forms have no chance to adapt to the newly emergent conditions in which they find themselves and therefore perish.[103] Human beings are far more adaptable than other species, but we still 'remain dependent on the earth's biological and geochemical systems' – minimally the oxygen, food and water we take from it, the production of which is part of a vast and inextricable web beyond our full comprehension – and there is a rate of change to which adaptation becomes impossible, even for the most privileged humans.

In terms of posing an existential threat to humanity as a species, climate change has only one precedent: the threat of nuclear destruction that hung over the earth during the Cold War. Both share the fact of being directly attributable to human actions and in that sense can be thought of as fatally auto-destructive, suicidal – though in neither case is the agency distributed evenly through humankind, nor are the effects limited to our own species. These similarities aside, however, the differences between the two threats serve to highlight the major challenges of conceptualization, comprehension and response posed by climate change. I do not mean to lessen the terror or gravity of the threat of nuclear war, but it is, I would suggest, *easier to think about*.

Perhaps the most significant difference is the fact that the nuclear threat remains a *potential* threat, whilst climate change is *already happening*. Claire Colebrook calls the Anthropocene 'post-apocalyptic', because, she writes, 'there will not be complete annihilation but a gradual witnessing of a slow end' and suggests 'that we are already at that moment of witness, living on after the end'.[104] In contrast, as Derrida writes in 1984, under the shadow of the Cold War, 'a nuclear war has not taken place: one can only talk and write about it'; it remains speculative, fictional.[105] (Writing now in 2020, a nuclear war still has not taken place, but nine nations – including the UK – continue to maintain nuclear weapons and, it must be assumed, the will to use them: so we still live under this fictional threat, even if it is today a story told less often.[106]) Nuclear armament is a nation's ultimate expression of power, a planetary threat that issues from geopolitical agency. Climate change, conversely, belies a more generalized human impotence: no amount of money or power can assert itself alone to avert it; instead, a global level of cooperation would be required to drastically transform the way that we interact with the planet. While both nuclear warfare and climate change are anthropogenic, the *anthropos* at the genesis of the latter is as widely dispersed in space and time as the 'thing' itself. There is no one individual, or small group of individuals, to whom climate change can be attributed – or by whom it could be averted. Finally, the potentialities of nuclear war are, Derrida writes, 'dominated by an economy of speed'; it is the threat of a cataclysm that would happen in an instant: 'a gap of a few seconds may decide, irreversibly, the fate of what now and then still calls itself humanity – and to which the occasion demands that we add a few other species'.[107] The 'actual' event, that is to say, would have a concentrated location and duration: the pushing of a button; the attainment of supercritical mass within the physical structure of the bomb; the detonation (though, of course, its material, psychological and philosophical effects would be far more dispersed in space and time). It is *cinematic*, narrativizable, imaginable. If I were in the right place at the right time (or the wrong place at the worst possible time), I could see the explosion. The threat of anthropogenic climate change, meanwhile, is characterized by what seems to be a tedious perpetuation. Again, Rob Nixon's notion of 'slow violence' is apt here: it is 'a violence that occurs gradually and out of sight, a violence of delayed destruction that is dispersed across time and space, an attritional violence that is typically not viewed as violence at all'.[108] While not all of the effects of climate change are slow – indeed, the increased floods, droughts and fires befalling parts of the world are nothing short of local cataclysm – the causal logic behind them *is* slow: these events are indirect effects of actions taken in other places at other times, so that culpability remains invisible to the naked eye.

Climate change stretches far into the past and future, and it is impossible to pinpoint the 'moment' of its event, or of its fatal tipping point. When did it start? When the concentration of carbon dioxide in the atmosphere began to rise at unprecedented rates? When humans first began to burn the fossilized remains of ancient life forms for energy? When we stopped foraging and started farming? When we hunted megafauna to extinction? When will it end? Will it end? What will survive? As Tom Cohen writes, climate change is not of a human other, does not occur in a flash, cannot occur in the name of 'the Name' (and, in essence, is un-name-able). It requires no decision, unless that be the elusive counter-decision against what today accelerates its vortices – a 'decision' to throw the brake on, say, hydro-carbon emission in the illusion of a sovereignty that is non-existent (Copenhagen). It is without the agency of war explicitly, but folds all war into itself (resource wars).[109]

Climate change is an event of extremely extended and, therefore, non-human, temporality. It has no determinable location smaller than the atmosphere: it is everywhere at once. We are – temporally and spatially – *within* it and cannot simply catalogue its duration or its spread. This is why nuclear annihilation is easier to think about – if not any less harrowing. We could characterize nuclear war as a Ptolemaic threat and climate change as a Copernican one: the former is localizable, temporalizable, has an identifiable point around which everything turns (the pushing of a button); the latter is radically without centre, without horizon. It can be thought of in terms of what Timothy Morton calls 'hyperobjects': 'massively distributed entities that can be thought and computed, but not directly touched or seen'; they are 'non-human entities … that are incomparably vaster and more powerful than us', in which 'our reality is caught'.[110] One quality of hyperobjects, Morton notes, is that they 'invert what is real and what is only appearance' – so that the local, perceptible effects of climate change (crop failure, for example) are 'mere' manifestations of an object or event that defies apprehension and, therefore, representation.[111] The Copernican revolution demonstrated that experience is bounded by an arbitrary limit – the beyond of which bespeaks the limits of perception, rather than the limits of reality – and a hyperobject like climate change is so widely dispersed in space and time, has so many expressions, that its totality remains beyond our grasp. At the same time, however, we might also think of climate change as irresistibly opening or facilitating a strange kind of telepathy, or what Derrida describes as 'distance against menacing immediacy'.[112] Is the catastrophe of climate change very far away or very close, everywhere at once? How can we begin to think what it has done to our sense of 'here' or 'now'?

The inversion of what is 'real' and what is 'appearance' also applies to the *speed* of climate change. Above I quoted Kolbert stating that all mass extinction events have in common the speed or abruptness of change that triggers them. Then I said that climate change, in comparison to the threat of nuclear war, is characterized by a tedious slowness. This apparent contradiction is again an effect of scale, in which what is true at one scale becomes false on another. On the geological timescale, the rate of climate change is extraordinarily fast: in the last half century it has accelerated to 170 times the previous rate of temperature change.[113] Kolbert notes that 'by burning through coal and oil deposits, humans are putting carbon back into the air that has been sequestered for … millions of years. In the process, we are running geologic history not only in reverse but at warp speed.'[114] What *appears* to be a fundamental difference between the threat of nuclear war and climate change – that of speed and slowness – is a symptom of reading at different scales. At the evolutionary scale, species have no more time to adapt to newly hostile conditions than human beings in the blast zone of a nuclear bomb would have to run away. Just as the Copernican shift demanded a conception of a universe much larger and much older than ever before imagined, the dawn of the Anthropocene necessitates a radically different perception of place and time.

Civilization in deconstruction

The threat of nuclear war rests on the 'decision' of those in power to press a button which would destroy everything – so for the majority of people, the threat comes from *outside* their lives, even if that outside is another human being or nation state. Climate change, in contrast, is a force of destruction that grows out of the way that a large proportion of human beings in the developed world currently live their lives. In the Anthropocene, as David Collings writes, 'our way of living threatens *itself*.'[115] 'Where the nuclear led us to affirm ordinary life virtually without reserve, climate change forces us to imagine how it can be transformed so it will no longer undermine itself'; 'it splits our reality to the core, forcing us to live at once with and against our ordinary lives, to cherish what we must also change.'[116] Nicholas Royle recognizes how deconstruction works through a 'strange, even contradictory combination of description and transformation' – both explicating the complexity of what is being read, but also transforming it, making it *do* things.[117] Likewise, climate change both 'describes' the human relation to the planet – revealing in an unprecedented way the destructive and unsustainable nature of the dominant human way of life – and transforms it: either by making us choose to live very differently or by changing the conditions on which current civilization depends. Things that were taken to be markers of stability (such as sea levels or average temperatures) prove to be mobile, erratic. What was considered to be 'progress' or 'development' (air travel, industry, increasing human populations) is revealed to be the disruptive force that demands we rethink the very concepts upon which we have built and measured 'civilization'. As Wallace-Wells writes, when we consider that the 'epic era once derided as "prehistory" accounts for about 95 percent of human history', the 'entire history of civilization ... look[s] less like an inevitable crescendo than like an anomaly, or blip' – an anomaly that, nevertheless, 'has brought us to the brink of a never-ending climate catastrophe'.[118] Climate change reveals how far the ideological assumptions of a capitalist economy (the 'need' for constant growth, the right to endless extraction, the assumption that such extraction will be without ramification) *are* merely ideological and reveals how far the paltry and myopic responses to the crisis are also embedded within such a logic. The hegemony of this view (for while it is not universal, it is certainly dominant) is shown to be self-destructive by the fact that the continued existence of the human species is put under threat by such actions. Climate change reveals, in no uncertain terms, that the planet and its systems are not *for* us and thereby reverberates the radically decentring force of the Copernican blow. As Bruno Latour and Timothy Lenton write, the recognition of the Anthropocene is not just a geophysical event but rather also necessitates 'a cultural paradigm shift', 'affecting science as well as politics, morality, and the arts'.[119] It necessitates, just as the Copernican revolution did, a radical transformation of thinking that changes not just what is observed but the point of view from which any observation is made.

Living on: After the end of the world

The mystic, the visionary, walked the beach, stirred a puddle, looked at a stone, and asked themselves 'What am I?' 'What is this?'

Woolf, To the Lighthouse, 143

Let us return one last time to Woolf. *To the Lighthouse*, published in 1927, speaks in strange ways to parts of Heidegger's 1929–30 lecture series, *The Fundamental Concepts of Metaphysics*. Heidegger sets out 'three guiding theses': that 'the stone is worldless, the animal is poor in world, man is world-forming',[120] thereby employing, as Derrida points out, general terms for human beings and other animals ('man'; 'the animal'), but using a specific example of an inanimate thing ('the stone'):

> Why does he take the example of an inanimate thing, why a stone and not a plank or a piece of iron, or water or fire? One of the reasons, no doubt, is that the generality 'inanimate,' with no example, would have raised the question of

life, which Heidegger does not wish to raise here as such, and which would leave hovering the ambiguity of vegetables and plants, which are more animate and living than the stone, and about which one might wonder ... would Heidegger have said that the plant is *weltlos* like the stone or *weltarm* like the living animal?[121]

The fact that Heidegger uses a stone to stand in for 'the' inanimate implies that, as Derrida suggests, the category resists such generalization. The other examples in Derrida's list are all a bit 'less' inanimate than a stone: a plank was once living wood and is still mutable, biodegradable; a piece of iron will rust, taking oxygen from the air spontaneously, of its own accord; water flows around and can transform into ice or vapour; fire consumes carbon and oxygen, moving and growing as it does so. Heidegger attempts to sidestep the question of in/animacy but instead underlines it: for by choosing the stone as an exemplary inanimate object, he is silently suggesting that it is *most* inanimate, that it is *more* inanimate than other things, and inadvertently admitting that there is, then, no rigorous opposition between the animate and the inanimate but instead a scale: degrees of more or less animacy.

One thing, Heidegger asserts, is certain: 'A stone cannot be dead because it is never alive' (197). Opposed to this eternal non-life are two categories of life: human beings and other animals. The latter category, 'the animal', is bestowed with a multiplicity of examples – a lizard and a beetle and a woodpecker, to name a few (196, 198, 277) – for his thesis (that the animal is poor in world) includes, he tells us, '*all* animals, *every* animal' (186). Except, of course, humans. Heidegger is more concerned with what separates human beings from other animals than with questions of life as such (as his choice of a stone to represent 'the' inanimate demonstrates). Derrida discusses this at length in *The Beast and the Sovereign*, and it is not my aim here.[122] I was making my way, you remember, towards another creature: a wolf, or, rather, a Woolf. I have just one more stop to make in Heidegger's text: at a lizard, 'basking in the sun on its warm stone' (197) – although the possessive form ('its stone') is to be quickly withdrawn:

> When we say that the lizard is lying on the rock, we ought to cross out the word 'rock' in order to indicate that whatever the lizard is lying on is certainly given *in some way* for the lizard, and yet is not known to the lizard as a rock. ... [It] is not accessible to it *as a being*. (198)

The lizard is 'poor in world', because it cannot access its world 'as a being'. And though Heidegger has chosen to use a specific example here, it is not to refer to some specific relation to the world had or not had by the lizard (all non-human animals are '*equally*' 'poor in world', for, as Derrida notes, Heidegger asserts that 'poverty in world does not mark a degree and does not admit of a hierarchizable more or less, of superior and inferior'[123]), but merely, it seems, to enliven his prose. The generalized world-poverty of 'the animal' leads Heidegger to conclude that 'the animal cannot die in the sense in which dying is ascribed to human beings but can only come to an end' (267). Humans have a relation to the world 'as such' and to death 'as such' of which other animals are deprived.

Now let us turn to Woolf. To a scene in which a man, a lizard and a stone appear. We have been there already. The man is Mr Ramsay, walking the terrace and beset with anxiety about human transience ('The very stone one kicks with one's boot will outlast Shakespeare'), and about his work – which, he worries, will be swiftly forgotten. He is concerned that his 'contribution' has not been *enough* to be remembered and that he is therefore a 'failure':

> For if thought is like the keyboard of a piano, divided into so many notes, or like the alphabet is ranged in twenty-six letters all in order, then his splendid mind had no sort of difficulty in running over those letters one by one, firmly and accurately, until it had reached, say, the letter Q. … But after Q? What comes next? … A shutter, like the leathern eyelid of a lizard, flickered over the intensity of his gaze and obscured the letter R. In that flash of darkness he heard people saying – he was a failure – that R was beyond him. He would never reach R. (39)

The mode of 'thought' in which Mr Ramsay is failing to progress any further is philosophical thought. Philosophy is, Heidegger says, 'not some mere gathering of knowledge that we can easily obtain for ourselves at any time from books, but … something to do with the whole, something extreme, where an ultimate pronouncement and interlocution occurs on the part of human beings' (4). It is, then, proper to man. It has to do with human beings having a world 'as such' that they can philosophize about, a capacity through which they can differentiate themselves from other animals. Perhaps he is right. I'm still not sure what it means to have a world 'as such'. All I know is that if we 'have' a world, it is not really 'ours'. And it is at risk. Bits of it are disappearing, irretrievably. If, as Heidegger says, philosophy is an activity so bound up with what it means to be human, it seems to me significant that Mr Ramsay cannot reach the letter of his own name, his own identity: R. And it seems significant too, that it is the eye of a lizard – the animal Heidegger chose to represent the generalized lack of relation to the world 'as such' of which he deprives all non-human animals – that flickers over Mr Ramsay's vision, preventing him from reaching self-knowledge, as if there is a kind of animal rejoinder to man's hierarchizing quest for 'truth'.

Indeed, stuck at Q, unable to reach R, we read that Mr Ramsay 'knocked his pipe out … on the ram's horn which made the handle of the urn' (39). So absorbed in his thoughts that he does not heed his surroundings, unable to utter the letter that starts his own name, he misses that there in front of him is the animal with which he shares that name: a ram. He cannot see the animal, and therefore he cannot see.

What I mean to do by putting Woolf and Heidegger alongside each other like this is merely to note that they represent two very different ways of looking at the world and the human place in it, and to gesture how being alive in the age of anthropogenic climate change might disturb our thinking on such matters. Heidegger writes that 'the animal is confined to its environmental world, immured as it were within a fixed sphere that is incapable of further expansion or contraction' (198). This is, is it not, precisely the situation we now find ourselves in, and which threatens our very existence? Meanwhile the stone, destined to, as Mr Ramsay says, 'outlast Shakespeare' – along with all other living things – looks set to inherit the world it apparently does not, and can never, 'have'. Traces left in rocks, the sedimented remains of our existence, will survive every animal. The complication of what 'living' is that we find in Woolf's writing – and that is so staunchly denied by Heidegger – asks us to recognize a post-Copernican cosmos with neither human beings nor life itself at its centre. The survival of traces is, as I have been saying, a kind of living that is not reducible to organic life, and one which reading Woolf helps us to apprehend. Sarah Wood puts it as follows:

> The thought of the trace is compelling precisely because it has no proper habitat. It belongs with affect no more than it belongs with reason or any other continuity. It migrates between contexts. It refers to a going away that is not a kind of event we know: not the departure of a guest, not a migration, not the end of a day, or of a year, or even of an individual life. It gives us to think these things, and when these things are written without mastery – written on us, and not merely by us – the writing that results may take us some way towards the thought of the trace, and towards what it is necessary to experience, to feel and not-feel, in order to imagine an extinction.[124]

It may not be possible, finally, to 'imagine an extinction'. To imagine, that is to say, the gaining of a loss, the presence of an absence, the past deprived of its future. And yet, with each day that passes, as thousands of forms of life disappear forever, the attempt becomes increasingly necessary. Mrs Ramsay perhaps knew how to feel the kind of 'going away' of the trace, the strange experience of being alive in a world that is forever disappearing:

It was necessary now to carry everything a step further. With her foot on the threshold she waited a moment longer in a scene which was vanishing even as she looked, and then, as she moved … and left the room, it changed, it shaped itself differently; it had become, she knew, giving one last look at it over her shoulder, already the past. (121)

3

Animals at the End of the World: The Evolution of Life and Language

Probably all the organic beings which have ever lived on this earth have descended from some one primordial form, into which life was first breathed.

Charles Darwin[1]

Animots

Here I was a different animal. Have you ever watched a deer walking out from cover? They step, stop, and stay, motionless, nose to the air, looking and smelling. A nervous twitch might run down their flanks. And then, reassured that all is safe, they ankle their way out of the brush to graze. That morning, I felt like the deer. Not that I was sniffing the air, or standing in fear – but like the deer, I was in the grip of very old and emotional ways of moving through a landscape, experiencing forms of attention and deportment beyond my conscious control. Something inside me ordered me how and where to step without me knowing much about it.[2]

'Here I was a different animal.' Already we have a reciprocal relation of place and being: there is something about this place, *here*, that changes the self, that transforms the 'I' into a *different animal*. Different from the one that is writing, reflecting, autobiographically looking back at an experience of inhabiting – or being inhabited by – a different self, a different animal. Which animal? A deer, 'walking out from cover'. An animal that, while it is not perhaps *ashamed* of its nakedness or nudity, can still uncover itself, can feel the vulnerability of being uncovered, can feel its mortality. Yet this is not a real deer: 'a deer' is here 'any deer', an exemplary deer that stands in (or walks out) for deer-in-general. 'Like the deer', the speaker feels herself 'in the grip of' some qualities or characteristics presumably common to all deer: 'old and emotional ways of moving through a landscape', 'forms of attention and deportment beyond … conscious control'. The invariant plural (a deer, some deer), so common in animal names (bison, boar, buffalo, fish, fowl, sheep, etc.) compounds this effect, as the English language enacts its strategic violence against individuals.

I open with this passage as it gathers together so many of the aspects that must animate our thinking as, with and of animals – human and otherwise: identity and difference; the vitality and mortality of what lives; the power of movement and the capacity to be moved, e-motionally or otherwise; the 'old' inherited ways of being that have us in their 'grip', beyond, perhaps, conscious control; and the 'forms of attention and deportment' that will be so necessary in guiding everything I want to say – and these two words alone already announce so much. 'Attention', from the Latin *tendĕre*, 'to stretch', is not only the directing of the mind towards something – listening, heeding, considering – but 'to attend to' something or someone also carries senses of 'to look after' or 'to care for', as well as 'to follow', 'to accompany'. Attention is a subservient tendency, a consideration for or heeding of the other. The noun 'deportment' refers to the way in which one behaves or carries oneself (from the French *porter*, 'to carry'), but its verb form, 'to deport', bears within it conflicting senses: the modern sense of 'to banish or exile' and an older, now obsolete sense of 'to bear with, to be forbearing towards; to treat with consideration, to spare' (*OED*). Both of these senses open the bearing of the 'port' towards others, turn it into a *portal*, perhaps, as thinking concerning non-human animals is bound to do – though it appears today that human relations with other animals are severely lacking in this latter sense.

Readers of Jacques Derrida's *The Animal That Therefore I Am* will have recognized in the foregoing paragraphs many of the themes that he approaches there: nudity and alterity, humanity and inhumanity, the violence of generalization enacted by the syntagm 'The Animal' and our following, carrying and thinking as, of and with animals. You may have also noted that the animal with which I opened is one to which I am very close, to which I feel a particular kinship or affinity, thanks to the name we share – the name that precedes and outlives me and all other deers[3] (and, as Derrida points out, thinking about non-human animals has to do with the power and the capacity of naming or being named, a fact to which I will shortly return). I also pause to note that the human ancestors from whom I inherit my name would have been named *after* deers – both at a later time and in memory of – so deers are, more than any others, the animals that I am following, even if I have never been on such a hunt. The word 'deer' now refers to the family of ruminant quadrupeds – four-legged, antlered herbivores who chew the cud (and, later in this chapter, I will also be returning to the relation or contradiction between eating and thinking that the word 'ruminate' carries) – such as reindeers, red deers and fallow deers. In an earlier incarnation, however, the word 'deer' was a more general term, denoting *any* 'beast', 'usually a quadruped, as distinguished from birds and fishes' but also, 'sometimes, like *beast*, applied to [all] animals of lower orders' (*OED*). A deer is, then, an appropriate creature with which to begin thinking about those animal others that we perceive to be not just different from humans, but *lower*, and therefore less worthy of our care, attention or respect – those animal others that are supposedly *beastly*, as well as about the bestiality of the human.

The word 'deer' comes from the Old English *díor* or *déor*, and like the modern German word for animal (*Tier*), it comes from the pre-Germanic root *dhus*, 'to breathe'. Like the word 'animal', which, as I outlined in the first chapter, comes from the Latin root *anima* ('air', 'breath', 'life', 'soul', 'spirit'), a 'deer' is also that which *breathes*. In Genesis, God names this commonality too; both human beings and other creatures are described as having שֶׁפֶנ (Hebrew, *nephesh*), 'the breath of life'. At Gen. 1.20, 1.21, 1.24 and 1.30, it is used to refer to non-human animals, and at 2.7 to man: 'the Lord God formed man of the dust of the ground, and breathed into his nostrils the breath of life; and man became a living soul [*nephesh*].'[4] Life is, in the biblical account, the animism of non-living matter (the dust of the ground).

While the roots of the words 'animal' and 'deer' attest to the common breath of human beings and other animals, we have somehow conspired to forget this essential kinship, as the terms have come to denote those beings assumed to be distinct from humans. Now more than ever, it is also necessary to hear the homonym 'dear' – from the Old Norse root *dýrr* ('worthy', 'precious', 'costly') – for as we witness the accelerated extinctions I discussed in the last chapter, those animal others that for so long have been deemed inferior, expendable and worthless must now be recognized as immeasurably dear to us: we must attend to the great worth and precious irreplaceability of the other forms of life with which we live and breathe. Humans evolved from and with other life forms, and we depend upon many of them for the oxygen we breathe and the food we eat. As David Krell asks, what would it mean 'if our planet suddenly were bereft of the life-forms that were already here long before we were, lending the Earth its shape and texture? We realize by now that as more and more of these life-forms become extinct human beings do not become safer.'[5] This chapter will be attempting to lay out some of the reasons why this is the case, attending to the different forms of life and the living – not all of them organic – that interrelate to animate the world. For now, consider this passage from biologist Nick Lane, who troubles the assertion that viruses are not alive, by underlining the extent to which human beings, just like viruses, rely upon other forms of life:

> Why would a virus not be alive? Because it does not have any active metabolism of its own; it relies entirely on the power of its host. That raises the question – is metabolic activity a necessary attribute of life? The pat answer is yes, of course; but why, exactly? Viruses use their immediate environment to make copies of themselves. But then so do we: we eat other animals or plants, and we breathe in oxygen. Cut us off from our environment, say with a plastic bag over the head, and we die in a few minutes.[6]

That 'plastic bag' might be replicated by the Sixth Mass Extinction, which could 'cut us off from our environment' by putting it – and eventually us – to death. We evolved *with* the world, in all its living and non-living manifestations, and we cannot, therefore, live without it.

There is one more name, then, that it is necessary to bring to the table: the name that signifies the second of Freud's blows to human narcissism – that of Charles Darwin. The name 'Darwin' comes from the Old English *déor-wine*: the *déor* we have met already (a 'beast' or 'deer'), and *wine* means 'friend' or 'kinsman'. Meanwhile, 'Charles' comes from the Old Norse *karl*, meaning 'man', so 'Charles Dar-win' translates as 'Man Beast-Friend' or 'Man Animal-Kin' – an etymology that perhaps auto-bio-graphically voiced itself in his life's work: his writing of life.[7]

In the beginning

I have been making assertions about origins, digging for the roots of modern English words, to say what they 'mean' at bottom. Yet I have been misleading you, for surely the 'origins' I have named (*déor, dhus, dýrr*, etc.) did not spring into existence like the heavens and the earth, the night and the day that God calls into being in Genesis. They have their own murky histories, or rather pre-histories, the traces of which have not made it into written records. These traces might to an extent be deduced, but they are, fundamentally, lost to time. The roots I name here owe their existence in turn to older roots, and those to older still: the study of origins is always a matter of buried genealogies, dark and radically abyssal. As Derrida notes in *Of Grammatology*, 'the concept of origin has merely a relative function within a system situating a multitude of origins in itself, each origin capable of being the effect or the offshoot of another origin'.[8] There is an unfathomable generativity at root, sprouting, spreading in the dark.

The blow to human narcissism around which this chapter will turn is also a matter of lost or untraceable origins. Darwin's title, *The Origin of Species*, is somewhat misleading – as what his work actually tells us is that species do not exist as distinct sets and that the distinctions between them are arbitrary categories made for the convenience of taxonomy: 'Our classifications,' he writes, 'will come to be, as far as they can be so made, genealogies', and we shall then be 'freed from the vain search for the undiscovered and undiscoverable essence of the term species'.[9] The origin of species, then, is no origin: only differences, infinitesimal and innumerable differences that, over the incomprehensible vastness of deep time, add up to what today we see as the distinctions between species – and the distinction between life and non-life.

The real force of Darwin's revelation is that it accounts for the production of complexity without agency. All that is required is chance, time and death. The fluctuations of chance automatically accumulate to produce the staggering complexity we see around us, giving the appearance of intelligent design – which is why so many cultures tell creation stories. Darwin too, he admits, finds it 'difficult to avoid personifying the word Nature' – though he emphasizes that this is a 'merely' metaphorical expression.[10] Noting the relative brevity of the human species' existence on earth, he writes the following:

> Can we wonder, then, that Nature's productions should be far 'truer' in character than man's productions; that they should be infinitely better adapted to the most complex conditions of life, and should plainly bear the stamp of far higher workmanship?
>
> It may metaphorically be said that natural selection is daily and hourly scrutinizing, throughout the world, the slightest variations; rejecting those that are bad, preserving and adding up all that are good; silently and insensibly working, whenever and wherever opportunity offers, at the improvement of each organic being in relation to its organic and inorganic conditions of life.[11]

The animism implied by the phrase 'natural selection' – that there is some agency doing the selecting, 'silently and insensibly working' – gains rather than loses force through its explicit metaphoricity. The complexity of life was not created by a deified Nature but merely through the accumulation of mindless automatic processes.[12] That this produces 'far higher workmanship' than human intelligence gives a keener edge to the blow struck to human narcissism by the theory of evolution: not only are humans shown to be descended from animals, but the level of intelligence humankind attribute only to themselves and to a presumed 'higher power' – a god that created everything – is revealed, in the case of natural selection, to be far more 'mindless' and irrational than the 'lower' forms of life from which humans had thereby distinguished themselves. The interminability of evolution (constant adaptation as opposed to completion) also radically undermines teleological conceptions of history, and, therefore, any notion that human beings represent the pinnacle of existence.[13]

Evolutionary interactions also work to destabilize the subject/object distinction upon which humans base much of their sense of agency, as well as dethroning consciousness from its (self-ascribed) position of superiority. In *The Botany of Desire: A Plant's Eye View of the World*, Michael Pollan describes his realization that the sense of intention and agency of a human gardener or farmer is more of an effect of perspective, more of 'a self-serving conceit', than an absolute fact.[14] He notes that when we observe co-evolutionary relationships between other species, we recognize the reciprocal – and unconscious – nature of the transaction: 'the two parties act on each other to advance their individual interests but wind up trading favors: food for the bee, transportation for the apple genes. Consciousness needn't enter into it on either side, and the traditional distinction between subject and object is meaningless.'[15] When we observe processes of agriculture and domestication, however, we see them as radically different from the relationship between the bee and the apple tree: we assume that humans have the upper hand, that we manipulate other species to wholly serve our own ends. But taking a 'plant's eye view', as Pollan's book endeavours to do, can engender a radical shift in perspective that recasts agriculture as 'something certain plants and animals have done to us, a clever evolutionary strategy for advancing their own interests' (i.e. spreading their genes).[16] For instance, he notes how the 'edible grasses (such as wheat and corn)' have 'incited humans to cut down vast forests to make more room for them', whilst certain other plant species (the examples he explores in the book are apples, tulips, marijuana and potatoes) have for generations employed human labour and ingenuity to ensure their widespread and continuous propagation.[17] Seeing his garden in this strange new light, Pollan remarks that 'all these plants, which I'd always regarded as the objects of my desire, were also, I realized, subjects, acting on me, getting me to do things for them they couldn't do for themselves'.[18] Plants also get us to do things which are not necessarily for our own benefit. As Yuval Noah Harari recognizes, the demands of agriculture completely and permanently transformed the human way of life – and this change was not altogether for the better: 'It did not offer a better diet' (foraging provided many more nutrients), nor did it 'give people economic security' (farmed crops are more susceptible to pests and unpredictable weather), or even 'security against human violence' (farms attracted raiders).[19] Agriculture did not even provide *more* food: because every increase in yield was matched or outpaced by an increase in human mouths to feed. 'We did not domesticate wheat,' says Harari, 'it domesticated us.'[20]

Such a radical change in perspective is also what is being called for in the Anthropocene. What would happen if we were to look at our current predicament from the perspective of, for example, capital – the primary concern of which, like that of the gene, is to increase and multiply? How might the continued extraction of fossil fuels, the deregulation of industry and the seemingly suicidal sociopolitical support for such an economy look if we were to inhabit the viewpoint of neoliberal capitalism (which, like most cultural artefacts, is a meme and therefore the product of natural selection)? This is not to say that petro-capitalism is a conscious being – no more than Pollan thinks his potatoes are conscious – but rather to recognize that consciousness is not a necessary prerequisite for agency. Mindless or unconscious processes are perfectly capable of doing things, of making things happen, as the respective work of Darwin and Freud incontestably shows. In fact, what is becoming increasingly apparent is that consciousness does not even guarantee agency – it just does a very good job of creating the illusion of agency in those beings who find themselves possessed of (or, perhaps, by) it. As Jane Bennett writes,

> No one really knows what human agency is, or what humans are doing when they are said to perform as agents. In the face of every analysis, human agency remains something of a mystery. If we do not know just how it is that human agency operates, how can we be so sure that the processes through which nonhumans make their mark are qualitatively different?[21]

In the beginning was the Word

Darwin writes of language in terms exactly transferred from his theory of organic life: 'no philologist now supposes that any language has been deliberately invented; each has been slowly and unconsciously developed by many steps', and the 'survival or preservation of certain favoured words in the struggle for existence is natural selection'; the two processes, he notes, are 'curiously the same'.[22] (In fact, as Daniel Dennett remarks, 'the idea that languages evolve, that words today are the descendants in some fashion of words in the past, is actually older than Darwin's theory of [the] evolution of species'.[23]) The evolution of language and the evolution of organic life do work as particularly snug metaphors for each other: both involve the production of complexity without agency, the extinction of some forms and the survival and/or mutation of others, and the interrelation and interdependence of forms. Gillian Beer asks, 'Is knowledge … an organic process, its accretions and transformations more than metaphorically like that of the organism?'[24] She is here thinking text in terms of organic life, but, as her phrase 'more than metaphorically' attests, we can just as readily think organic life in terms of text. The discovery of DNA explains the 'curious' similarity that Darwin perceived between the development of language and the development of life: it shows that the evolution of life *is*, at bottom, an evolution of text or code. As Lane writes, 'biology is information, genome sequences are laid out *in silico*, and life is defined in terms of information transfer'.[25] Given that verbal language is considered, as Darwin writes, 'one of the chief distinctions between man and the lower animals', the fact that language derives its force from a trait not exclusive to it, but at work before and beyond it, rather undermines the 'distinction' it is supposed to mark, as I will be discussing.[26]

While a textual basis for the production of the complexity of life gives new significance to the first chapter of the Gospel of John – 'In the beginning was the Word' (1.1) – the same cannot be said for the beginning as told by the Old Testament. Darwin's work undermines the notions that God created each of the species 'according to their kinds' (i.e. in fixed, immutable forms) and gave man 'dominion' over them (Gen. 1.20-8), as well as rendering false the age of the earth implied in the Bible. Even so, the values and hierarchies of Genesis still underpin many Western societal assumptions – regardless of religious faith or lack thereof. The most prominent of these include not only the subjugation of animals but also the subjugation and vilification of women, a retributive logic of crime and punishment, and the valuing of light over dark which informs notions of racial supremacy and the idealization of 'enlightenment' science (the word 'light' appears thirteen times in Genesis 1, 'darkness' only four, and the former is explicitly said to be 'good'). All of these assumptions grow out of the notion of a monotheistic, patriarchal god, who created earth and all the life forms on it *for* Man. Though the human authors of the Bible may have framed their story as if 'God created man in his own image' (1.27), the writing of the text was in fact Man creating God in his own image – looking to the heavens and seeing, like a certain Narcissus, his own likeness reflected there. 'God' is perhaps man's first autobiography, the Bible its Echo. Any supposedly 'God-given right' is mere self-affirmation: it is a right attributed to man *by* man.

Humanimals

There is no fundamental difference between man and the higher mammals.
                                                              Charles Darwin[27]

The distinct difference between human beings and other animals laid out by Genesis has formed or corroborated, as Derrida notes in *The Animal That Therefore I Am*, the classical thinking of non-human animals:

> Philosophers have judged that limit to be single and indivisible, considering that on the other side of that limit there is an immense group, a single and fundamentally homogeneous set that one has the right, the theoretical or philosophical right, to distinguish and mark as opposite, namely, the set of the Animal in general, the Animal spoken of in the general singular. It applies to the whole animal kingdom with the exception of the human.[28]

On this basis, violence towards non-humans is justified or ignored and has, over the last two centuries, reached '*unprecedented* proportions' (25). Such violence is enabled and normalized by the general singular term, 'the Animal', which, as Derrida describes above, operates in two ways. First, it enacts a homogenization of all non-human living creatures into one immense set, ignoring the infinite differences between them – many of whom are more different from each other than they are from humans. 'The Animal' simultaneously designates, for example, elephants (one of the so-called charismatic megafauna that we anthropomorphize even as we raze their habitat) and sponges (which have no face, are hermaphrodites and have no distinct circulatory, respiratory, digestive and excretory systems). Second, the human/animal opposition implies that humans are radically distinct from other animals, obfuscating our common ancestry and the characteristics we all share: the facts of being able to breathe, move and leave traces, and the capacity for feeling, in particular the capacity for suffering.

Recognizing that we cannot rigorously distinguish between human beings and other animals 'does not, of course,' as Derrida goes on, 'mean ignoring or effacing everything that separates humankind from the other animals', but, rather, attempting to think a limit that 'no longer forms a single indivisible line' (47, 31). He is concerned with 'what sprouts or grows at the limit, around the limit, by maintaining the limit, but also what *feeds the limit*, generates it, raises it, and complicates it', and so his work 'will consist, certainly not in effacing the limit, but in multiplying its figures, in complicating, thickening, delinearizing, folding, and dividing the line precisely by making it increase and multiply' (29). There is animism at the limit: it increases and multiplies just like the life forms inhabiting both sides of its supposed division. The limit drawn between humans and other animals has a purpose – it is 'the bordercrossing from which vantage man dares to announce himself to himself, thereby calling himself by the name that he believes he gives himself' (12). Human identity, that is to say, is both constructed and deconstructed by this internally divided and mobile limit. Or, as Giorgio Agamben puts it, '*Homo sapiens* ... is neither a clearly defined species nor a substance; it is, rather, a machine or device for producing the recognition of the human'.[29]

Of the many limits that are used to distinguish between humans and other animals – conceptual language, reason, history, politics, self-consciousness, possession of a soul, upright stance, laughter, cooking, religion, law, shame and war (to give a list both incomplete and contradictable) – one that has been a favourite in the history of Western philosophy is that of the *word*. Walter Benjamin, in 'On Language as Such and on the Language of Man', writes that 'there is no event or thing in either animate or inanimate nature that does not in some way partake of language', but '*the language of man speaks in words*'.[30] Benjamin does not deny language to non-human or even non-living entities. On the contrary, he recognizes that every 'event' and every 'thing' – whether animate or inanimate – leaves, produces, receives or stores traces of some kind: it 'partake[s] of language'. Even verbal language, then, which is, he asserts, exclusive to man, is not unique in its *modus operandi*. In recent decades, such thinking has developed into the field of biosemiotics, which elaborates how, as Thomas A. Sebeok puts it, 'the process of message exchanges, or *semiosis*, is an indispensable characteristic of all terrestrial life forms'.[31] Such a recognition operates at multiple levels. It refers to the signs interpreted by animals with sophisticated sense organs (including verbal language, calls and cries, scents, gestures, posture, etc.), the chemical communication practised by plants, the processes of signification between an organism and its environment (made up of other organisms and inorganic things such as minerals and weather), and also to the sign processes essential to life right down to the cellular and molecular levels.[32] As Sebeok writes elsewhere, 'biosemioses between bacterial entities started more than a thousand million years ago and are thus at the root of all communication'.[33] Such radical semiosis complicates the distinction made between human beings and other living things on the basis of verbal language. The division opened between signifier and signified, between mark and meaning, between name and named, is a general trait that precedes human language. As

Derrida writes, 'as soon as there is, there is *différance* (and this does not await language, especially human language ... only the mark and the divisible trait)'.³⁴

In Genesis, to signal his dominion, Man names the other animals: 'whatsoever Adam called every living creature, that was the name thereof' (2.19). Benjamin suggests that this act had a certain 'purity of name' that was lost after the Fall: 'The paradisiacal language of man must have been one of perfect knowledge, whereas later all knowledge is again infinitely differentiated in the multiplicity of language.'³⁵ Before the Fall, knowledge is 'perfect', undifferentiated; later it splits and fractures, flawed forever after. A maculate conception:

> The Fall marks the birth of the *human word*, in which name no longer lives intact and which has stepped out of name-language, the language of knowledge, from what we may call *its own immanent magic*, in order to become expressly, as it were externally, magic. The word must communicate *something* (other than itself). In that fact lies the true Fall of the spirit of language.³⁶

Paradise is a garden of im-mediate words: Adam calls each of the animals in turn and the names are, according to Benjamin, 'intact', unbroken, undivided. Before the Fall, the name *is* the named, signifier and signified are one. After the Fall, the 'immanent magic' of words breaks out, begins to ex-press itself and become 'other than itself'. The 'Fall of the spirit of language' is not a decreased but an *increased* potency – but it is a potency that is no longer human, that has taken on a life of its own, an animistic magic. The 'language of man' is not faithful to him and will not be subdued. The language of man may speak in words, as Benjamin says, but not before the language of words speaks in man.

The schema of pre-Fall identity and post-Fall alterity of words that Benjamin attempts to lay out is untenable, for the division of the trace, as I said above, is the condition rather than the capacity of naming. What allows a name to survive its bearer is already at work in the structure of every trace. Every word, every mark, is always internally divided from the moment of its inscription, and so, even before the Fall, there can never have been the 'purity of name' in which Benjamin trusts.³⁷ Before Adam names the animals, he has already received his own name (though we should note that in the English version, he receives his name *as* a proper name – he is 'Adam' – yet in the Hebrew text he is simply 'the man', *hā-ādām*). At Gen. 1.26, we read, 'God said, Let us make man [*ādām*] in our image', and, at 2.7, 'the Lord God formed man [*hā-ādām*] of the dust of the ground [*adamāh*]'. Man is named after the ground from which he is taken, and the Hebrew Bible repeatedly remembers the material unity of living and non-living matter, of human beings, other animals and the dust of the ground: 'out of the ground [*adamāh*] made the Lord God to grow every tree that is pleasant to the sight, and good for food' (2.9); 'out of the ground [*adamāh*] the Lord God formed every beast of the field' (2.19); man will toil 'till thou return unto the ground [*adamāh*]; for out of it wast thou taken' (3.19); 'the Lord God sent him forth from the garden of Eden, to till the ground [*adamāh*] from whence he was taken' (3.23); 'the Lord said, I will destroy man [*hā-ādām*] whom I have created from the face of the earth [*adamāh*]' (6.7). Man is taken from the earth literally and figuratively, in being and in name. Adam is named *after* the ground; his name precedes him and will survive him. Even if man distinguishes himself from other animals by speaking or giving names, he is no less subject to their power – no less subject to what Benjamin calls the 'immanent magic' of language.

Foreign language: The necessity of metaphor

To face another animal – especially a non-human animal – is to come up against what Derrida calls a 'vertiginous untranslatability'.[38] Its 'bottomless gaze' is, he writes, 'uninterpretable, unreadable, undecidable, abyssal and secret. Wholly other, like the every other that is every (bit) other [*tout autre est tout autre*]' (*A*, 12). Though Derrida here sees himself 'seen' in the eyes of a non-human other, we should remember, too, that there are also countless forms of life on earth with whom such a specular relation is not possible, that do not have eyes to meet our gaze, whose alterity resides at an even greater distance and yet whose place within the genealogy of forms is no less important, whose fundamental relation and relatedness to human beings is no less significant – indeed, perhaps in this greater difference it is more so. Human language reflects the ocularcentrism of our species – we have *insights*, we make *observations*, we *speculate*, we *look* (albeit myopically) into the future or the past – and it struggles or fails, therefore, to translate the worlds of creatures whose experiences are primarily sonic, haptic, olfactory or electroreceptive (or indeed whose sense of sight far surpasses our own). We cannot begin to imagine such perspectives (and again, 'imagine' and 'perspective' both come back to sight, from the Latin *imāgō*, 'visible form', and *specere*, 'to look') in a language and thought that resides in a different world, a world foreign to these non-human others. Human language cannot but miss its mark; it is a mode of apprehension incommensurable with its object – like trying to harpoon rainbows. Sarah Wood suggests that 'the success of thinking is to keep missing what it aims at, not as one misses a target – once and for all – more in the way that one misses a person'.[39] Thinking about non-human others is necessarily characterized by this kind of insatiable and asymptotic yearning towards something irreducibly other, irreducibly distant, un-representable – and this is not thinking's failure, but rather, as Wood says, its success.

Writing about other animals often employs negative terms: 'uninterpretable, unreadable, undecidable' – unable to say what *is*, we can only say what is *not*. This is the case even (or, perhaps, especially) when the language comes in positive terms. Responding to the work of Emmanuel Levinas, Derrida remarks how the 'unthinkable truth of living experience' cannot be encompassed by or reduced to language, which thus 'progress[es] by negations, and by negation against negation' (and this is, I think, the only possible mode of approach towards non-human others): The 'proper route' of language, Derrida suggests, 'is not that of an "either this ... or that", but of a "neither this ... nor that". The poetic force of metaphor is often the trace of this rejected alternative, this wounding of language. Through it, in its opening, experience itself is silently revealed.'[40] Language moves towards, without ever touching, what remains ineffable. The 'wounding of language' in metaphor, its silent negation even in affirmation, opens itself to reveal experience. The wound is the mark of a non-identity, a rupture or difference between language and the 'truth' of that to which it cannot be reduced ('meaning'). Metaphor, then, makes manifest the 'vertiginous untranslatability' of non-human animals, the alterity which cannot be reduced to language. In that respect, metaphor could enable what we might think of as *ethical* writing about non-humans – writing that would work to oppose the bipartite violence of the general singular term 'the Animal' (i.e. the notion of an absolute distinction between human beings and other animals, and the homogenization of all non-human life into one category). It would entail a careful attention to the experiences of being common to all living things (including humans), whilst maintaining an utmost respect for the untranslatable and heterogeneous alterity of non-human lives: the strange and intractable asymmetrical specularity of living others, that can only be approached via metaphor.

You recall that in my first chapter I suggested that the life of metaphor – or what Derrida calls 'the animality of the letter'[41] – is a metaphor for life, and not just the other way around. To reiterate: not only does the automotoric life of living beings help us to think the life of language, but the strange and irrepressible life of language – beyond any conscious intention or authorial control – can perhaps also help us to think the otherness of non-human animals (and, to be clear, this is a different – although undoubtedly related – point to the one I made earlier about the similarities between the development or evolution of organic life and verbal language). Whether we read the 'life' of language to be a generalization of, or a 'mere' metaphorization of, the concept of 'life', it accounts, I think, for the force behind Derrida's suggestion that 'thinking concerning the animal, if there is such a thing, derives from poetry'. To elaborate: he further suggests that such 'poetic thinking' is what philosophy has 'had to deprive itself of' (*A*, 7). Philosophy's deprivation here has in part to do with the effacement of metaphor described in 'White Mythology': 'metaphysics has erased within itself the fabulous scene that has produced it, the scene that nevertheless remains active and stirring'.[42] If philosophy grounds itself upon the assumption that there is 'proper meaning' in opposition to metaphorical meaning (an assumption already undone by, for example, the 'ground' of its grounds), it sacrifices or excludes the 'animality of the letter' (that is, metaphor), acting as a sterile and disinfected laboratory environment, that could, in principle, 'master and analyze polysemia': a place of knowledge as opposed to *thinking*.[43] It remains for poetry – or, I suggest, what we call literature more generally – to be the habitat or territory for both the animality of the letter and the thinking of animal life.

The myriad incarnations of the otherness of non-human animals perhaps pose the greatest challenge to human comprehension, being, as they are, 'at the infinite distance of the animal'.[44] Wood, in *Without Mastery*, 'risk[s] the claim' that 'literature offers the most advanced way of thinking about thinking'.[45] This claim, I suggest, can be made on the following bases: that literature inhabits a strange threshold between the 'real world' and its other, the place that disturbs the opposition between fact and fiction; that literature is a space for the freest of speech (as Derrida notes in 'This Strange Institution Called Literature', it allows one 'to *say everything*'[46]); and that reading literature is an experience of inhabiting, or being inhabited by, a certain otherness. If literature offers the most advanced way of thinking about thinking, then it certainly offers the most advanced way of thinking about non-human animals. This is not to say that literature closes that 'infinite distance', allowing us to think *how* non-human animals 'think', or even making non-human animals thinkable. Rather, it is to realize that while science and classical philosophy consistently fail (or fail even to try[47]) at animal thinking, literature perhaps fails better, *advances* a little further along the infinite distance, which remains nonetheless untraversable.

Animal writing: Neither fish nor fowl

Two works that venture toward the alterity of non-human worlds are Helen Macdonald's *H is for Hawk* (2014) – a passage from which opened this chapter – and Nicholas Royle's *Quilt* (2010). These books both turn upon the loss of a father and encounters with non-human animals, both are touched by madness and disappearance, and both disturb the threshold between fiction and non-fiction writing. *H is for Hawk* is Macdonald's memoir of working through the grief of losing her father – whilst or by training a goshawk. Royle's *Quilt* tells the tale of a man who, after his father's death, adopts – into the latter's former home – four South American freshwater stingrays. Although *H is for Hawk* is 'non-fiction' and *Quilt* a novel, the two works share many concerns: confluence and incongruence between human and non-human animals; problems of representation; the life of language; the experience of grief and loss; and a preoccupation with or by the auto-bio-graphical, with what Derrida calls 'the writing of the self as living' (*A*, 47).

Let us proceed then, carefully, towards some animals. Here is the first sustained description of Mabel, the goshawk of *H is for Hawk*:

> The feathers down her front are the colour of sunned newsprint, of tea-stained paper, and each is marked darkly towards its tip with a leaf-bladed spearhead, so from her throat to her feet she is patterned with a shower of falling raindrops. Her wings are the colour of stained oak, their covert feathers edged in palest teak, barred flight-feathers folded quietly beneath. And there's a strange grey tint to her that is felt, rather than seen, a kind of silvery light like a rainy sky reflected from the surface of a river. She looks new. Looks as if the world cannot touch her. As if everything that exists and is observed rolls off like drops of water from her oiled and close-packed feathers. And the more I sit with her, the more I marvel at how reptilian she is. The lucency of her pale, round eyes. The waxy yellow skin about her Bakelite-black beak. The way she snakes her small head from side to side to focus on distant objects. Half the time she seems as alien as a snake, a thing hammered of metal and scales and glass. But then I see ineffably birdlike things about her, familiar qualities that turn her into something loveable and close. She scratches her fluffy chin with one awkward, taloned foot; sneezes when bits of errant down get up her nose. And when I look again she seems neither bird nor reptile, but a creature shaped by a million years of evolution for a life she's not yet lived.[48]

From the first sentence, we are in the realm of representation: newsprint, paper, stain and mark: the world of surface and trace. Mabel has been drawn upon (and we should remain alert here to the multiple senses of 'drawn'), her feathers are 'marked darkly' and 'she is patterned with a shower of falling raindrops'; just as the words paint an image of the bird for the reader, her features are described as though they have been painted on, reminding us that our view of her is not an objective reality but a reading effect, created by the observer as much as by the observed. There is, however, more than the visual here: 'there's a strange grey tint to her that is felt, rather than seen, a kind of silvery light like a rainy sky reflected from the surface of a river.' This line subtly introduces repeated 'R's and 'S's before its palindromic mirroring of the Rainy Sky *reflected* from the Surface of a River: the specular arrangement of the letters miming the play of light that refracts through the image – from sky to river and back again, each colouring the other just as reader and text are reciprocally brought into being. The image disturbs the concept of an 'environment' as that which environs: the rainy river scene that we automatically see the hawk *within* emanates out of the 'strange grey tint' of Mabel herself (likewise, we hear the rain before it arrives in the sentence, voicing itself in the 's*trainge grey*' tint); hawk and surroundings haunt each other from the outset.

The hawk arrives to sight as an event: 'She looks new. Looks as if the world cannot touch her. As if everything that exists and is observed rolls off like drops of water from her oiled and close-packed feathers.' What is seen and what is refused to sight infect each other: her feathers refuse the water that rolls off her, just as the attempt to verbalize the experience of seeing her will never quite *stick*. The 'looking' in the above lines splits itself into the two conflicting senses of 'having an appearance' and 'directing one's sight', so Mabel looks or appears *to* us 'as if the world cannot touch her', but she also looks *at* us 'as if the world cannot touch her': she is not just seen but *seeing*. The repeated *as if*s here mark out the necessity of fiction for this encounter – and I'll be returning to the power of the 'as if' in the next section.

Struggling to verbalize her experience of the hawk, the narrator stoops from different angles: Mabel is both reptilian, 'as alien as a snake' and 'ineffably birdlike', though also 'neither bird nor reptile'; she is rigidly unyielding, 'a thing hammered of metal and scales and glass' with her 'Bakelite-black beak', and also in soft motion, snaking her head around, scratching her fluffy chin. The seeming redundancy of the description of a bird as 'ineffably birdlike' is testament not only to her resistance to description but also to the limits of linguistic description as such. It is not that she *is* or *is not* birdlike – 'like' a bird – but rather that the category of 'bird' is itself made unstable or chimærical in the presence of what we suppose it to signify: for how can these four shapes on the page – 'b', 'i', 'r' and 'd', or indeed the phoneme 'bəːd' – correspond to, or be 'like', the living thing that faces us? The word 'bird' is a metaphor too.

Inevitably, then, metaphors proliferate. The animality of the letter is let loose. 'She is a conjuring trick. A reptile. A fallen angel. A griffon from the pages of an illuminated bestiary. Something bright and distant, like gold falling through water. A broken marionette of wings, legs and light-splashed feathers' (53). Later she is a 'cappuccino samurai': not only, perhaps, a coffee-coloured warrior (her '*café-au-lait* front streaked thickly with cocoa-coloured teardrops'), but also one that is made to wear a falcon hood, 'to keep [her] from fearful sights' (65, 53) – the cappuccino coffee being named after the Capuchin, or 'hooded', friars (from the Italian *capuche*, 'hood'). Mythical and magic, the hawk conjures language as language conjures the hawk: a dis/appearing trick performed interminably, without smoke and mirrors. The image of gold falling through water recalls the tale of Zeus impregnating Danaë in her subterranean chamber – the hawk falls to us from elsewhere, 'bright and distant', altering us from the inside: a precipitate semination. The 'broken marionette' is here not a damaged lifeless puppet but something that will not submit to human direction or control. Derrida writes that metaphor 'is the moment of possible meaning as the possibility of non-truth', 'the moment of the detour in which the truth might still be lost'.[49] It is the moment, perhaps, when the 'conjuring trick', 'reptile', 'angel' and 'griffon' – the unavoidable detours on the approach to the 'meaning' or 'truth' of the hawk – all turn into a 'broken marionette' in your hands.

If we turn now to *Quilt*, we find here too a proliferation of metaphor, a faltering of language around the rays: four South American freshwater stingrays, *Potamotrygon motoro* – to give them their 'scientific name' – from the Greek ποταμός (*potamos*), 'river', and τρῠγών (*trygon*), a 'dove' or 'fish', and the Latin *motor*, 'person who (or thing which) moves or causes to move' (*OED*). I use inverted commas here to question the phrase 'scientific name', which seems to assume that this name is more accurate, more stable, more objective, than any other that we might employ, and also to alert us to the links between the historical practice of taxonomy and a certain (Western, Judaeo-Christian, Victorian) relationship to non-human life on earth – though the Greek-Latin hybridity of *Potamotrygon motoro*, as well as the fish-fowl hybridity of *trygon* (dove or fish), tells us that we are already dealing with an unclassifiable chimæra of sorts. In English, they are called 'ocellate river stingrays', or 'peacock-eye stingrays', and, as *Quilt* tells us, 'are distinctive for the beautiful eyespots on their backs, like leopards, peacocks, chameleons or butterflies, and their bellies white as ghosts'.[50] Speed, seduction, disguise and transformation on one side, spectres on the other – words will have their work cut out:

> Neither fish nor fowl, they move like moles in the gravel of the substrate, burrowing and blowing up air, like animated pancakes, or stay at rest on the bottom, half-hidden dark moons. ...

> How to talk about them? They are eerie machines for creating and overturning words. Every time you think you have come up with an appropriate way of describing them, a submarine bird or robotic frittata or psychodelic beret, you are undone. You're mere bystanders. They're Teflon: nothing sticks because in reality they are the cooks, the makers, somnifluent agents of provocation and alterity in a maddening game with invisible rules in operation before you set eyes on them and being perpetually revised. (93–4)

Just as 'everything that exists and is observed rolls off like drops of water from [Mabel's] oiled and close-packed feathers', here too 'nothing sticks'. The negation of terms (neither fish nor fowl, and certainly neither sense of *trygon*) followed by the increasingly ridiculous and oxymoronic descriptions (animated pancake, dark moon, submarine bird, robotic frittata, psychodelic beret) attest to the intractable strangeness of these creatures that elude language even as they provoke it: 'They are eerie machines for creating and overturning words.' To see is to be hypnotized: these 'somnifluent agents' call up a dream world in which the 'invisible rules' change imperceptibly, like the dangerous pull of an undertow, invisible at the surface.

The end of the world

Human language falters when faced with non-human animals because they are not *things*, static and immutable 'objects', but *beings*. Moving, growing, breathing, feeling: they inhabit, experience and create a world. Not *the* world – the singular fractures and proliferates as soon as multiple subjectivities come into play – but *a* world. In *The Beast and the Sovereign*, Derrida offers three theses regarding 'the community or otherwise of the world':

> 1. Incontestably, animals and humans inhabit the same world, the same objective world even if they do not have the same experience of the objectivity of the object.
> 2. Incontestably, animals and humans do not inhabit the same world, for the human world will never be purely and simply identical to the world of animals.
> 3. In spite of this identity and this difference, neither animals of different species, nor humans of different cultures, nor any animal or human individual inhabit the same world as another, however close and similar these living individuals may be (be they humans or animals), and the difference between one world and another will remain always unbridgeable, because the community of the world is always constructed, simulated by a set of stabilizing appearances, more or less stable, then, and never natural, language in the broad sense, codes of

traces being designed, among all living beings, to construct a unity of the world that is always de-constructible, nowhere and never given in nature. Between my world ... and any other there is the space and the time of an infinite difference, an interruption that is incommensurable with all attempts to make a passage, a bridge, an isthmus, all attempts at communication, translation, trope, and transfer that the desire for a world or the want of a world, the being wanting a world will try to pose, impose, propose, stabilize. There is no world, there are only islands.[51]

These three theses move from *unity* (of *the* world), to *difference* (between *the* human world and *the* animal world – a distinction which again relies upon a generalization of the heterogeneity of non-human animals into one group), to *unity-in-difference* (each individual world has its infinite difference in common with all others). As Derrida remarks later, 'no one will ever be able to demonstrate, what is called *demonstrate* in all rigor, that two human beings, you and I for example, inhabit the same world, that the world is one and the same thing for both of us'.[52]

In order to protect ourselves from the 'infinite anxiety' that grows out of 'the irremediable solitude without salvation of the living being', we act *as if* there 'must be a certain *presumed, anticipated* unity of the world'.[53] We put our faith, that is to say, in a fiction of 'the world': '*as if* we were inhabiting the same world and speaking of the same thing and speaking the same language, when in fact we well know – at the point where the phantasm precisely comes up against its limit – that this is not true at all'.[54] Wood comments that the 'as if' 'exposes the fictions we live by, necessary fictions that allow for the very profound connections that exist between how we understand ourselves' – and, I might add, *others* – 'and the acknowledged fictions of creative writers'.[55] Non-human animals live beyond the horizon of human comprehension, even as they infect and disturb the coherence of our 'identity'. Language can *act* (in the various performative senses of to *do* and to *simulate* or *mime*) *as if* this were not the case, *as if* we could step beyond that horizon – even if such a step must always be taken with extreme care, for you cannot know what might lie underfoot. Because what Derrida calls 'the logical-rhetorical fiction of "as if"', 'affects all language and all experience with *possible* fictionality, phantasmaticity, spectrality',[56] the rigorous distinction between 'to step' and '*as if* to step' – between 'fact' and 'fiction' – becomes untenable. Fiction conditions every experience and necessarily inhabits every relation to others. Michael Naas points out that the 'endless multiplication of worlds' of Derrida's third thesis calls into question 'the very horizon and meaning of the word *world*'.[57] It is revealed to be, that is to say, irreducibly fictional.

The word 'world' has a very human history. Its earliest senses refer specifically to human existence, coming from, as I noted in the introduction to this book, the Old Danish *wærœld*, meaning literally 'age [*œld*] of man [*wær*]' (which makes it an older word for what we are now calling the Anthropocene). Given this etymology, one might assume that, strictly speaking, a non-human could not inhabit what we call a 'world'. But such an assumption is falsified in two ways. First, as we have seen, there is no rigorous dividing line between humans and other animals: there could be no 'age of man' that was not already an age of animals – and there would certainly be no 'age of man' *without* other animals. Second, even if this were not the case – even if humans were extricable from or independent of other animals – right from its very early uses in Old English, the word 'world' evolved to denote the entire planet and everything on it. This semantic 'globalization', even if anthropocentric in its motive (bringing the whole planet under man's rubric) cannot but recognize that there is no world without the earth – that the 'age of man', as an event, is *of* the earth. This latter sense further developed to denote an individual's environment or experience, the 'world' in which they live – which, 'incontestably', as Derrida says, is what non-human animals also inhabit. To say 'my world' is to recognize a temporal and spatial plane beyond myself that I can sense, influence or be influenced by, to a greater or lesser extent. Or, to put it more simply, there are things outside of myself that are not myself. My world is not mine. This is the kind of world of Derrida's third thesis, characterized by solitude and 'infinite difference'. It is the kind of world that cannot do without fiction, without 'translation, trope, and transfer', without the 'as if' that allows us to construct a community of the world – as if we could traverse 'the abyss between the islands of the archipelago and the vertiginous untranslatable'.[58] And without the fiction of the world, without the relations to others it facilitates, it is hard to see how one would avoid total psychic death. What would 'I' mean if there were no others to see and know it?

Through the looking glass

Even if you want to argue, as so much of the Western philosophical tradition has done, that non-human animals' experiences of the world are somehow *less* than human ones (and we should note the value judgement contained within this *less*, and its anthropocentric origin), you cannot deny that non-human animals have some kind of sensuous experience – and in many cases, that experience is *richer* than the human one. Many non-humans have access to spectra of light, sound and smell imperceptible to us, and in these cases, it is humans that are, to put a different spin on Heidegger's term, 'poor-in-world'. The assumption that non-humans have a 'lesser' experience depends upon what is essentially tautological reasoning. It runs roughly as follows: non-human animals, being non-human, cannot experience the world as human beings do, ergo their experience of the world is pitiably lacking in human flavour, which, as far as we *Homo sapiens* are concerned, must be the best. What this formulation forgets is that all its terms – world, experience, lack – issue from *within* a particular horizon *outside* of which they are assumed to be able to signify with such finality. It forgets, that is to say, the fiction of 'the world'. Derrida notes how such discourses identify in all non-humans

> a lack, defect, or general deficit, a deficiency that is nonspecific except to say that it is a lack that is incommensurable with lack, with all our lacking, all the deficiencies or impoverishments, all the privations that can affect us, even in cases of debility or madness. What the animal lacks, in its very perfection, what its defect is, is incommensurable with what is lacking in human imperfection, which in turn draws from this lack, from this incomparable defect, its superiority. (*A*, 81–2)

In ascribing a 'lack' to non-human animals, we fall prey to the lure of a solipsistic anthropocentrism: we mistake our world for *the* world. We posit ourselves as superior to something to which we have no access – to something that *we* lack. An octopus may 'lack' certain qualities, characteristics and abilities that define my existence and experience, but equally I lack the qualities, characteristics and abilities of an octopus. (And if we recall Pollan's 'plant's eye view' that I discussed at the beginning of this chapter, we might need to entirely redress the notion that non-humans lack agency or manipulative capacity.) Difference is not lack, is not privation – and to recognize this is to render Heidegger's notion that non-human animals are poor-in-world meaningless. Difference is life itself. The evolution of more and more complex forms of life is down to *differences* in the copying of genetic material, differences which cumulatively produce diverse new forms. As Beer puts it in *Darwin's Plots*, evolutionary theory is an order based on 'difference, plenitude, multifariousness', 'so that the exigencies of the environment [are] persistently controverted by the genetic impulse towards variety and by the multiformity of environmental responses as well'.[59] If we apprehend difference not as lack but as life itself – as the condition for life, for the movement and development of life, and for temporality (as the Second Law of Thermodynamics shows) – we might be better able to heed, if not to comprehend, the alterity of other forms of life.

Both of the texts I have been reading with you are attentive to living difference, aware that humans are not the only subjectivities in the world, aware that the human world is not the only world. They exhibit what Kari Weil calls 'a concern with and for alterity, especially insofar as alterity brings us to the limits of our own self-certainty and certainty about the world'.[60] Macdonald writes of Mabel the goshawk:

> The world she lives in is not mine. Life is faster for her; time runs slower. Her eyes can follow the wingbeats of a bee as easily as ours follow the wingbeats of a bird. *What is she seeing?* I wonder, and my brain does backflips trying to imagine it, because I can't. I have three different receptor-sensitivities in my eyes: red, green and blue. Hawks, like other birds, have four. This hawk can see colours I cannot, right into the ultra-violet spectrum. She can see polarised light, too, watch thermals of warm air rise, roil, and spill into clouds, and trace, too, the magnetic lines of force that stretch across the earth. The light falling into her deep black pupils is registered with such frightening precision that she can see with fierce clarity things I can't possibly resolve from the generalised blur. … I'm standing there, my sorry human eyes overwhelmed by light and detail, while the hawk watches everything with the greedy intensity of a child filling in a colouring book, scribbling joyously, blocking in colour, making the pages its own. (98)

Mabel's world is *unimaginable* – in the strong sense – to human beings. Her world 'is not mine': both radically different and nonappropriable. Her sense organs give her not a different 'picture' of the world – there is no world beyond that given by our senses – but a different world. In the presence of the hawk, in the distance and proximity of her alterity, Macdonald is made to realize how 'sorry' her human eyes are in comparison. For all our ocularcentrism, none of us have the eyes that could produce a hawk-world: those 'pages' are its own.

Take now the following passage from *Quilt*, in which the narrator finds himself looked at by the four rays, Taylor, Audrey, Hilary and Mallarmé:

> Watching is also to be watched, the singular oddity of bearing witness to these creatures sometimes buried and virtually out of sight in the substrate, eyes nonetheless kept free, pricked up like cats' ears, at attention in the quartz sand, again and again picked out after the event the realisation of another creature realising you, and at other times electrically surging, … ghost birds flapping up through the water, plapping at the surface and looking, yes, from the wings, in alary formation, indisputably on the watch at you, at where you are if not *at* you, the body rising through the water seen in its pulsing forcing resurrecting

swoop, showing its creamy white underside, the gill slits and mouth organised as a smile returning to the world dolphin-like yet phantasmic, the rearing up of a living white sheet of ventral alien face, then the superbly fickle jilting gesture, surfacing or retreating, the flip and show of the dorsal view, the waving through the water of backs dark and gorgeous spotted, another world of eyes, the ocellate gliding, neither peacock, leopard, butterfly nor chameleon, but *motoro*, the rays all four the same variant or morph, name unknown. (80–1)

The sense of specular alterity here is strong, as each experience of seeing is explicitly mirrored: watching is to be watched, to realize is to be realized, to look is to be looked at – 'another world of eyes' is also, manifestly, another world of 'I's. Even when the rays are 'buried and virtually out of sight', their eyes are 'kept free', so you might be seen before you see. Indeed, the meeting of gazes is 'again and again picked out after the event' – which is to say there is delay, deferral, the event is divided for consciousness, an animal after-effect. Watching has a time-lapse in its wake. The word 'watch' comes from the Old English *wæcc-*, 'wake' – to watch is to wake or to be awake. It is the kind of looking or looking out that you do at night, on guard, vigilant. If 'watching is ... to be watched', it is also a wake-up call, opening your eyes to a world on another level of consciousness.

The whole passage quoted above is one sentence, clause after clause pouring at the reader, its excess attesting to the impossibility of de/termination when it comes to these animals. Surging, flapping, plapping, looking, rising, pulsing, forcing, resurrecting, rearing, jilting, surfacing, retreating, waving, gliding: the prose is in incessant motion. Samuel Weber writes of the 'uncanniness of the present participle', suggesting that it performs 'a reiteration that is forever incomplete ... always open to change', and the repeated use of it here marks the intractable and always-altering otherness of the rays, these 'phantasmic' 'ghost birds'.[61] The trebled impetus of 'pulsing forcing resurrecting' is made even more potent by the lack of punctuation, and the final verb of the triad, 'resurrecting', is particularly resonant. A resurrection is the rising or exhumation of the dead, and while these creatures are most certainly alive, they do repeatedly bury themselves, and are, as the novel puts it later, 'irreproachably creatures of elsewhere' – so the image is also suggestive of a coming up from an underworld or an otherworld, transgressing the usual boundaries between life and death, here and elsewhere (93). The passage ends by recalling the four comparisons that had been made earlier, but this time negating them: 'neither peacock, leopard, butterfly nor chameleon, but *motoro*', coming to rest on an abbreviation of their scientific name, *Potamotrygon motoro*. The abbreviation here is apt: is this *motoro* perhaps an underwater incarnation of the *primus motor*, the prime mover: setting language in motion, initiating its maddening chase after these eternally elusive creatures?

The specularity of the relation goes beyond the mere fact of recognizing another subjectivity that recognizes you – there is a deeper identity which we cannot see but which Darwin's great revelation made clear: the infinite distance between animals is also an intimate relation. Noting the 'ludicrously anthropomorphic ego-projective perception of everything' that people have when faced with nonhuman animals, the narrator of *Quilt* gives us the following:

> [People] can't so much as glance at a fishtank without thinking of being them, inhabiting a watery world of swimming, floating, shimmying through the depths. What must it be like, you think to yourself, to have the constant noise of that water-pump and filter system, the endless inanity of nosing up and down and burrowing in the substrate, and eating whatever is provided when it is provided, and flopping on a fellow-creature if that's how the mood takes you, or burying yourself in gravel: what sort of a life is *that*? And then at the same time you come to experience this quite different thing, the murky registration that, in terms of deep time, in terms of the actual timeframe of life on the planet, half a hiccup ago you were a lungfish yourself. You were decidedly less imposing-looking, but you were a not dissimilar sort of creature yourself. At which point you dimly sense a sort of vast retelling, a turning shadow cast out over the waters in the flickering light of which the projection actually goes *the other way*, and the refractively aleatory antics of Mallarmé with Hilary, no different now from how they would have been a couple of hundred million years ago, show us frankly what or who we are. (107)

The experience of facing the rays begins by trying to comprehend or inhabit their ways of being, their ways of living life: 'What must it be like, you think to yourself … what sort of a life is *that*?' This anthropomorphic mode of facing animals presumes that one *could* imagine oneself in the other world, presumes that human language might come close enough to imitate the experience. Yet the presumption is swiftly (or 'at the same time') undercut by a more uncanny realization: that not too long ago, in the grand scheme of things, 'you were a lungfish yourself'. The strangeness of this other life (what sort of a life is *that*?) folds itself into your 'own'. These few sentences perhaps describe something like the vertiginous realization that Darwin must have had, as it became clear to him that human beings were descended from other animals – the realization that prompted him to begin his own 'vast retelling' of a story that had formed the basis of so many of the assumptions upon which his society was grounded. Here, the 'turning shadow cast out over the waters' explicitly recalls the second verse of Genesis: 'And the earth was without form, and void; and darkness was upon the face of the deep. And the Spirit of God moved upon the face of the waters' (1.2). Both tales – the one told by the Bible and the one told by the experience of facing the rays – tell the story of the origin of life, but one includes a divine vindication of hierarchy and all the violence and subjugation it is used to justify, while the other, in which 'the projection [of the anthropomorphic ego] actually goes *the other way*', shows human beings that they are intimately related to all life on earth, and that there is no rigorous distinction (god- or man-given) to declare otherwise.

Darkness upon the face of the Deep: Time, and the undoing of identity

The common ancestry of all life recognized by evolutionary theory is, as Elizabeth Grosz puts it, 'never based on a given unity but on a broad community-in-difference and common history which could be understood as biological "memory," as the present traces and supercessions of the past'.[62] This simultaneously augments and impoverishes human identity. On the one hand, what Grosz calls the 'community-in-difference' enfolds the entire vastness of deep time *into* our sense of identity. As Darwin puts it, when we understand 'all beings' to be 'the lineal descendants of some few beings which lived long before the first bed of the Cambrian system was deposited, they seem to ... become ennobled'.[63] The line in its entirety is untraceable, thanks to the impermanence of species and the inevitable gaps in the fossil record. Nevertheless, human beings (and all currently living creatures) *are*, in a very real sense, living manifestations of the past. On the other hand, this 'community-in-difference' could also be read as a community *indifferent*: humans are afforded no special place within the entangled branches of the evolutionary genealogies.

Darwin's next sentence reads as follows: 'Judging from the past, we may safely infer that not one living species will transmit its unaltered likeness to a distant futurity.'[64] The notion of species identity – and, therefore, individual identity, because we may also 'safely infer' that no individual will 'transmit its unaltered likeness to a distant futurity' either – is, then, something momentary, something that cannot survive or live on. Darwin's statement, though it does not specifically mention human beings, does obliquely refer to them (via the phrases 'all beings' and 'living species'), and this implication-without-mention exactly mimes the undoing of the centrality of the human that any understanding of evolution must effect. As Beer writes, 'the human' is 'everywhere and nowhere in his argument'.[65] We are there, but undifferentiated. Evolution is driven by survival, but identity or sameness – including human identity – by definition cannot survive. It meets with the future by being altered, becoming-other. This is perhaps best demonstrated by cloning, which, Beer writes, could be considered 'the contrary of evolution':

> It replicates; it refuses deviance; it is the strongest form of artificial selection yet invented since it allows humankind to select whole organisms for absolute replication. But already difference is emerging. The cloned creature is born into a new generation. Its conditions vary from those of the mother. … As Borges foresaw, to write *Don Quixote* now produces a different text even if it is word for word identical with the original. And that applies to Dolly the Sheep and her like too.[66]

Again, we see the textual nature of organic life brought to the fore – the cloning of an organism is a matter of iterability, of repetition that is always also difference. Even if life or human life survives into the far future, the condition for its survival will be difference. If life survives, it will be not as we know it.

The radical undermining of the possibility of identity is, then, the irresistible effect of thinking about deep time – which is, to quote *Quilt*, 'at once somewhere no one will ever be visiting' *and*, unavoidably, 'the substrate of the present' (32). Or, as Jeremy Davies puts it in *The Birth of the Anthropocene*,

> the claim that the history of the human species is confined within the blink of an eye of geologic time is a boast disguised as self-deprecation. … The truth is that simply because they are an evolved species, humans have always belonged in deep time, even before the environmental crisis … turned that belonging into a politically urgent reality. The Anthropocene, in other words, does not fasten human beings into a geological chronology from which they had previously been separate. There never was any such separation, although it is true that the timescales of plate tectonics once had very little practical relevance to the timescales of political economy. What the Anthropocene provides is a way to conceptualize human societies' participation in deep time, a participation that had always existed, and that has taken on practical salience under the peculiar circumstances of the present day.[67]

No now without the preceding aeons, no present that is not divided abyssally into a past and a future much larger than the scope of human comprehension.

It is a thought, as Davies recognizes, provoked not only by an understanding of geologic reality but also by an understanding of evolution. A thought that might be provoked, then, by any encounter with non-human life.

In *H is for Hawk*, Macdonald recalls an experience of a bird (before Mabel appears) that rouses within her a sense of deep time: 'it occurred to me that this goshawk was bigger than me and more important. And much, much older: a dinosaur pulled from the Forest of Dean. There was a distinct, prehistoric scent to her feathers; it caught my nose, peppery, rusty as storm-rain' (19). It is an olfactory encounter, which, along with related gustatory experiences, can be distinguished from the visual and haptic by a strange capacity to powerfully invoke the past, whilst also being difficult to recall or imagine at will. One cannot very well bring a certain smell or taste to mind, but, uncalled for, a smell or taste can bring associated memories irresistibly back. (The incident with the madeleine in Marcel Proust's *In Search of Lost Time* is the famous literary example of this phenomenon.) Indeed, smell is the sense most related to memory, thanks to the direct connections between the olfactory bulb and the amygdala and hippocampus (areas of the brain that are strongly implicated in emotion and memory) – whilst visual, auditory and tactile information does not pass through these areas.[68] It is not surprising, then, that it is the smell – rather than the sight or sound – of the hawk that provokes a feeling not dissimilar to the 'vast retelling' sparked by the rays in the passage from *Quilt* above: a feeling that this bird is something ancient, a still-living dinosaur, whose being recalls a past beyond the scope of individual or 'rational' human comprehension, a past of deep time.

'To follow this yarn', we are told towards the beginning of *Quilt*, 'you have to go back into what is called deep time (as if there were any means of doing so)'. We are then given a whirlwind evolution of the ray, starting 'over 220 million years ago', 'long before the dinosaur or anything of ragged claw' and, indeed, 'before the creation of the Andes', when the ray already 'ranged' the ocean. It was the raising up of the aforementioned mountain range, the passage continues, that led to the evolution of the freshwater variety. The passage ends by reminding us that 'all of this took place in what is called deep time (as if there were any other)' (21-2). The parenthetical *as ifs* that frame the passage mark the necessity of fiction for thinking and not thinking deep time: we cannot 'really' go there, but, at the same time, we cannot 'really' separate ourselves from it. Situated between two sections of domestic grief – the man learning about the death of his father and then collecting the latter's belongings from the hospital – this passage is itself a fish out of water, *unheimlich* in a literal sense, invading the home with its strangeness and thereby miming the way that deep time is both inseparable and inaccessible from what we think of as 'reality'. We cannot truly separate 'now' – which we might claim with a reasonable confidence as, if not 'ours', at least available to perception – we cannot separate this 'now' from the vast magnitude of the altogether in-experienceable abysses of deep time.

Animal products

In both the texts I have been discussing, the non-human animals are *bought* by humans. The goshawk and the rays have a particular market value, the tendering of which facilitates the exchange of these beings from one human owner to another. These animals, that is to say, are commodities, objects understood to be or do something *for* humans, to be possessions or property that can be acquired in exchange for money. The narrator of *Quilt*, while complicit in the system, expresses his discomfort at the situation:

> Then there are the online dealers. Replaceable ray, dish of the day, this one or that! Initially set you back a hundred dollars, my friend, but if it arrives damaged or dead, refund guaranteed, we'll dispatch another one within twenty-four hours! If, on the other hand, you get it home and it acclimatises and seems happy but after three weeks begins to develop fin curl or abrasions from that gravel you selected for the substrate, or if it turns out the creature never really developed an appetite and has succeeded in starving itself, such apparently suicidal behaviour not unknown, if it dies it dies: just think of it as one of those balloons that go flat, simply pick up the phone or get online and order another one! (86–7)

Voicing the exclamatory tone, false familiarity ('my friend') and fast pace of a TV or radio advertisement, this passage highlights the way in which a living creature that is 'for sale' takes on the qualities of a mass-produced item. The dying breath (or *anima*) is reduced to the puff of air that escapes a punctured balloon, the living body reduced to a disposable or 'single-use' item. An animal as commodity is shorn of all individuality: 'it' is entirely replaceable, 'this one' is apparently just the same as 'another one'. Meanwhile, the human as consumer is shorn of all responsibility: 'if it dies it dies', no big deal, it's not your fault, you can 'simply' get another one, dispatched right away! To 'dispatch' is not only to send something quickly, it is also to kill, to do away with by putting to death, a double meaning which darkens still further the promise to 'dispatch another one within twenty-four hours'.

In *H is for Hawk*, the animal-cash transaction is also made strange. '*I'm meeting a man I don't know off the Belfast ferry and I'm going to hand him this envelope full of paper in exchange for a box containing a goshawk.* It seemed the unlikeliest thing imaginable' (50). The recognition of money as paper (which is, after all, almost worthless) serves to underline the radical incommensurability of the items for exchange. The money can be counted, it has a certain value. The thing in the box – the living bird – seems to resist any such accountability. Indeed, when the narrator goes to collect the bird, there are in fact two boxes, two goshawks (one for a different buyer). And what is emphasized in this scene is precisely how different they are: having encountered both and finding out which is to be hers, the narrator is dismayed: 'I didn't recognise her. *This isn't my hawk*' (54–5). Her feeling is so strong that she convinces the breeder to give her the other.

While the sale of non-human animals in these texts is by definition commodification, the purchased creatures are treated with utmost responsibility, respect and care. The rays and the goshawk are allowed to live, and to live without suffering. This, unfortunately, is not usually the case where the commodification of animals is concerned. Whether as food and drink, clothing and footwear, or as the victims of habitat loss or pollution, non-human animals are sacrificed by the billion before the altar of consumerism. The commodification of once-living beings enacts something of a conjuring trick as the dead corpse is reanimated through the appearance of a mystical market value – what Marx calls the 'fetish-character' of the commodity, the 'magic' that haunts and animates it.[69]

Fetishism is a form of animism, where 'inanimate' objects are understood to have 'inherent magical powers' or to be 'animated by a spirit' (*OED*). Taking the term from Charles de Brosses's early anthropological work *Du Culte des Dieux Fétiches* (1760), Marx used it in order to liken the transmutation of products of labour to what happens in 'the misty realm of religion' where 'the products of the human brain appear as autonomous figures endowed with a life of their own'.[70] Just as Freud finds animistic tendencies in certain aspects of 'modern' culture, Marx finds animism at the very heart of capitalist relations. As Keston Sutherland notes, Marx's use of fetishism constitutes a 'violent resituation of the term', transforming it from a word that 'celebrates the enlightenment of European culture' to one that 'expose[s] that same culture's fundamental injustice' by satirizing not only 'superstitious thinking and behaviour, but [also] the centuries-long continuity of bourgeois civilized disgust at "superstition" itself'.[71]

Marx's example of this now-quotidian magic is a table, and before we set any animals upon it, we would do well to pay a little attention to the table itself. Marx writes of a wooden table (once a living tree, I might add) that appears to be just 'an ordinary, sensuous thing', but as soon as it 'emerges [*auftritt*, comes on stage] as a commodity', it becomes more than itself, 'it changes into a thing which transcends sensuousness'.[72] So while the table may *appear* to stand 'with its feet on the ground', there is more than meets the eye: 'it stands on its head' (it has a head!) 'and evolves out of its wooden brain grotesque ideas'.[73] The images of these various body parts pre-empt the recognition in the next paragraph that the 'mystical character of the commodity' arises from the 'expenditure of human brain, nerves, muscles and sense organs' that has been required for its production.[74] As Sutherland remarks, this list of body parts is in turn 'a gruesome satirical echo of the allegorical account of abstract human labour as *Gallerte*'.[75]

In a chapter that discusses Marx's use of *Gallerte* at length, Sutherland explains how what is translated into English as 'congealed quantities of homogeneous human labour' is in German a much more specific – and disgusting – image: the '*bloße Gallerte unterschiedsloser menschlicher Arbeit*', or 'the pure *Gallerte* of undifferentiated human labour'.[76] *Gallerte* (which comes from the same root as 'gelatin') is, as the German encyclopedia that Sutherland quotes tells us, a 'semisolid, tremulous mass', made from 'meat, bone, connective tissue, isinglass, stag horns, etc'.[77] The force of this image, Sutherland suggests, is to reduce the 'living hands, brains, muscles and nerves of the wage labourer' into 'mere "animal substances," *ingredients* for the feast of the capitalist'.[78] As such, the 'consumption of use value … is in every case an act of cannibalism':

> The object of Marx's satire on abstract human labour is not the worker reduced to a condiment but the bourgeois consumer who eats him for breakfast. It is the bourgeois consumer who suffers by the influence of Marx's satire on abstract human labour, because the satire makes his unavoidable daily acts and his very survival disgusting. … Can the bourgeois consumer exit the stage of this satire, protesting his abstinence or his vegetarianism? No, he cannot, because the rendering of human minds and bodies into *Gallerte* is not, on the terms of Marx's satire, an abuse of wage labour … but the fundamental law of all wage labour.[79]

The table-as-commodity is not, despite appearances, just an inert surface off of which you will eat your meal. In Marx's image, it is not only made *by* humans, but is also made *of* humans – of bits of humans boiled down into jelly, rendered unrecognizable. The table-as-commodity becomes, then, what we might call an 'animal product': a thing derived from the body of an animal – in this case, a human.

And don't things become even more complex when there are animal products *on* the table, as is so often the case? Let us take a specific example: a glass of milk, from a dairy cow in the United Kingdom – one of 1.88 million such creatures at the last count.[80] As an animal that is non-native to Europe, her presence here is undeniably anthropogenic, though it has not always been a question of market value. Cows were perhaps one of the first species to be domesticated by humans, about 10,500 years ago, and so human consumption of dairy products predates capitalism by many millennia.[81] Market value enters, quite literally, when cows become *cattle*. The word 'cattle' comes from the Latin *capitāle*, 'head', and was used in medieval times in the sense 'principal sum of money, capital, wealth, property'. The earliest recorded usage is *c.*1275, in the now obsolete sense of 'property, substance; strictly personal property or estate, wealth, goods' (*OED*). The later sense of 'cattle' as 'a collective term for live animals held as property, or reared to serve as food, or for the sake of their milk, skin, wool, etc.' is first recorded in 1325, and the modern sense, of specifically bovine animals, in 1555 (*OED*). Not only does the invariant plural 'cattle' enact a violent homogenization of many individual creatures – a bit like the reduction of human labour into *Gallerte* – but it also lumps them in with goods, wealth and profit-making more generally (and such associations have been again made material by the Bank of England's new five- and ten-pound notes, which contain beef tallow: cattle are, once again, literally money).[82]

The inherent violence of the commodification of living creatures aside, for much of this history, the domestication of cows and the consumption of dairy products was possible without the degree of cruelty and destruction it necessarily involves today. It is – once again – a question of scale. Modern dairy farming is *worse* than meat farming, both in terms of the suffering caused to the animals and in the environmental impacts. A cow produces milk, just like a human female, to feed her young, and so will only lactate after giving birth – usually for about ten months, although modern dairy cows have been bred to lactate for sixteen or more. The calves are separated from their mothers at birth, causing distress to both animals, and then most calves are killed for veal – though some females are raised as the next generation of dairy cows. These calves are fed a milk substitute, as their mothers' milk is for human consumption – *naturally*. A cow usually goes through this relentless cycle of artificial insemination, pregnancy, separation and extended lactation (which increases incidence of painful udder infections and sores) four or five times before she begins to produce less milk, at which point she, too, will be slaughtered for meat. The notion, then, that the dairy industry is even separable from – let alone less cruel than – the meat industry is entirely untenable: the vast majority of dairy cows and their offspring end up being eaten, and they suffer a great deal before reaching slaughter. Such widespread and unacknowledged torment casts any sense of the peaceful prosperity of the modern world into stark relief. As Harari writes,

> we can congratulate ourselves on the unprecedented accomplishments of modern Sapiens only if we completely ignore the fate of all other animals. Much of the vaunted material wealth that shields us from disease and famine was accumulated at the expense of laboratory monkeys, dairy cows and conveyor-belt chickens. Over the last two centuries tens of billions of them have been subjected to a regime of industrial exploitation whose cruelty has no precedent in the annals of planet Earth. If we accept a mere tenth of what animal-rights activists are claiming, then modern industrial agriculture might well be the greatest crime in history. When evaluating global happiness, it is wrong to count the happiness only of the upper classes, of Europeans or of men. Perhaps it is also wrong to consider only the happiness of humans.[83]

If the human race survives the next century, our descendants may well look back at factory farms as the worst form of barbarism and wonder how so many people chose not to know or care.[84]

Putting animal welfare aside for a moment (as much of society does all of the time), let us turn to the environmental effects of the industry. Cows kept indoors are usually fed on maize, the production of which causes flooding and strips the soil of nutrients.[85] Cows that graze outside, while no doubt happier and healthier, also require more land, food and water, putting further pressure on these already limited resources. On a planet where the human population is set to hit ten billion by the end of the century, we must use the land and water that we have in the most efficient way possible in order to be able to feed everyone – and, for example, producing a plant-based diet for humans in the United Kingdom would require less than a third of the land that we currently farm.[86] Further, the run-off from dairy farms – 'slurry', or 'manure in fluid form' as the *OED*'s vivid gloss puts it – is the worst polluter of water in the country.[87] Finally, animal agriculture is a huge emitter of carbon dioxide, methane and nitrous oxide – the latter two having a much stronger greenhouse effect than the former – making it a significant contributor to emissions that cause global warming.[88] Meanwhile, the UK dairy industry is subsidized by the government (or, rather, the taxpayer), and the consumption of dairy products is promoted by the media as a 'healthy' food source, despite evidence to the contrary.[89]

Back to our glass of milk. Symbol of innocence and purity, the white liquid before us (the 'ordinary, sensuous thing') can no longer be thought of simply in terms of its nutritional content (its use-value). As a commodity, it is imbued with a fetishistic market value, but, more than this, as a product of twenty-first-century industrial farming, it is also imbued with the complex of cruelty, suffering and destruction that makes its presence possible: the drudgery and premature deaths of the dairy cows from which it was taken; the slaughter of the calves and the anguish of their separation; the multiple environmental impacts of the industry. It also contains the long-ingrained assumptions that humans have a 'right' to these 'animal products', that our consumption of them is 'natural' and that the suffering of animals is admissible in the name of feeding human beings.

Homo sapiens: Ruminant bipeds?

The dinner table is, then, the place where *Homo sapiens* both asserts and loses its so-called humanity. In a 'carnophallogocentric' culture such as ours – to borrow Derrida's term from 'Eating Well' – the consumption of flesh is one of the ways in which human beings maintain the hierarchy that places the life of non-human animals in a different category from that of humans.[90] At the same time, this consumption also calls into question the very hierarchy upon which it relies. The taxonomical term for the human species names our apparently superior intelligence: *Homo sapiens* is *wise*, man is the rational animal. However, the Latin *sapĕre* means not only 'to be sensible or wise' but also 'to have a taste or savour' (*OED*). Similarly, the action of 'rumination' – as I noted at the beginning of this chapter – can be both meditative contemplation and chewing or mastication. In a time when huge proportions of land and resources are used – contrary to economic and ecological sense – to raise excessive amounts of livestock, while billions of people worldwide still do not have enough to eat, I wonder whether these links between taste and wisdom, chewing and contemplation, can really be upheld? The drives to eat and drink are common to all animals, and given that such drives so often surpass our supposed rational powers, the assured potency of the latter begins to tremble. Most consumers of animal products are *at least* minimally aware of the cruelty and environmental impacts of the industry, yet choose not to know more. As Derrida writes, 'no one can deny seriously any more, or for very long, that [people] do all they can in order to dissimulate this cruelty or to hide it from themselves; in order to organize on a global scale the forgetting or misunderstanding of this violence, which some would compare to the worst cases of genocide' (*A*, 25–6).

The consumption of animal products is banal: a daily, mindless habit, assumed to be a 'right' (explicitly God-given or otherwise) and rarely or never appreciated for what it truly is – the sacrifice of a living creature whose death is a gift that maintains the life of the consumer and which should therefore inspire an infinite gratitude. Instead, meat is just one more product, packaged in plastic and placidly stacked on supermarket shelves, the life, pain and suffering at its origin both invisible to and unlooked-for by the complicit consumer. This systematic dissimulation of cruelty and violence is built on the unquestioned assumption that 'The Animal' is merely another resource to be exploited. As David Wood writes, 'the masses of animals industrially slaughtered for food die without names, many even without numbers. Their individuality is pre-eclipsed as stuff.'[91]

Mock turtle soup: Food and fellows in Wonderland

Derrida remarks early on in *The Animal That Therefore I Am* that, given time, he would have 'liked to inscribe [his] whole talk within a reading of Lewis Carroll' (7). Although we 'can't be certain' that he did not in fact do that, 'silently, unconsciously, or without your knowing', I will devote some time here to the Alice books, to their preoccupation with both consumption and the living, and to the multiple animal encounters that trouble assumptions about what it means to eat and what – or who – is meant for eating.

The crossings that Alice makes in her adventures – going first underground and then through a mirror – are crossings of thresholds, movements from, perhaps, the *mundane world* to *a world undone* (to play anagrammatically with 'wonderland'), a world of alterity, where things are upside down or back-to-front. Wonderland: a land of 'wonder' (etymology unknown), a place of astonishment, marvels and the supernatural, of bewilderment and perplexity, of the extraordinary and inexplicable, where the 'grounds' of rationality and logic have been upended or reversed (and you know Alice's adventures originally happened 'under Ground').[92] It is also a place for *wondering* – for questioning and curiosity. 'I wonder if I shall fall right *through* the earth!', Alice thinks to herself as she plummets down the rabbit hole, 'How funny it'll seem to come out among the people that walk with their heads downward! The Antipathies, I think –'.[93] Alice's malapropism here is ironically appropriate (an optimalapropism, perhaps – to pack two meanings up into one word), 'antipathy' coming from the Greek ἀντί (*anti-*, 'against') and πάθος (*pathos*, 'feeling'). In Wonderland, it is not just feet ('-podes' being the suffix Alice has misremembered – she has lost her footing in more ways than one) but *feelings* that are opposite, flipped upside down, undone or transformed.

Living things in Wonderland – Alice included – are sometimes 'who', sometimes 'it'. They are sometimes food (potential or otherwise) and sometimes friends. Most (but not all) have the power of speech. Some are fabulous and chimærical, others seem 'normal' – if such a word can retain any sense in Wonderland. Some have human faces, yet are less than humane (the Duchess and her cook, for example), while some non-human animals seem to fulfil criteria we often reserve for the human (talking, standing upright, wearing clothes, delivering letters, having tea parties, and so on). The effect of all of this is to complicate the distinction between human beings and other animals.

Take the scene shortly after the Caucus-race, in which Alice's company includes 'a Duck and a Dodo, a Lory and an Eaglet, and several other curious creatures' (23). The Mouse has been telling its tale/tail, but has walked away, insulted:

> 'I wish I had our Dinah here, I know I do!' said Alice aloud, addressing nobody in particular. '*She'd* soon fetch it back!'
>
> 'And who is Dinah, if I might venture to ask the question?' said the Lory.
>
> Alice replied eagerly, for she was always ready to talk about her pet: 'Dinah's our cat. And she's such a capital one for catching mice, you ca'n't think! And oh, I wish you could see her after the birds! Why, she'll eat a little bird as soon as look at it!' (29)

In a party composed of a mouse, several birds and two crabs, this utterance causes 'a remarkable sensation' (29). The animals interpret Dinah as a predatory threat, though of course as readers we know that Alice is one too: she eats eggs (as she tells the Pigeon later) and would probably also, unlike Dinah, dine upon the crabs. We should note that Dinah, alone among the animals in this scene to be given a proper name, is not just 'a cat' but '*our* cat' – her name is a sign that she is the property of humans, a common example of the way in which many humans in their day-to-day lives make an exception to the strict human/animal divide and recognize certain non-humans as their fellows: for no one would think to bake their pet in a pie. Meanwhile, although the rest of the animals are called only by their species' name, these are capitalized (Duck, Dodo, Lory, Eaglet, etc.), thereby also disturbing the border between a noun and a proper name (not unlike the movement in Genesis, as discussed earlier, from the noun *ādām*, 'man', to the name 'Adam'). Dinah and the crabs are given gendered pronouns ('she'), whilst the rest of the animals in this scene are referred to as 'it'. Other characters, such as the Rabbit, and Bill the Lizard, are called both 'it' *and* 'he': 'it' by the narrator and 'he' by Alice or the other characters (31–7). Meanwhile, the Duchess's baby boy, who is for Alice initially a 'he' ('Oh, there goes his *precious nose!*' cries Alice as the cook flings a saucepan), is for the narrator and the Duchess an 'it' (she sings 'a sort of lullaby to it … giving it a violent shake at the end of every line'), and then – *before* transforming into a pig – the baby becomes an 'it' for Alice too (54–5).

The metamorphosis of the baby into an animal seems to begin well before the actual 'moment' of transformation (though, as we will see, there is no 'moment' as such). First, in the middle of a conversation with Alice, the Duchess, with 'such sudden violence', addresses the baby (still as a baby) with the word 'Pig!' (53) – though whether we are to interpret this as a name or an admonition or even an instruction is not made clear. Shortly after this, the cook 'at once set to work throwing everything within her reach at the Duchess and the baby – the fire-irons came first; then followed a shower of saucepans, plates and dishes', and as 'the baby was howling so much already, … it was quite impossible to say whether the blows hurt it or not' (53). Because the baby is engaged in a generalized howling and unable to speak, it is apparently 'quite impossible to say' whether he is suffering as a barrage of metal rains down upon him. This sounds strikingly similar to the arguments used by those that support industrialized meat production – of pork, for example. The baby at this point, though still ostensibly in the form of a baby, seems to have already begun to be at least a little bit pig. A living creature, a 'little thing' who/that cannot speak, who/that cannot express him-/its-self: to be carried and nursed, or to be slaughtered and eaten? This is the dilemma Alice next faces. The Duchess leaves, 'flinging the baby' at Alice, who carries him/it outside, where he/it changes into a pig in Alice's arms:

> 'If I don't take this child away with me,' thought Alice, 'they're sure to kill it in a day or two. Wouldn't it be murder to leave it behind?' She said the last words out loud, and the little thing grunted in reply (it had left off sneezing by this time). 'Don't grunt,' said Alice; 'that's not at all a proper way of expressing yourself.'
>
> The baby grunted again, and Alice looked very anxiously into its face to see what was the matter with it. There could be no doubt that it had a *very* turn-up nose, much more like a snout than a real nose ['*there goes his precious nose!*']: also its eyes were getting extremely small for a baby: altogether Alice did not like the

look of the thing at all. 'But perhaps it was only sobbing,' she thought, and looked into its eyes again, to see if there were any tears.

No, there were no tears. 'If you're going to turn into a pig, my dear,' said Alice, seriously, 'I'll have nothing more to do with you. Mind now!' The poor little thing sobbed again (or grunted, it was impossible to say which), and they went on for some while in silence.

Alice was just beginning to think to herself, 'Now, what am I to do with this creature when I get it home?' when it grunted again, so violently, that she looked down into its face in some alarm. This time there could be *no* mistake about it: it was neither more nor less than a pig, and she felt that it would be quite absurd for her to carry it further. (55–6)

This is a remarkable passage. There is no instant of transformation, and yet, before we know it, everything has changed. We go from 'this child' to 'this creature', from 'murder to leave it behind' to 'absurd … to carry it further', from ambiguity (between sobbing and grunting – 'it was impossible to say which') to certainty ('*no* mistake about it: it was neither more nor less than a pig'). A grunt is, according to Alice, 'not at all a proper way of expressing yourself', revealing an assumption that 'proper' self-expression is limited to human language, to what non-human animals supposedly lack. Though it is not specified in the text, I think we can safely assume that Alice eats pork (or pigs, if we were to lose the euphemism). She is certainly not vegetarian – she mentions eating eggs ('I *have* tasted eggs, certainly'), lobster ('Alice began to say "I once tasted –" but checked herself hastily') and whitings ('I've often seen them at dinn –'), and would quite happily carve a slice of the Mutton if the Red Queen didn't have it swiftly taken away ('"May I give you a slice?" she said, taking up the knife and fork') – though the aposiopeses of the second and third examples perhaps mark the beginning of an unease with carnivorous habits in the face of so many animals (48, 88, 91, 234). If we assume that Alice eats pork (or at least that she is fed pork – for few children are vegetarian unless their parents are as well), then the passage above describes the transition of the baby from fellow to food. While the 'little thing' is still perhaps 'more [or] less than a pig' (I wonder, was the baby *more* than a pig? or *less*?) – that is to say, not quite yet absolutely unmistakeably pig – Alice still feels an obligation towards it, a responsibility of care, represented by her carrying it in her arms. Yet when all uncertainty has gone, not only is the obligation released, but it also becomes 'absurd'. This is precisely the certainty that human beings have about the distinction between themselves and other animals – a certainty that allows them to justify, condone and wilfully blind themselves to violence against non-humans. It is significant, I think, that it is the *cook* that plays such a violent role in this scene, for it is predominantly with regards to the production of food, as I have discussed, that we allow violence against animals to occur on a scale that beggars belief – if or when we think of it.

There are two other characters in Wonderland whose appearance further makes salient the deleterious effects of humankind on other animals: the Dodo and the Mock Turtle. The dodo, of course, has come to symbolize anthropogenic extinction, having been exterminated shortly after humans first colonized Mauritius in 1644. While its extinction was not solely attributable to hunting by humans – the arrival of the colonizers' non-native animal entourage was probably more to blame – it was, nevertheless, to be found on dinner plates.[94] The head and foot of one are in the Oxford Museum of Natural History (which Charles Dodgson visited[95]) and are the most complete remains of a single dodo now in existence. Its fragmentary survival – the rest of the bird was improperly preserved and therefore had to be burnt – could stand in for the bungled approach that seems to characterize human attempts at conservation. Further, given that – as I said at the beginning of this chapter – Darwin thought of the survival and extinction of words in the same terms as life, it is perhaps significant that it is the Dodo who speaks in archaic language that the others cannot understand – 'Speak English!' the Eaglet says, 'I don't know the meaning of half those long words, and, what's more, I don't believe you do either!' The Dodo is, that is to say, a symbol for more than one type of extinction (25).

The Mock Turtle also invokes the rapacious attitude of humans towards other species: 'Once', as he tells Alice with a deep sigh, he 'was a real Turtle' (84). His demoted status is a matter of soup. Turtle soup was such a popular dish in the eighteenth and nineteenth centuries that green sea turtles were hunted to near extinction. While the turtle was not quite as dead as a dodo, its scarcity forced cooks to come up with mock turtle soup, which was made from the head and feet of a calf, and accounts for the strange chimærical appearance of the Mock Turtle in the original illustrations to the book. The character makes an ironic reference to this practice of animal substitution when, on suggesting that they 'try the first figure' of a Lobster Quadrille, he notes that they 'can do without lobsters, you know' (89). The bizarre interchangeability of species implied is reminiscent of the modern practice of 'biodiversity offsetting', in which biodiversity loss is 'made up for' elsewhere, as if the singularity of species' relationships with their ecosystems is quantifiable and exchangeable – that is, commodifiable.

Thou shalt not kill – who or what?

Whether something is 'it' or 's/he', 'what' or 'who', food or fellow, comes down to an opposition we think we can make between an object and a subject, a thing and a being. This opposition has always been made from the point of view of a subject, where the assumed self-identity and auto-deictic relation to itself are taken as given. In 'Eating Well', Derrida calls into question both sides of the certainty upon which the 'classical determination of the subject' relies.[96] This determination, as he explains, depends upon the assumptions that, on the one hand, we can identify a subject (and this would always be an auto-deictic identification) that is self-identical, present and separable from *its* world (I underline the possessive here to note that, as a subject, it is presumed to have a relation to its world *as such*), and, on the other hand, that there are beings that lack this kind of subjectivity. Leaving this untenable distinction behind, he rethinks the notion of subjectivity in terms of relation to the other, in terms of, that is to say, *responsibility*:

> The singularity of the 'who' is not the individuality of a thing that would be identical to itself, it is not an atom. It is a singularity that dislocates or divides itself in gathering itself together to answer to the other, whose call somehow precedes its own identification with itself. ... Here, no doubt, begins the link with the larger questions of ethical, juridical, and political responsibility around which the metaphysics of subjectivity was constituted.[97]

A subject is constituted through its relation to others. The failure of Western philosophy has been, in any ethical calculations, to recognize only the fellow human as other and thereby to maintain a responsibility only to human others. Derrida goes on to discern 'a place left open, in the very structure of these discourses' for 'the executions of ingestion, incorporation, or introjection of the corpse'.[98] While this may be a symbolic incorporation of a human corpse (in a Catholic Communion, for example), when the corpse is that of a non-human animal, the act is 'as real as it is symbolic' – the symbolic nature revealing itself when we recognize the non-necessity of the act, for 'who can be made to believe that our cultures are carnivorous because animal proteins are irreplaceable?' he asks.[99] The sacrificial structure Derrida identifies again relies on an assumed human/animal distinction, in which responsibility towards the other (upon which, let us not forget, the subjectivity of the subject is based) does not extend to non-humans.

> The subject is responsible for the other before being responsible for himself as 'me'. This responsibility to the other, for the other, comes to him, for example (but this is not just one example among others) in the 'Thou shalt not kill'. Thou shalt not kill thy neighbour. Consequences follow upon one another, and must do so continuously: thou shalt not make him suffer, which is sometimes worse than death, thou shalt not do him harm, thou shalt not eat him, not even a little bit, and so forth. ... 'Thou shalt not kill' is addressed to the other and presupposes him. It is destined to the very thing that it institutes, the other as man. ... The 'Thou shalt not kill' – with all its consequences, which are limitless – has never been understood within the Judeo-Christian tradition ... as a 'Thou shalt not put to death the living in general.' ... The other, such as this can be thought according to the imperative of ethical transcendence, is indeed the other man: man as other, the other as man.[100]

The great contradiction of the edict 'Thou shalt not kill' – in its exclusion of non-human animals – was, as Derrida identifies in *The Animal That Therefore I Am*, anticipated in Genesis with the story of Cain and Abel (4.2-4). Cain offers God 'the fruit of the ground', while Abel offers an animal sacrifice: 'And the Lord had respect unto Abel and to his offering: But unto Cain and to his offering he had not respect' (4.3-5). Cain, understandably perturbed by God's preference for Abel's offering, decides (less understandably) to kill Abel, and then is cursed, punished and exiled by God. Right from 'the Beginning', then, the slaughter of non-humans (as enacted by Abel) is permissible, even admirable, while the slaughter of humans (as enacted by Cain) is unlawful and must be punished (unless you are God cleansing the earth with a deluge a few generations later, of course).

Alice says at one point in her adventures, 'I suppose I ought to eat or drink something or other; but the great question is "What?"' (39). *What*, precisely, not *who*: for animals-as-food are always 'what' – always, that is to say, denied the possibility of subjectivity. Yet the distinction between 'what' and 'who' is quite as troubled in Wonderland as it is in 'Eating Well'. When Alice grows extremely tall after eating some of the Caterpillar's mushroom, a Pigeon mistakes her for a serpent that has 'come wriggling down from the sky' (48):

> 'But I'm *not* a serpent, I tell you!' said Alice. 'I'm a – I'm a – '
>
> 'Well! *What* are you?' said the Pigeon. 'I can see you're trying to invent something!'
>
> 'I – I'm a little girl,' said Alice, rather doubtfully, as she remembered the number of changes she had gone through that day.

> 'A likely story indeed!' said the Pigeon in a tone of the deepest contempt. 'I've seen a good many little girls in my time, but never *one* with such a neck as that! No, no! You're a serpent; and there's no use denying it. I suppose you'll be telling me next that you never tasted an egg!'
>
> 'I *have* tasted eggs, certainly,' said Alice, who was a very truthful child; 'but little girls eat eggs quite as much as serpents do, you know.'
>
> 'I don't believe it,' said the Pigeon; 'but if they do, why then they're a kind of serpent, that's all I can say.'
>
> This was such a new idea to Alice, that she was quite silent for a minute or two, which gave the Pigeon the opportunity of adding 'You're looking for eggs, I know *that* well enough; and what does it matter to me whether you're a little girl or a serpent?'
>
> 'It matters a good deal to *me*,' said Alice hastily; 'but I'm not looking for eggs, as it happens; and if I was, I shouldn't want *yours*: I don't like them raw.' (48)

Here the usual relation has been inverted: instead of a human regarding an animal as a 'what', it is the other way around. '*What* are you?' says the Pigeon to Alice. Alice is no better able to answer this question than the 'Who are *you*?' posed to her earlier by the Caterpillar (40). 'I can't explain *myself*, I'm afraid, sir', she says, 'because I'm not myself, you see' (41). Identity is precisely *not* self-identical, present, or rigorously separable; instead, it is shown to be determined by the relation of self to world and to others. Alice may declare that she is not a serpent, but if 'little girls eat eggs quite as much as serpents do', then, for the Pigeon, 'they're a kind of serpent' too. Alice is quite startled by the pronouncement, for, having grown up in a Christian culture, she will naturally have imbibed the 'enmity' towards snakes dealt by God in Genesis (3.15). Yet for the Pigeon, a serpent is an eater-of-eggs – and a serpent by any other name ('little girl', perhaps) would still be as predatory, even if she 'doesn't like them raw'. It is through this last statement that Alice attempts to reassert her humanness (if not her humanity), as cooking is of course a particularly human practice. Later, when Alice *is* looking for eggs – when she decides to buy one from the Sheep's shop – the food/fellow distinction is again troubled as the egg grows 'larger and larger, and more and more human', turning at last into Humpty Dumpty: the *what* becomes a *who* (185). Becoming annoyed at Alice's 'chattering', Humpty Dumpty insists that she introduces herself – 'tell me your name and your business,' he says (186). At this point, we must assume that the human-egg can no longer be food, for as the Red Queen tells Alice later, 'it isn't etiquette to cut any one you've been introduced to' (234).

Let's return to the original vilification of serpents alluded to above, which also has to do with the assertion or reassertion of humanness. It is, as Robert Alter comments in the notes to his new translation of the Bible, 'the first moment in which a split between man and the rest of the animal kingdom is recorded'.[101] When God finds out about Adam and Eve's transgression in Genesis, he punishes the serpent *first*, cursing it, and putting 'enmity between thee and the woman' (3.14-15). The serpent was forever condemned to be a symbol of evil in the Judaeo-Christian tradition, punished *before* Adam and Eve, despite the fact that its wrongdoing seems trivial in comparison: they disobey an explicit order from God not to eat the fruit, whereas the serpent's 'crime' is merely to talk to Eve. She tells the snake that God has forbidden the fruit of a certain tree – 'Ye shall not eat of it, neither shall ye touch it, lest ye die' (3.3) – to which the serpent replies, 'Ye shall not surely die: For God doth know that in the day ye eat thereof, then your eyes shall be opened, and ye shall be as gods, knowing good and evil' (3.4-5). So the serpent does not really deceive Eve: it tells the truth. Indeed, though it is introduced as 'more subtil than any beast of the field' (3.1), the highly negative connotations of the word 'subtil' – crafty, cunning, sly, treacherous – are perhaps too strong. The word translated here as 'subtil' is the Hebrew עָרוּם (*arum*), elsewhere translated in the King James Version as 'prudent' (see Prov. 12.16, 12.23, 13.16, 14.8, 22.3, 27.12), and is also a word for 'naked': 'And they were both naked [*arumim*, עֲרוּמִּים], the man and his wife, and were not ashamed' (Gen. 2.25). In fact, the two passages just quoted are directly juxtaposed, so as one reads the last verse of the second chapter followed by the first verse of the third (Gen. 2.25–3.1), the nakedness (*arumim*) of Adam and Eve is echoed in the subtlety/prudency (*arum*) of the snake.[102] The serpent's words are naked; they do not lie or dissimulate: Adam and Eve do not die after eating the fruit, and indeed, as promised, 'the eyes of them both were opened, and they knew that they were naked' (3.7). The crime comes down to the very human – and, perhaps, prudent – realization that they are naked. Unashamed nudity, 'being naked without knowing it', is, as Derrida identifies, 'the property unique to animals, what in the last instance distinguishes them from man' (*A*, 4–5). Meanwhile, the serpent's crime relies upon its having the power of speech – another characteristic proper to man – without which it would not have been able to tempt Eve. Both crimes – that of the serpent and that of Adam and Eve – are crimes of becoming-human, which is perhaps why 'sin' (or the capacity for sin) is 'original', or at the origin, of the Judaeo-Christian conception of humanity.

Life after the end of the *wærœld*

'*Die Welt ist fort, ich muß dich tragen*.' 'The world is gone, I must carry you.'[103] This is the last line of a poem by Paul Celan, to which, as I said in my first chapter, Derrida returns time and time again. It describes a moment of relation between self and other (I, you), of obligation and responsibility (I *must* carry you) and of a disappearance of the world. The 'infinite inappropriability of the other' is what at once cannot, yet *must*, be carried. Here we encounter 'the immediacy of the abyss that engages me on behalf of the other wherever the "I must" – "I must carry you" – forever prevails over the "I am," over the *sum* and over the *cogito*'. Responsibility prevails over *auto-deixis*: 'Before *I am*, I carry. Before *being me*, I carry the other.'[104] Of course, this other, the 'you' of the poem, can refer to *any* 'living being, a human or non-human animal'.[105] As Wood writes, this 'you' is 'a You-not-identifiable, You on another scale, negligibly small as well as huge, finite, elastic with its own elasticity, its own breaking-points. A You felt with the intimacy of love, fear and resistance. It's also animal, and non-living.'[106]

This 'you' then, in its radical alterity, is the kind of 'you' we need for the Anthropocene. In this age of mass extinctions (so many worlds already *gone* forever), we have a responsibility to, for and of *life*. Earlier I suggested that the word 'world', in its etymological sense of 'the age of man' (*wær-œld*), could be read as an older word for the Anthropocene. But in the face of the responsibilities undeniably provoked or invoked by climate change and the concomitant threats to life on earth, I would instead argue that the Anthropocene is precisely the call for, or necessity of, the end of the world/*wær-œld*. Worlds have already ended because of climate change, as species are lost forever in the Sixth Mass Extinction. As Derrida remarks, 'each time, and each time singularly, each time irreplaceably, each time infinitely, death is nothing less than an end of *the* world'.[107] It is time now for an apocalyptic apocalypse, for the end of the *wær-œld* as such – not, one can hope, for the extinction of the human but for the end of a world in which human beings think themselves separable from or independent of other animals and forms of life. Could the end of the *wær-œld* be the beginning of responsibility to others beyond the human? If the *wær-œld* is gone, I *will* carry you.

4

Hatching: Psychoanalysis and the Textual Unconscious

I no longer understand the state of mind in which I hatched the psychology.
Sigmund Freud[1]

Reading beyond consciousness

What I need to write about now resists thinking. It is not available to consciousness and yet underlies its every move. As Sigmund Freud writes, 'psycho-analysis cannot situate the essence of the psychical in consciousness'.[2] What is conscious is only 'the *surface* of the mental apparatus'.[3] Given that this surface is all that is available to direct observation, empiricism cannot help us make sense of what moves below. Instead, we will need a practice that makes invisible connections, that is sensitive to force as well as to form, that is creative and receptive, lawless and inventive, and that allows things to emerge or hatch out. We will need, that is to say, the practice of reading.

The alterity which divides every 'I' before it thinks or thinks it thinks, is what, as Jacques Derrida writes, Freud gives the 'metaphysical name, the unconscious', and is

> definitively taken away from every process of presentation in which we would demand for it to be shown forth in person. In this context and under this heading, the unconscious is not, as we know, a hidden, virtual, and potential self-presence. It is differed – which no doubt means that it is woven out of differences, but also that it sends out, that it delegates, representatives or proxies; but there is no chance that the mandating subject 'exists' somewhere, that it is present or is 'itself', and still less chance that it will become conscious.[4]

If we are dealing with a thing, it is a thing of nothing. The unconscious 'sends out' representatives or proxies, but it does not 'exist' as a sender, as a 'mandating subject'. As such, Derrida continues, 'the language of presence or absence … is in principle inadequate'.[5]

The unconscious appears as a foreign agency at work in or through the 'self', without, precisely, being identifiable with it: all its 'acts and manifestations', writes Freud, 'must be judged as if they belonged to someone else'.[6] This is an agency that disrupts every agency from within. It produces effects without any identifiable or locatable cause. We might say it is *only* its effects, except that it is also *not* these effects, being always temporally prior to – and therefore different from – them.[7] It is characterized 'by irreducible aftereffects, by delayed effects'.[8] Temporally disjointed (*nachträglich*, as Freud would say), traceable only in being untraceable, the unconscious does not bear thinking; thinking is, precisely, the work of the conscious mind – even if and when it is subject to unconscious operations. The moment that the unconscious is translated into consciousness – and Freud often spoke of psychoanalysis in terms of such translations, as we will see – it is, precisely, no longer 'itself', no longer unconscious. Its translation is, then, both impossible and unavoidable.

Psychoanalysis and climate change

The work of psychoanalysis formed the third and 'most wounding' of the blows to 'the universal narcissism of men' identified by Freud.[9] It comprised 'two discoveries – that the life of our sexual instincts cannot be wholly tamed, and that mental processes are in themselves unconscious and only reach the ego and come under its control through incomplete and untrustworthy perceptions'.[10] Psychoanalysis sought, then, to 'prove to the ego that it is not even master in its own house'.[11] The previous two blows are described in more literal terms (the first showed that 'our earth was not the centre of the universe', and the second 'proved [humankind's] descent from the animal kingdom'[12]), but, in describing psychoanalysis, Freud's language becomes overtly figurative. He turns to an image of a house, of which the ego finds it is 'not even' the master. Implicit in this 'not even' is the idea of a more generalized mastery – that stretches outside of the domestic sphere to social, political and environmental spaces – and that is entirely undone when the ego is shown that 'even' at home, 'even' in its 'own' house, it is not in charge. An image of a house or home is apt, for the blow struck to human narcissism by Freud's 'discovery' of the unconscious reverberates through the domains of mastery and sovereignty; interior and exterior spaces, the psychic and the corporeal; the *oikos* (Greek, οἶκος, 'house') of ecology and economics – at both individual and global scales (the libidinal economy, the unconscious workings of ecology). It also has to do with the *Unheimliche* or the uncanny: forces which disturb the home from the inside, unsettling the comfortable domain of the ego.[13]

The opening of William Vollmann's *Carbon Ideologies* pointedly captures the limits of human rationality as revealed by the climate crisis: 'Someday, perhaps not long from now, the inhabitants of a hotter, more dangerous and biologically diminished planet … may wonder what you and I were thinking, or whether we thought at all.'[14] The repressions, denials, self-destructiveness and pathological relations that characterize human responses to climate change all call to be thought psychoanalytically, as does the possibility of responding more effectively. Individual and societal responses to climate change are not – in the vast majority of cases – determined by knowledge (there is no lack of data); they are determined by political narratives and by desire: desire for profit, for consumption or for a reality in which climate change is not a threat. A better understanding of the perverse power of human irrationality, and of the ways in which narrative and emotions shape belief, has the potential not only to cast light on our failure to act but also to facilitate a radical change in behaviour.

Indeed, psychoanalytic knowledge was already used to facilitate a widespread behavioural change in the latter half of the twentieth century – although this change, in hindsight, was not for the better. An understanding of unconscious desires was instrumental in creating the culture of consumerism which not only now hinders effective response to climate change but was also a key factor in causing the crisis. As Eli Zaretsky puts it in his book *Political Freud*,

> Premised on the view of the individual as infinitely desiring rather than capable of satisfaction, psychoanalysis was indispensable to an epoch that sought to expand consumption. It revolutionized advertising, which shifted from addressing perceived needs to addressing unconscious wishes. … Overall, psychoanalysis helped change the way in which capitalism was understood, from a mode of production to a mode of distribution and consumption.[15]

While there were other social and economic factors which influenced the growth of consumer capitalism in the mid-twentieth century, the role of new psychoanalytic knowledge was pivotal in changing the tactics (and, therefore, the effectiveness) of marketing strategy. In an essay discussing the links between psychoanalysis, fascist propaganda and the rise of American consumerism,

Lawrence Samuel describes how a growing understanding of unconscious desires came to revolutionize the way that products were advertised and sold.[16] Samuel identifies three key players in the change, all of whom used a psychoanalytic understanding of human behaviour to understand – and transform – consumer culture: Edward Bernays, Paul Lazarsfeld and Ernest Dichter. Bernays, credited with being the 'father of public relations', was Freud's nephew, and, starting in the early 1920s, he put his uncle's theories to work in advising corporate clients for more than four decades.[17] Bernays realized that consumer decisions were driven by suppressed desires and that this knowledge could be used to control the masses, to 'manipulate public opinion' and to 'engineer consent', as he put it.[18] Lazarsfeld and Dichter were Austrian psychologists who both moved to America in the 1930s. Lazarsfeld is credited with the invention of 'motivation research' (the analysis of the role of the unconscious in people's behaviour), while Dichter, one of his students, would go on to put the method to use for explicit corporate gain in market research.[19] Such analyses enabled companies to 'forecast and control consumer behaviour'.[20] This, as Samuels notes, was 'an idea nothing less than revolutionary in the mid-1930s' and became 'a powerful tool for Big Business in the postwar years'.[21]

In the context of climate change, the growth of consumer capitalism is doubly pernicious. First, the proliferation of disposable goods and planned obsolescence necessary to maintain a consumer economy based on infinite growth is in direct contradiction to sustaining life on a finite planet; and second, the seductive charm of consumer culture works to distract citizens from the existential threat that now poses itself, thereby facilitating and prolonging inaction.

In *Psychoanalysis and Ecology at the Edge of Chaos*, Joseph Dodds recognizes that just as psychoanalytic understanding was instrumental in creating consumer behaviour, it might also 'be turned to the task of developing pro-environmental behaviour'.[22] Dodds's book – along with George Marshall's *Don't Even Think About It: Why Our Brains Are Wired to Ignore Climate Change*, Kari Norgaard's *Living in Denial: Climate Change, Emotions, and Everyday Life* and Sally Weintrobe's *Engaging with Climate Change: Psychoanalytic and Interdisciplinary Perspectives* – represents a growing recognition of the ways in which unconscious forces determine individual and societal behaviour in the context of global warming.[23] In *Don't Even Think About It*, Marshall gives a survey of psychological research on the factors that determine our reactions or responses to climate change (including risk perception, social and political biases, apathy, decision-making, anxiety-response, etc.). The key to reconfiguring these 'hardwired' responses, Marshall concludes, is narrativization: 'Stories perform a fundamental cognitive function: They are the means by which the emotional brain makes sense of the information collected by the rational brain. People may hold information in the form of data and figures, but their beliefs about it are held entirely in the form of stories.'[24] The only way, then, to counter the repressive response to climate change and engage people in action is to tell compelling stories – something a certain father of psychoanalysis knew how to do.

Textual unconscious

Freud's turn to metaphor in describing the third blow (the ego 'is not even master in its own house') signals the necessity of *fiction* for psychoanalysis. While he always wanted to think of it as a science, the fact that its object was unavailable for direct study foreclosed the possibility of empiricism. Indeed, in *Beyond the Pleasure Principle*, Freud admits he has no choice but to stray into a realm of 'speculation, often far-fetched speculation', as he attempts to reckon with 'the most obscure and inaccessible region of the mind'.[25] Elsewhere, he states that 'The theory of the instincts is so to say our mythology. Instincts are mythical entities, magnificent in their indefiniteness. In our work we cannot for a moment disregard them, yet we are never sure that we are seeing them clearly.'[26] The house of psychoanalysis plays host to the meetings of science and mythology, theory and fiction, observation and speculation, the literal and the metaphorical. The cross-contamination of these supposedly opposing realms ties the work of psychoanalysis to the practices of reading and writing – as Freud was well aware. A subterranean play of unconscious forces underwrites text and consciousness, animating them in often incalculable ways. As Derrida writes, 'the difficulty of distinguishing conscious from unconscious is at its most obscure when the issue is one of language or of the use of language'.[27]

There are innumerable examples of Freud's linguistic figuration of mental processes and the world of dreams. He writes, for instance, how the elements of dreams are like the syllables or words of a language, which when taken together 'are no longer nonsensical but may form a poetical phrase of the greatest beauty and significance'.[28] He writes of the symptoms of hysteria as 'fragments', 'numerous inscriptions, which, by good luck, may be bilingual, reveal an alphabet and a language, and, when they have been deciphered and translated, yield undreamed-of information'.[29] He writes how dream-thoughts and dream-content 'are presented to us like two versions of the same subject-matter in two different languages' and how 'dream-content seems like a transcript of the dream-thoughts into another mode of expression, whose characters and syntactic laws it is our business to discover by comparing the original and the translation' – yet of course there is no 'original' text to consult here; it can only be inferred, from what is already a translation of a translation (the waking recollection of the dream).[30] I am reminded of Derrida's comment in 'Force and Signification': 'Force is the other of language without which language would not be what it is.'[31] The 'dream-thoughts' are the unconscious 'other' of the 'dream-content', radically inaccessible, yet essential, compelling.

The unconscious can only ever be read *in translation*, for as soon as it becomes an object for consciousness, it has – inevitably – been rendered in language foreign to it. In 'Des Tours de Babel', Derrida writes that 'meaning does not allow transport without damage into another language' – a fact which makes for 'the necessary and impossible task of translation, its necessity *as* impossibility'.[32] One must translate what is untranslatable. Translation operates, he goes on, via a 'mode that renders present what is absent, that allows remoteness to approach as remoteness, *fort/da*. Let us say that translation is experience, which one can translate or experience also: *experience is translation*'.[33] It is not fortuitous, I think, that Freud's own necessary-impossible work of translation, *Beyond the Pleasure Principle*, should make this striking dis/appearance here (in the *fort/da* which appears without citation or elaboration: Derrida's essay does not once mention Freud or psychoanalysis by name). First, both texts are concerned with detours or *Umwege* (and given Derrida's fascination with the 'detours' of *Beyond*, it is perhaps not surprising that the text was playing on his mind when he came to write his own text on detours, or 'des tours' of Babel).[34] Second, the fact that the *fort/da* that appears in Derrida's text remains in German, unannounced, unexplained, untranslated, perhaps allows its 'remoteness to approach as remoteness', thereby calling up without calling up the whole strange discourse of the text in which Freud elaborates his theory of the death drive, his mythology of the instincts. Derrida writes that 'what fascinates and orients the work of the translator' is the 'always intact, the intangible, the untouchable'[35] – and this could readily be a description of the work of psychoanalysis. Indeed, as Derrida recognizes by saying that 'experience is translation', the operation of *carrying across* that translation effects (from Latin *trans-*, 'across', and *-latus*, 'to bear', 'carry', 'bring') can be generalized beyond senses relating to the translations between verbal languages. There is a generalized translation that is essential to being, that is happening all the time, even in the 'same' language, even before or beyond verbal language, and which is essential, that is to say, to any relation to otherness, including that otherness which resides in the 'self'.

What follows, then, will be concerned with the two senses of what Hélène Cixous calls the 'textual unconscious' – both the unconscious operations of text and the textual operations of the unconscious, and the translations such operations effect or necessitate.[36] While the texts I mentioned in the previous section (by Dodds, Marshall, Norgaard and Weintrobe) look to think through the ways in which unconscious forces interface disastrously with climate change, this chapter will be concerned with elaborating the strange animisms of this bipartite textual unconscious and will then suggest how such an understanding might disturb or transform the ways in which we read the writing of the Anthropocene and the narcissisms of the human.

Magic words

As I discussed in my first chapter, Freud conceived of animism as the first in a three-stage progression of human thought, which developed from animism to religion and then to science. He also aligned these cultural progressions with the development of the individual, so that animistic belief in the omnipotence of thoughts corresponds to the narcissistic phase of childhood, which, in his view, should have no place in a scientifically enlightened and psychologically 'mature' culture:

> The scientific view of the universe no longer affords any room for human omnipotence; men have acknowledged their smallness and submitted resignedly to death and to the other necessities of nature. None the less some of the primitive belief in omnipotence still survives in men's faith in the power of the human mind, which grapples with the laws of reality.[37]

Indeed, as I noted in my first chapter, he admits that animistic beliefs also persist 'as the living basis of our speech, our beliefs and our philosophies' and 'in the field of art'.[38] Derrida notes that the attempt to reduce 'art's magic into a mere animist remnant' not only disrupts the progressive schema that Freud attempts to posit but also relies upon 'an utterly insufficient and inconsistent, traditional concept of art … as an illusion, purely and simply a representational and reproductive mimicry':

> Freud acts as if, first of all, 'effects of the affect' were not real events, as if the 'as if' had no real effect. What Freud seems strangely ignorant of, which comes down to misunderstanding nonrepresentational art – or nonconstative art, productive art, the poietic dimension of art – is the knowledge and power of

language in general, in the order of psychoanalysis in particular, on the side of the analyst and of the analysand, of theory, practice and the analytic institution, where performative power acts and produces always according to ways that are at once rational, technical, *and magical*. The effect, both affective and effective, of a performative, is always magical in appearance. It always operates as if by an enchantment. In practice and in theory, in technique – in particular, that of psychoanalysis. Who better than Freud himself at once showed it, illustrated it, and ignored it?[39]

The practice, theory and technique of psychoanalysis, then, operate through the enchanting magic of (performative) language, through an animistic potency that troubles the purely 'fictional' character of the 'as if'. As Freud himself writes, 'there are no indications of reality in the unconscious, so that one cannot distinguish between truth and fiction that has been cathected with affect'.[40]

Psychoanalysis deals with, or in, animism. It is, in fact, all in the name: psycho-analysis. While in English, the prefix 'psycho-' has come predominantly to denote what relates to the mind, the word has other facets of meaning. The Greek word *psyche* (ψυχή) means not only 'mind' but also 'breath', 'life', 'soul' or 'spirit': it is inhabited by the confluence of these meanings that is found in so many languages, as I discussed in my first chapter. Given that *psyche* and *anima* are so often taken as translations of each other, it is perhaps not surprising to find a certain animism at the heart of psychoanalysis. In 'Psychical (or Mental) Treatment', Freud describes the word with which he has named his work as follows:

> '*Psyche*' is a Greek word which may be translated 'mind' [*Seele*]. Thus 'psychical treatment' means 'mental treatment' [*Seelenbehandlung*]. ... 'Psychical treatment' denotes ... treatment taking its start in the mind [*Seele*], treatment (whether of mental [*seelischer*] or physical disorders) by measures which operate in the first instance and immediately upon the human mind [*Seelische des Menschen*].[41]

Where the English translation gives the words 'mind' or 'mental', the German has the word *Seele* and its derivatives, which, like the Greek *psyche*, also means 'soul', 'spirit' or 'pneuma' (the English 'soul' of course has the same root as *Seele* – the Old High German *sēla*, 'soul' or 'life'). While in English the words 'mind' and 'soul' have come to have quite distinct connotations, in Greek as well as German, one term encapsulates both concepts and so they are not separable in the same way. What is rendered in English as 'mental treatment', is, in German, *Seelenbehandlung*, and so could also be 'soul treatment'. Further, though 'soul' and *Seele* denote the 'spiritual' attributes of life in opposition to the corporeal or physical, the work of psychoanalysis begins to break down that opposition: *Seelenbehandlung*, as Freud states, can be used to treat both 'mental or physical disorders [*seelischer oder körperlicher Störungen*]'. While in 'earlier times', he continues, physicians 'seemed to be afraid of granting mental life [*Seelenleben*] any independence [*Selbständigkeit*]' – as if that would be, he says, 'an abandonment of the scientific ground on which they stood' – in fact, as psychoanalysis recognizes, the 'relation between body and mind [*Leiblichem und Seelischem*] ... is a reciprocal one'.[42] The life of the mind/soul is potent and autonomous (*selbständig*), and it can affect the body, and vice versa. And what is the treatment that can work with or through this reciprocal relation? It is language – 'words are the essential tool of mental treatment':

> A layman will no doubt find it hard to understand how pathological disorders of the body and mind can be eliminated by 'mere' words. He will feel that he is being asked to believe in magic. And he will not be so very wrong, for the words which we use in our everyday speech are nothing other than watered-down magic. But we shall have to follow a roundabout path [*Umweg*] in order to explain how science sets about restoring to words a part at least of their former magical power.[43]

Fifteen years later, in *Beyond the Pleasure Principle*, Freud elaborates his theory of the death drive, the unconscious forces within an organism that cause it to strive along its own 'circuitous paths [*Umwege*]' towards 'an old state of things, an initial state' (38/40), and this is also a text in which, as I will show, Freud finds himself, consciously or unconsciously, restoring the 'magical power' of words.

More strange return: What Freud owes literature[44]

Tomorrow shall I beg leave to see your kingly eyes: when I shall, first asking your pardon, thereunto recount the occasion of my sudden and more strange return.
Shakespeare, *Hamlet*[45]

It is well known that Freud was a master storyteller, that his work was described as 'theoretical fiction', and often goes by way of literature.[46] Literature comes before and goes beyond Freud's oeuvre; as Derrida writes, 'Freud often said about poets and artists – even as he attempted to include their lives and works within the horizon of psychoanalytic knowledge ... – that they had always anticipated and exceeded the discourse of psychoanalysis'.[47] Ann Wordsworth writes that

152   *Radical Animism*

Freud's 'wish to found psychoanalysis as a positive science' subordinates 'the possibility of chance … to two series of causality: psychical/physical, internal/external'; there is, however, 'also a Freud who chances, one who knows how to be caught in a certain speculative overflow', which 'indebts him to literature'.[48] There is a tension between Freud's desire for a boundedness, a horizon (the word 'horizon' coming from the Greek ὅρος, boundary, limit), for psychoanalysis – which would be necessary for it to be a 'positive science' – and the fact that there is 'a certain speculative overflow' in which Freud 'knows how to be caught' – an overflow between, for instance, the supposedly clearly distinguishable 'worlds' of psychoanalysis and literature. Wordsworth distinguishes two Freuds: the scientist and the one 'who chances': 'The chancer works without a horizon, thrown by the divisibility of the mark, and falling across his text are the chances – examples and citations from a repressed network of descendence.'[49] Wordsworth's 'chancer' here is Derrida, but I would like to cast Freud – another chancer – in the role and begin to speculatively trace something of a 'repressed network of descendence' in *Beyond the Pleasure Principle*, bringing to light what he might owe a certain series of 'O's that fall in the text. In so doing, I also hope to allow something of what I mean by the 'textual unconscious' to come through.

Act One Scene One: A house in Vienna

In the second chapter of *Beyond*, after a brief summary of the 'normal' economy of pleasure and unpleasure in the human psyche, Freud introduces the behaviours associated with traumatic neuroses, which, in their apparent contradiction of the pleasure principle, invite reflection upon 'the mysterious masochistic trends of the ego' (14). He quickly proposes to leave this 'dark and dismal subject', however, and pass on to the 'normal' activity of child's play, telling the now-famous story of the game of *fort/da*: 'a little boy' (who is in fact Freud's grandson Ernst – though Freud chooses not to reveal this autobiographical element) playing a game of disappearance and return with his toys. This 'good little boy', who, we are told, 'was greatly attached to his mother',

> had an occasional disturbing habit of taking any small objects he could get hold of and throwing them away from him. … As he did this he gave vent to a loud, long-drawn-out 'o-o-o-o', accompanied by an expression of interest and satisfaction. His mother and the writer of the present account were agreed in thinking that this was not a mere interjection but represented the German word '*fort*' ['gone']. I eventually realized that it was a game and that the only

use he made of any of his toys was to play 'gone' with them. One day I made an observation which confirmed my view. The child had a wooden reel with a piece of string tied round it. ... What he did was to hold the reel by the string and very skillfully throw it over the edge of his curtained cot, so that it disappeared into it, at the same time uttering his expressive [*bedeutungsvolles*, meaningful, significant] 'o-o-o-o'. He then pulled the reel out of the cot again by the string and hailed its reappearance with a joyful '*da*' ['there']. This, then, was the complete game – disappearance and return. As a rule one only witnessed its first act, which was repeated untiringly as a game in itself, though there is no doubt that the greater pleasure was attached to the second act. (14–15/12–13)

Freud interprets the game as a repetition of a traumatic experience outside of the boy's control: the mother leaving. The game allows Ernst to 'stage' – and this is Freud's word (*inszeniert* in the German, with the same theatrical connotations) – the disappearance (*fort*) and the return (*da*) of his mother in a way that gives him mastery over the situation – particularly over the return: 'the greater pleasure was attached to the second act'. Everything is being relayed in the language of the theatre: the *staging* of the game; the first and second *acts*; later we are told that it is Ernst's 'great cultural achievement [*Leistung*, also 'performance']'; that he 'set the scene [*Szene setzte*]'[50] and played an '*active* part [*aktive Rolle*]' (15, 16/13). Keeping in mind little Ernst's dramatic 'O's, for we are to return to them, let us read on and remind ourselves of where Freud was heading when he decided to share this child's play with us.

Scene Two: In the dark

The scene of disappearance and return is how Freud introduces – via the compulsion to repeat and the drive for mastery – the notion of the death drive. This is not merely or no longer about satisfying the pleasure principle but is instead a symptom of the instinct of all living matter to return to 'an earlier state of things' (37). In Derrida's meticulous and revelatory reading of *Beyond*, he notes how the game of *fort/da* not only describes the manifest effects of the death drive but also mimes or mirrors what he calls the 'athesis' of Freud's text.[51] The word 'thesis', which comes from the Greek τιθέναι, 'to put, place', has not only the common sense of 'a proposition laid down or stated' but also originally referred to 'the setting down of the foot or lowering of the hand in beating time' (*OED*). Freud's text is without thesis in both these senses. Derrida suggests that it has a 'nonpositional structure', a lack of a definitive position or statement with regards to the death drive, and that it is an ambulatory text that never actually sets down a foot or takes a step: the text, says Derrida, 'mimes walking, does not cease walking, regularly sketching out one more step without gaining an inch of ground'.[52] It is a text in motion that never gets anywhere, proceeding as it does 'down the singular path of speculation' – a path which is both created and destroyed at once, in the 'pathbreaking of athetic writing'.[53] We should be alert here to the double meaning of 'pathbreaking', where the 'breaking' is both constructive and deconstructive: the path is broken, the trail is blazed, the way is shown for the very first time. But, in the same instance, the path is broken, the trail is blazed and you cover your tracks, as if to hide that you went this way at all. The detour (or *Umweg*) of athetic writing, that ends where it begins, that makes or breaks no ground – for 'despite several marching orders and steps forward, not an inch of ground is gained' – is, as Derrida describes, also the detour and return of instinctual life (294). The content of Freud's narrative directs its form, consciously or unconsciously. He writes,

> It would be in contradiction to the conservative nature of the instincts if the goal of life were a state of things which had never yet been attained. On the contrary, it must be an old state of things, an initial state [*Ausgangszustand*] from which the living entity has at one time or other departed and to which it is striving to return by the circuitous paths along which its development leads. If we are to take it as a truth that knows no exception that everything living dies for internal reasons – becomes inorganic once again – then we shall be compelled to say that '*the aim of life is death*' and, looking backwards, that '*inanimate things existed before living ones*'. (38/40)

After developing along 'circuitous paths', you are destined to end up returning to where you started. The German *Ausgang* (literally a 'going-out'), which can be a starting point, a beginning, a way out, can also be the opposite: an outcome, a conclusion, an ending. *Fort* and *da*: departure and return signalled by one word. The path from *Ausgang* to *Ausgang*, from going-out to outcome, from exordium to denouement, is not just circuitous but circular, and ends where it begins. We cannot then distinguish between the drive towards or away from death – and this is perhaps why, as I will go on to discuss, Freud finds it so difficult to definitively separate the life and death instincts and their supposedly opposed creative and destructive tendencies. What is here translated as 'looking backwards' is the word '*zurückgreifend*', which is not, unlike the English translation, a metaphor of sight. The verb '*greifen*' is to grip, grasp or seize: Freud is not *looking* backwards but is grasping in the dark for something that he cannot see, as he later reiterates: 'in no region of psychology were we groping more in the dark' (51).

Perhaps what lurks there is beyond comprehension: impossible, finally, to grasp. One can only speculate about what moves in the darkness:

> The attributes of life were at some time evoked [*erweckt*, awoken] in inanimate matter by the action of a force of whose nature we can form no conception. It may perhaps have been a process similar in type to that which later caused the development [*entstehen ließ*, which let the emergence happen] of consciousness in a particular stratum of living matter. The tension which then arose in what had hitherto been an inanimate substance endeavoured to cancel itself out. In this way the first instinct came into being: the instinct to return to the inanimate state. (38/40)

The inconceivable forces that rouse first life and then consciousness are more passive in the German than in the English. Where Strachey's translation describes a force 'evoking' life in lifeless matter, and 'caus[ing]' consciousness in living matter, in the German it is not the prime mover: the force instead awakens and lets emerge something already there but dormant, lying in wait. There is not *only* an inconceivable force but also something before or beyond it. Something like a radical animism, perhaps. David Wills notes how the analogy that Freud sets up here is based on 'a principle of contradictability' that 'relates two processes, one of which is the reverse of the other'. This, he goes on to suggest, 'amounts to a catastrophic redefinition ... of the animate-inanimate opposition. The death drive will oblige him to abandon, correlatively, the anteriority of either life or death, the causal consecution between life and death, and the binary opposition of life and death.'[54]

Intermission: More to life than death

Freud's description rests upon a series of oppositions – lifeless/life; inanimate/animate; sleep/waking; unconscious/conscious; non-being/being – where the latter term of each pair is the detour, the increase in tension, and the former is the return or release. These oppositions rely on a clear distinction between terms: no life-in-death and no death-in-life, but two strictly separable states. Yet, as Wills's book elucidates (and as Freud perhaps obliquely recognized), there is an undeniable contamination between terms – it is the supposedly 'lifeless' that gives rise to life:

> What we call life begins as a rupture vis-à-vis itself, an interruption of inanimate by an animate that has somehow lain inert, or inanimate, within the inanimate. We cannot, from that point of view, conceive of the animate without the inanimate. Even in scientific terms, defining where animate begins – say, with the chemistry of nucleic acids – means negating, or repressing, the inanimate but still chemically active, and in a sense 'animated,' prehistory of life.[55]

The terms 'life' and 'death' are not only conceptually mutually constitutive but also infect or inhabit each other in a more radical sense. The 'tension' of Freud's oppositions could be rethought in terms of an interplay of forces that does not so readily conform to a dualistic schema, leaving us with a death drive that is, then, not so much 'beyond' the pleasure principle but that fundamentally transforms it from within. Samuel Weber remarks that he prefers 'to translate *Jenseits* as "other side" in order to emphasize that this side is not fully separate from or in contradiction with Freud's notion of the "pleasure principle," but rather can be seen as its radicalization'.[56] Indeed, as Freud goes on to concede, if 'we are not to abandon the hypothesis of death instincts, we must suppose them to be associated from the very first with life instincts. But it must be admitted that in that case we shall be working upon an equation with two unknown quantities' (57). Such an equation cannot, by definition, be solved, and yet Freud was prepared to speculate.

If, as Freud postulates, '*the aim of life is death*', why does it always go via such 'circuitous paths' (38)? This is when mastery comes on stage, in order to ensure that equilibrium is achieved *internally*: each organism 'wishes to die only in its own fashion' (39). As Caroline Rooney points out, this means 'the death drive is paradoxically characterized by its conservative, life-conserving nature. The paradox is that this makes it rather close to, even identical with, what is posited as the self-preserving life instincts.'[57] She goes on to note that Sándor Ferenzci, while retaining Freud's notion of a primary self-destructive instinct, develops it into something that 'cannot be isolated from an interconnection with other forces in the world and also from a self-creation', where the 'self-destructiveness' (i.e. the death drive) can only be thought of in terms of a response to 'a destructiveness or, better, a *forcefulness* beyond [the] self'.[58] In this conception, creativity and life-death instincts primarily owe their existence to otherness – as that which is beyond the self but that also brings it into being. The beyond (of life, death, the pleasure principle) constitutes what is not beyond, just as a borderline is determined not merely by what it encloses but also by what it excludes. Rooney writes,

> In Ferenzci's summary, a partial destruction that comes from an external environment leads to self-constructing recovery: generation as originally regeneration; origination as creative construction. ... The so-called death drive (repeating, compelled originally to re-create) would rather be either a creative partial self-sacrifice for the sake of life or a being mastered by or capitulating to a force or forces stronger than those of the self-preserving organism.[59]

This is, as Rooney's book argues, an animistic conception of life, where the dichotomies between subject and object, self and world, are reinscribed as reciprocally constituting relations. Whereas in Freud's conception the drives remain 'within' the organism, in Rooney's conception via Ferenzci, there is an expropriation of forces that serves to reinscribe creativity as an interaction between entity and world – calling into question the rigorous internal/external opposition of Freud's schema.

In 'Animism, Magic and the Omnipotence of Thoughts', Freud twice mentions what he calls 'animatism' or 'pre-animism': 'the doctrine of the universality of life'.[60] As Derrida comments, what Freud calls 'animatism' is 'not a mere belief in the spirits of the dead. It is something like a theory of living, of being-alive, of livingness, of universal being-for-life' that 'has no other side: there is no side for nonlife':

> What does [Freud] say about the experience of this *Belebtheit*, which is not life in inanimate things but the always living experience of all that enters the field of this life? What does he say about the experience, which can only encounter the life that it is, that it lives, its life, even when it has to do with the nonliving, when an eschatology is announced ... for which the death drive itself would be *for life*? ... What does he, Freud, say about this animatistic pre-animism? Well, nothing.[61]

Is a death drive that is *for life* still a death drive? Or, to put it another way, if experience is characterized by a 'universal being-for-life', does it make sense to think of the 'death drive' *as* a drive towards death? Or is it perhaps, as Peter Brooks suggests in 'Freud's Masterplot', more of a drive for *meaning* through closure? Reading *Beyond* 'as a text concerning textuality', he writes that the 'possibility of meaning plotted through time depends on the anticipated structuring force of the ending: the interminable would be the meaningless'.[62] Freud's theory is, he continues, a theory of 'the dynamic of the life-span, its necessary duration and its necessary end, hence, implicitly, a theory of the very narratability of life'.[63] This would resituate the eschatological aspect of the death drive within a drive towards *life* as meaningful.

Act Two: Translating those 'O's

Ernst is too young to pronounce the word *fort* (gone) and therefore merely gives 'vent to a loud, long-drawn-out "o-o-o-o"' – the interpretation of which was confirmed by the use of the opposing term *da* (there) (and again we have a scene of mutual constitution, where the gone-ness of the gone relies upon the there-ness of the there). Yet there is already more than one interpretation (*Deutung*) at work here (unsurprisingly, perhaps, considering that Freud has called the sound *bedeutungsvolle*: 'meaningful' or 'significant'). Freud not only translates the child's non-verbal locution into the form and meaning of the word *fort*, but he also translates it into a specific form on the page: 'o-o-o-o' (or, as it appears in the German text, with em-dashes rather than hyphens: 'o—o—o—o'), which is repeated each time that the child's inarticulate articulation is mentioned. Why four 'O's? Did Ernst give a four-part moan every time he played his game? No: we are told it is a 'long-drawn-out' sound, one long 'oooo', rather than the divided representation that we find on the page. Perhaps, then, each 'O' stands in for the letters of the word Ernst cannot say, like circular apostrophes, or blank spaces left for Freud's readers to fill with meaning. Or perhaps the 'O's could be read as a diagrammatic rendering of the primitive 'vesicles' that appear some pages later – the circular outline representing the surface or 'crust' that the organism forms in response to the 'stimuli' of the external world (26), represented by the dashes: 'o—o—o—o'. Or perhaps Freud just wanted to draw the little spool-train, that it 'never occurred' to Ernst to 'pull … along the floor behind him, for instance, and play at its being a carriage' (15).[64]

Enter Ernst, dressed as the Prince of Denmark

– *Or* (and now I am speculating), perhaps in his inscription of a series of four 'O's, Freud is consciously or unconsciously alluding to a moment in one of his favourite plays. The moment I refer to is Act 5 Scene 2 of *Hamlet*, when the eponymous prince speaks his last words. These are, famously, 'The rest is silence' – but in the Folio edition, the elegant poignancy of this line is followed by four groans: 'O, o, o, o'. Whether these were Shakespeare's 'O's or an actor's interpolation that found their way into the Folio has been contested, and most editors and actors now choose to leave them out or to translate them into a stage direction: '*He gives a long sigh and dies*'.[65] Just as Freud translated Ernst's 'long drawn-out' sound into a series of four 'O's, Hamlet's four 'O's get translated into 'a long sigh'. The choice in the stage direction of 'sigh' over, for example, 'groan' or 'moan', serves to rob the utterance of voice, and its appearance and disappearance, expression or repression in different versions of the play bespeaks a faltering uncertainty at what does not submit to verbal language.

Let us remind ourselves of why *Hamlet* was so important to Freud, of why he so often evoked the play in his psychoanalytic works. As I noted in my first chapter, Hamlet's remark that 'There are more things in heaven and earth ... / Than are dreamt of in our philosophy' was particularly resonant for Freud.[66] Freud perhaps saw the speculative work of psychoanalysis as an approach towards these 'more things', leaving empirical science to its limited dreams. More significant for the current reading, however, is the fact that the character Hamlet is for Freud an incarnation of the Oedipus complex. In *The Interpretation of Dreams*, he comments on Sophocles' *Oedipus Rex*, suggesting that when the 'poet' 'unravels the past', in 'bring[ing] to light the guilt of Oedipus, he is at the same time compelling us to recognize our own inner minds, in which those same impulses, though suppressed, are still to be found'.[67] Despite the fact that the Oedipus complex takes its name from Sophocles' character, Oedipus is, in Freud's view, just one example of a fundamental human desire that predates any dramatic rendering. Oedipus had an Oedipus complex – but he was not the first. (As Freud admits in a letter, 'I have found, in my own case too, [the phenomenon of] being in love with my mother and jealous of my father, and I now consider it a universal event in early childhood'.[68]) Freud recognizes that there is no progressive development of the psyche: the impulses of 'our own inner minds' have not changed from 'the past' that is being unravelled. What has changed, however, are the social conditions that that mind operates within, and so, as Freud goes on, it is Hamlet who better represents modern Oedipal desires:

> Another of the great creations of tragic poetry, Shakespeare's *Hamlet*, has its roots in the same soil as *Oedipus Rex*. But the changed treatment of the same material reveals the whole difference in the mental life of these two widely separated epochs of civilization: the secular advance of repression in the emotional life of mankind. In the *Oedipus* the child's wishful phantasy that underlies it is brought into the open and realized as it would be in a dream. In *Hamlet* it remains repressed; and – just as in the case of a neurosis – we only learn of its existence from its inhibiting consequences.[69]

Those 'inhibiting consequences', Freud continues, play out in Hamlet's inability to kill Claudius and thereby 'take vengeance on the man who did away with his father and took that father's place with his mother, the man who shows him the repressed wishes of his own childhood realized'.[70] *Hamlet* is, for Freud, primarily a drama of delay and deferral, caused by unconscious inhibitions.[71] This is not overtly expressed in the play, Freud says, but he has 'translated into conscious terms what was bound to remain unconscious in Hamlet's mind' (note that again we find psychoanalysis described as translation).[72] Perhaps aware of the problematic ascription of an unconscious mind to a fictional character, he goes on to tell us that 'it can of course only be the poet's own mind which confronts us in Hamlet', and so, Freud says, it is in fact Shakespeare who is autobiographically voicing – through Hamlet – his childhood feelings about his own father, which would have been, he asserts, 'freshly revived' by the latter's recent death.[73]

If the play (*Schauspiel*) *Hamlet* is an expression or realization of Shakespeare's repressed Oedipus complex, then the play or game (*Spiel*) of *fort/da* is Freud's restaging of the whole meta-drama – with little Ernst cast in the leading role. Although Ernst's father is not dead (he has just gone away to war), the child nevertheless 'made it quite clear that he had no desire to be disturbed in his sole possession of his mother' (16). Ernst's childhood naivety means that he has not yet learnt the necessary repression of these desires, and so, just as in Freud's reading of *Oedipus Rex*, 'the child's wishful phantasy ... is brought into the open and realized as it would be in a dream': *fort* and *da*. Yet, like Hamlet, who, when faced with the pain of being 'separated' from his mother by Claudius, is drawn to suicide, Ernst too has a fascination with 'making himself disappear': he begins to play the game *with*, and not just *by*, himself – 'Baby o-o-o-o!' – in an attempt to achieve mastery over the situation (15 n.1). Hamlet is Shakespeare is Oedipus is Ernst is Freud – and all are incarnations or translations of the fundamental unconscious desires that shape Freud's understanding of the human psyche.

That given, if we return to Hamlet's 'O's, which Freud was later to (consciously or unconsciously) put in the mouth of his grandson Ernst, what might their dis/appearance signify? (And perhaps it goes without saying that, in the ABC of psychoanalysis, 'O' is for Oedipus ...) Hamlet says, 'The rest is silence,' and then dies – either silently, or, as I noted above, rather noisily, with a long-drawn-out groan, a series of 'O's: 'O, o, o, o'. The rest is not silent then: there is a non-verbal excess infringing upon the terse eloquence of Hamlet's final lines, which some editors have found 'preposterous' and therefore left out.[74] But what if we were to read these non-verbal ejaculations as the untranslatable 'voice' of a certain beyond? The 'rest' of which Hamlet speaks is both the 'rest' of what remains or is still to come (only silence) and also the 'rest' or repose of sleep or of death. Yet when the 'O's appear after this declaration, they serve to undo it: the rest is *not* silence – though it may be beyond language, beyond the grasp of reasonable comprehension. These 'O's after the end, after what could or should have been the end, might well have appealed to Freud. Because, in *Beyond* as in *Hamlet*, the 'rest' is *not* silence – there is something at work beyond or before life. These 'O's might figure the threshold of life-death, neither *fort* nor *da*, untranslatable missives from that 'undiscovered country from whose bourn / No traveller returns'.[75]

Shuffling off the mortal coil

Reading *Hamlet* and *Beyond* side by side engenders many parallels. Ernest Jones expounded Freud's Oedipal reading of Hamlet into a full essay, in which he shows how the prince's 'internal conflict ... is inaccessible to his introspection' – though Jones's text strangely fails to make any comment on the notion of the death drive.[76] The omission is odd because, as Rooney notes, the prince 'illustrates very well what Freud says of the death drive: he does not have enough will to live and he does not have the will to kill himself, and thus ... he is caught within what can only be a paralysis'.[77] Hamlet's urge 'to take arms against a sea of troubles / And by opposing end them' (3.1.58–9) could be read as the 'tension' of living matter endeavouring 'to cancel itself out' (*BPP*, 38); the 'thousand natural shocks / That flesh is heir to' (3.1.61–2) would be the 'the ceaseless impact of external stimuli on the surface of the vesicle' (*BPP*, 26); and just as 'to die: to sleep' is 'a consummation / Devoutly to be wished' (3.1.59–66), 'an *old* state of things, an initial state' is what the 'living entity' is 'striving' to return to (*BPP*, 38). Meanwhile, Hamlet's famous phrase 'mortal coil' plays out in miniature the whole drama of *Beyond* (3.1.66). The noun 'coil' has decidedly negative connotations, referring to a 'noisy disturbance', a 'row', 'tumult, turmoil, bustle, stir, hurry, confusion': it is noise and movement to be endured, not to seek out – 'unpleasurable tension' in the language of *Beyond* (7), or the 'clamour of life' that is opposed to the muteness of the death instincts in 'The Ego and the Id'.[78] The rowdiness of the 'mortal coil' is counterposed by the silence and stillness of death, the release of the tension towards which the organism strives: 'The rest is silence'.

'For in that sleep of death what dreams may come / When we have shuffled off this mortal coil / Must give us pause' (3.1.65–7). Modern audiences hear the verb 'shuffled' in this line as referring to the subject of the sentence, and so the image evoked is of a dying man, 'shuffling off', dragging heavy feet, dying after his own fashion – even if it is not a very dignified one (not unlike, perhaps, a certain Freud who 'limps' off stage at the very end of *Beyond*: taking 'comfort' 'in the words of the poet': 'What we cannot reach flying we must reach limping'

(64)). Yet if we look at Shakespeare's other uses of the verb 'shuffle', it refers to the object, not the subject of the sentence, as in *Twelfth Night* when 'good turns, / Are shuffled off with such uncurrent pay' and in *The Merry Wives of Windsor* when Doctor Caius 'shall likewise shuffle her away'.[79] Indeed, the *OED* defines the phrase 'to shuffle off' as 'to get rid of or evade (something difficult, arduous, or irksome)', 'to dispose of evasively; to shirk (a duty or obligation)'. To 'shuffle off this mortal coil', then, is to shake off the irksome disturbance that surrounds living being – and I cannot now help but hear the other sense of 'coil', the circular looping of a rope, in rings or coils (round and round, *fort* and *da*), binding itself around being, tighter and tighter, increasing the tension, like a 'little fragment of living substance … suspended in the middle of an external world charged with the most powerful energies' (*BPP*, 27).[80] But the tightening coil is met with the hardening of the 'outermost surface' of the living matter into a 'protective shield' (27), which extends its life so that it can 'die only in its own fashion' (39) – or, if you will allow me to shuffle the phrase, to coil the course of its own mortality (another old sense of 'coil' is as an earlier form of 'cull', meaning to 'select' or 'choose') – only shuffling off the coil in its own time, a vesicular Houdini.

'For example, in tragedy'

I have been getting too caught up in all this Freud-Hamlet-Ernst-Oedipus drama. 'It may be asked whether and how far I am myself convinced of the truth of the hypotheses that have been set out in these pages. My answer would be that I am not convinced myself … Or, more precisely, that I do not know how far I believe in them' (*BPP*, 59). Nevertheless, as psychoanalyst André Green recognizes in *The Tragic Effect: The Oedipus Complex in Tragedy*, 'theatre is the best embodiment of that "other scene", the unconscious'.[81] And I *am* sure that Freud had the theatre in mind (you remember how Ernst 'staged' the first and second 'act' of his game, 'set the scene' and played an active 'part'), even if he was only playing with it as an example – 'the artistic play [*Spielen*] and artistic imitation carried out by adults, which … do not spare the spectators (for instance, in tragedy [*zum Beispiel in der Tragödie*]) the most painful experiences and can yet be felt by them as highly enjoyable' (17/15). Freud asserts, however, that such examples have nothing to do with the case in hand: 'They are of no use for *our* purposes, since they presuppose the existence and dominance of the pleasure principle; they give no evidence of the operation of tendencies beyond the pleasure principle, that is, of tendencies more primitive than it and independent of it' (17). And yet, for all Freud's insistence that this example is 'of no use for *our* purposes', is it not precisely the *Beispiel* of tragedy that gives evidence of the operation of tendencies beyond the pleasure principle, of tendencies more primitive than it and independent of it? Or at least gives them a name and a (dramatic) force? 'These reproductions, which emerge with such unwished-for exactitude, always have as their subject some portion of infantile sexual life – of the Oedipus complex, that is, and its derivatives' (18). The compulsion to repeat *always*, Freud says, can be traced back to Oedipus – or to the desires that are made to bear that name. Those 'O's in the mouths of Ernst and Hamlet seem so in/expressive. 'It may be, however, that I have overestimated their significance. ... One may have made a lucky hit or one may have gone shamefully astray' (*BPP*, 59). 'Well – I cannot deny that some of the analogies, correlations and connections ... seemed to me to deserve consideration' (*BPP*, 60).[82]

Because the death drive is so elusive and enigmatic, Freud can only lead by example: 'We must endeavour to draw a lesson from examples [*Beispielen*] such as this and use them as a basis for our metapsychological speculations' (30/30). And so the speculative meanderings are led by the examples of little Ernst's *fort/da* game (*Spiel*); of 'examples [*Beispiele*] from animal life' where 'the most impressive proofs of there being an organic compulsion to repeat lie in the phenomena of heredity and the facts of embryology' (37/38); and of a sadistic sexual impulse as a 'displaced' 'example [*Beispiel*] of the death instinct': where the drive to self-destruction is turned outwards (54/58). On the next page, Freud adds another loop to the coil, and the self-destructive instinct which has been thrown outwards to the object (sadism) turns back again to the self, which would 'in that case be a return to an earlier phase of the instinct's history, a regression', and so he concedes that 'there *might* be such a thing as primary masochism' (55).

Is it possible to get any closer to the death drive than these examples? I have been playing with the fact that the German word *Beispiel* contains the word *Spiel* ('play' or 'game') and thus ties together Freud's whole playful theatrics: the game and the plays which are 'merely' exemplary but also set the stage for the entire speculative discourse. However, the *spiel* in *Beispiel* is in fact a homograph. The *Bei-spiel* is not *bei*/by (in the sense of 'near' or 'about') the *game*, but by the *spell*. The *spiel* in *Beispiel* has the same root as the English word 'spell' – the Gothic *spill*, meaning 'recital, tale, narrative, legend, fable'.[83] (Indeed, according to the *OED*, the word 'byspel' for 'parable' or 'proverb' has recorded usage in English from the tenth to the thirteenth centuries and makes its way into the nineteenth century as a word for 'bastard' – and I leave it to you to make the connections between illegitimate descendance and speculative discourse.) The 'example' in German is by definition the literary example, the by-spell, that which is by-the-tale. In the path-breaking of athetic writing, every way must go by way of the by-way, never by the direct route, but via the detours, *Umwege* or 'circuitous paths' of the *Beispiel* – the athesis cannot be articulated beyond its variously displaced examples.

Casting spells

In English, the noun 'spell' has lost its more general sense of something spoken or recited and now denotes words possessed of magical or occult powers, charms or incantations that are able to alter or transform the world. (Though, of course, as Freud recognizes in the passage from 'Psychical (or Mental) Treatment' that I quoted previously, all words possess a certain 'magical power'.)[84] The transition from the former to the latter sense was a nocturnal metamorphosis: the original 'spell' as something spoken turned into a 'night-spell', intended as protection against – or to cause – harm at night, and then – *ta-da!* – the prefix vanished and left the word 'spell' changed forever (*OED*). A 'spell' in the modern, magical sense is an exemplary performative utterance, a locution designed and believed to *make something happen* – for example, when little Ernst casts away his spool and says 'o-o-o-o': I hereby pronounce you *gone*. Indeed, the *Spiel* of the spool is a game of spells: both the magic spell of making things disappear and reappear with a *fort*/'o-o-o-o' and a *da* – not forgetting the *coup de théâtre*, 'the child had found a method of making *himself* disappear' (15 n.1) – as well as being, not by chance, the by-spell or *Beispiel* of the whole fabulous discourse of Freud's text.

The whole movement of *Beyond*, then, could be read as a spell or a night-spell: a *ta-da* or *fort/da* that produces the athesis of the death drive, only to make it vanish once more, but also as a preventative measure, designed to ward off nocturnal dangers, spirits that move in obscurity and darkness – to ward off, perhaps, the 'mystical impression' produced by the theory of the death instincts: its fabulous and mythical elements (54). Rooney suggests that Freud's published work is concerned with preserving 'its decisive separation from anything too occult, shamanistic, magical', in what she calls a 'troubled and obsessive attempt to ward off precisely animism'.[85] This warding off of agencies beyond or before human control is, paradoxically, also an acknowledgement of their existence.

Sarah Kofman, in *Freud and Fiction*, describes how Freud's 'interpretations' of literary texts involve not just 'readings' of the original works but are rather 'rewritings which weave the thread of the elements in the original text into a completely new tissue, involving them by displacement in a completely different play'.⁸⁶ Kofman focuses on Freud's use of the poetry of Empedocles, Friedrich Hebbel's play *Judith*, Wilhelm Jensen's novel *Gradiva* and E. T. A. Hoffmann's story *The Sandman* – that is to say, works of which he offers overt interpretations. In each of his readings/rewritings, Kofman notes how Freud finds a place for the character of Oedipus and the primal drives he represents, not only providing a psychoanalytic interpretation of the texts, but also confirming his own theory that the Oedipus complex represents 'a universal law of human life'.⁸⁷ Kofman asks whether in Freud's 'desire to see literary fiction corroborate analytic truth' we can also 'recognize the workings of a fantasy of mastery and reappropriation of predecessors? A family romance in which ancestral prerogatives are recognized only in order to usurp them more successfully?'⁸⁸ Commenting on Freud's reading of Empedocles' poems, in which he finds a precursor to his theory of the death instincts, she writes,

> For whilst it is indeed the case that psychic reality is the true content of the myth, it could also be said that the Empedoclean myth serves as a substitute, a possibly provisional substitute, for a completely rational basis to Freud's final theory of the instincts. This can be imagined as a circle: the theory of instincts establishes the truth of the Empedoclean myth, which in turn acts as proof of the validity of the former. There is a reciprocal relationship between myth and theory in which each is the verification of the other: a circularity in which each retains its hypothetical character.⁸⁹

Freud sets up a similar reciprocally validating relation between his work and *Hamlet*. He proclaims in 'Psychopathic Characters on the Stage' that he is the first to have understood the repressed Oedipal desires that cause Hamlet to act in the way he does: 'After all, the conflict in *Hamlet* is so effectively concealed that it was left to me to unearth it.'⁹⁰ However, this unearthing of the secrets of *Hamlet* does not only provide an apparently definitive interpretation of the play but also, of course, corroborates Freud's own theories. *Fort* and *da*, 'the greater pleasure was attached to the second act', a reappropriation through which *Hamlet* both is elucidated by and confirms psychoanalytic theory, even if sometimes the restaging, as in *Beyond*, is done in silence (like, perhaps, a certain dumb show: the play-within-a-play, which, Hamlet says, 'is the image of a murder done in Vienna' (3.2.232)). Avital Ronell notes that 'the proper name "Psychoanalysis"' was patented by Freud, 'as if by chance, the year of his father's death' – an act which effectively inscribes the entire oeuvre signified by that proper name within Freud's own Oedipal drama: a patricide done in Vienna, albeit symbolically.⁹¹ As Derrida says, there is 'an immense autobiographical scene invested in this apparently theoretical writing, and it is doing *fort/da*'.⁹² To say whether Shakespeare ghostwrites Freud, or the other way around, would be a matter of 'groping ... in the dark' (*BPP*, 51) – for what it is that appears-disappears in these texts, like a certain ghost, '"Tis gone and will not answer' (1.1.51). But, given that both are haunted by the uncanny compulsions of desire, repetition and a drive towards death, would it be so far-fetched to speculate, as I have done, upon another more strange return for Hamlet in Freud's play-within-a-play, the *Spiel* or *Beispiel* within the *fort* and *da* play of a text that conceives of life itself on the basis of a drive towards its own more strange return? Would it be so far-fetched to speculate that the relations or resonances (the 'O's and echoes) that appear in these two texts are not merely fortuitous, not merely coincidental?

The hatch and disclose

It is not possible to ascertain whether the traces of *Hamlet* I have found in *Beyond* were consciously or unconsciously laid there by Freud – nor would it change what I am trying to say about language. For even if Freud had never read Shakespeare's work, the play of written traces cannot be reduced to what we might think of as conscious authorship. As Derrida writes, the 'iterability that forms the structure of every mark is doubtless what allows it to withdraw from a context, to free itself from any determined bond to its origin, its meaning, or its referent, to emigrate in order to play elsewhere, in whole or in part, another role'.⁹³ The mark frees itself of its own accord.

To speak of a 'textual unconscious' is not only to recognize that the unconscious and language *can* be thought of in terms of each other but rather that they cannot be thought of *except* in terms of each other. There is no unconscious that can be recognized or thought except in terms of language, and there is no language or text that is not subject to the play of unconscious effects. There are at least three ways that these interrelations come into play: First, the relations between the conscious and unconscious minds, rational thought and instinctual behaviours, waking life and the dream world are all analogous to the relation between the ways in which a person writes or speaks a language, 'using' it to communicate, and the way in which language writes or speaks them, creating, shaping and determining their thoughts and expressions – what Nicholas Royle describes as 'the strangeness of words operating by themselves within us'.⁹⁴ Second, the conscious/unconscious opposition, with its schema of visible and invisible, form and force, is analogous to the distinction between the text as written and what lies beneath or beyond it – but that does not 'exist' apart from it – its 'meaning/s' or that which is un/translatable. Third, there is an animism of language and letters, an automotricity at work not just at the level of sentences and words but also animating the letters and punctuation, the marks or traces on the page, so that the materiality of the text stirs in unforeseeable ways, doing things outside of the author's conscious control. As Sarah Wood asks, 'What ... freedom of the subject' can compare with the wild insistence of a fragment of writing?'[95] The fact that all of this is at work to more or less of an extent in every text – and text is, as I have been saying, not reducible to human language – accounts for the generative interminability of reading, and for the vital, irrepressible fertility of texts.

In *The Theory of Inspiration*, Timothy Clark elaborates how the composition of written texts can be understood to pose 'a crisis in subjectivity'[96] (and it is no coincidence, as we will see, that psychoanalysis can be conceived in precisely these terms):

> The subject of enunciation is a multiply contaminated one: the source of the work is neither a commanding conscious intentionality, nor the impulses and drives of the somatic or the unconscious, nor the structures and constraints of the discourse at issue, but the temporary and incalculable co-workings of all these factors in a non-linear space that, at its most extreme, may be experienced by the writer as a reversal of cause and effect.[97]

The 'subject of enunciation' – that is, the writer – is not a stable and self-defined entity but is rather 'contaminated' by the various factors that Clark identifies as infecting the scene of writing. First, there is the 'commanding conscious intentionality', the person or self who thinks that they are doing the writing (the 'I' that I think I know I am). Second, there are 'the impulses and drives of the somatic or the unconscious', which operate, by definition, below or beyond the level of consciousness, invisibly and ineluctably affecting what I think and do. Third, there are the 'structures and constraints of the discourse at issue', that is to say, the linguistic, grammatical and generic conventions that work to determine what I am saying and how I say it. And these three factors – the self, the unconscious and the discourse – co-implicate, in a 'temporary' and 'incalculable' fashion, to produce a written text: the interrelation of these factors happens each time differently and in a way that, even or especially after the event, cannot be ascertained. Finally, Clark notes that this process, 'at its most extreme, may be experienced by the writer as a reversal of cause and effect'. It can feel to the writer that the text has come from elsewhere, perhaps fully formed, and that the traditional or expected relations of cause and effect – the writer as cause and the text as effect – appear to have been reversed, so that the writer becomes an *effect* of the text, the writer only becomes the writer *in relation to* the text. Given the interrelation and intractability of all these factors, a question such as 'Which came first, the writer or the text?' eludes any simple logical answer and produces the 'crisis of subjectivity' that Clark's book elaborates. The writer and text are incessantly *altered*, made other, by the movement of their co-implication: 'Inspiration may bear a peculiar transitivity, one that confounds distinctions between self and other.'[98] There can, of course, be no theory of in-*spir*-ation that is not also a theory of animism, and so it is not surprising to find such correlations between the two.

With all that in mind, let us turn to 'The Egg and the Chicken', a short text by Clarice Lispector, which, as its title suggests, concerns itself with the strange disruption of cause and effect that the experiences of reading and writing can bring about. The scene is a kitchen, the domestic space of the home, which is of course Freud's chosen metaphor for the mind – the house in which the ego is not master. There is an egg in the kitchen, which the narrator of the text simultaneously sees and does not see. Defying narrativization and genre, the text's ten pages are concerned with creation and reproduction, agency and instrumentality, causality (which came first? the chicken or the egg?), identity, mothering, reading and writing. 'The Egg and the Chicken' is full of visible surfaces and hidden depths, lucidity and obscurity, and stages another scene of disappearance and return, a game of *fort/da* played with or by the egg and the text – and, as I will show, these two objects seem to be translations of one another. We also find ourselves faced with the dis/appearance of yet another series of 'O's. The first line in the Portuguese ends with the words '*vejo o ovo*': 'I see the egg', and, lost or obfuscated by the English translation, the Portuguese text is scattered with 'O's, lovely letter-eggs nestling in every sentence.[99] There are not only 'O's in the egg (*o ovo*) and in the 'the' (*o*), but everywhere you look (*olhar*), in every apostrophe (*você*, you), in 'the beginning' (*o começo*), in what is seen (*visto*) and lost (*perdido*), and there are 'O's all through the line: 'Like the world, the egg is obvious' (*Como o mundo o ovo é óbvio*) – and all these instances are from the first two pages (276–7/49). There are many more. The reader's attention is drawn to the material form of the text, to how it looks on the page: its 'shell and shape' (282). Cixous writes in *Reading with Clarice Lispector* that 'something is happening in Portuguese between the egg and the look. It is of the order of the 'O's'. Do you see the egg? Or do you see the 'O's? Cixous continues,

Clarice says that she looks at the egg in a single glance, and at the same time she does not see it. It is this necessary correction that is being made from one sentence to another and which gives us a bizarre feeling. The egg is permanently in eclipse. When it is being announced that one sees it, it is also being announced that one does not. ... It is the *fort-da* of the subject of the egg. The egg is presented and withdrawn, like all the subjects of the text.[100]

As you read, the body of the text – its form on the page, the little black marks (so many 'O's) – metamorphoses into the solidity of an egg lying on a table in front of you: 'In the morning in the kitchen on the table I see the egg' (276). As Clark remarks, the 'poetic' (and this applies to the literary in general) brings 'what it relates into being by force of its own event'.[101] The text turns into an egg. You see the egg. But then, before you know it, the egg has transformed itself into a metaphor for the very text which you are reading (its fragile yet obscure surface or shell; its perfect structure; its capacity to give birth to its own mother): 'Immediately' – and we should read this in the literal sense, *without mediation* – 'I perceive that one cannot be seeing an egg' (276).

Objectively, all that is there are the little black marks on the page. The transformations happen within you, the reader, where, as you take the text in, your eyes deceive you and you think you see an egg, or, further, a metaphor; the little black marks, not so different from *these* ones, are hidden in plain sight: 'an egg seen is an egg lost' (276). The text anticipates this too, when the narrator admits that 'the metamorphosis is happening inside me: I start not to be able to discern the egg any more' (281). The *fort/da* is played out interminably and on multiple levels. For just as the egg of the story appears and disappears – like Ernst's spool, or the athesis of *Beyond*, or Freud's autobiography, or the unconscious 'itself' ('The egg has no itself' (276)) – the narrator who initially appears as a woman who sees the egg seems to disappear into the symbolic and nonsensical play of the text, and each 'meaning' or interpretation at which we might arrive is also subject to destabilization and undoing. 'The egg is a suspended thing. It has never landed. When it lands, it is not what has landed. It was a thing under the egg' (277). The strange multiplication of tenses here (the proleptic retrospect of 'has never landed', the general present of 'when it lands', the present-past of '*is* not what *has* landed') recalls Derrida's recognition, quoted previously, of the 'passageway of deferred reciprocity between reading and writing'.[102] Text is a 'suspended thing' that has not, will never, will have never, landed, but that is always *landing*, each time anew.

'Clarice's attention,' writes Cixous, 'can pick up the murmur of every hatching, the infinitesimal music of particles calling to one another to compose themselves in fragrance.'[103] As this forcefully synaesthetic description attests, 'seeing' in 'The Egg and the Chicken' is not the ordinary kind of seeing, but the strange seeing and not-seeing that reading renders, the kind of seeing that happens in what Hamlet calls the 'mind's eye' (1.2.184). And indeed, it will be worth keeping *Hamlet* in your own mind's eye, for just as the egg in Lispector's text can be read as invoking the unconscious and its effects, in *Hamlet* we find images of eggs figuring the workings of the psyche. Claudius, on witnessing his wife's 'too much changed son' (2.2.36), proclaims, 'There's something in his soul / O'er which his melancholy sits on brood / And I do doubt the hatch and the disclose / Will be some danger' (3.1.163–6), and later the Queen likens Hamlet's 'madness' to a 'female dove' whose 'golden couplets' – her eggs – will be 'disclosed' (5.1.275–6).[104] The word 'disclose' is an obsolete synonym for 'hatch', but the uses of it in *Hamlet* also invoke its other meanings: to reveal or discover. Claudius does not yet know that his nephew-son is aware of his crime, but he senses 'something' developing 'in his soul' that threatens to hatch out and reveal itself to consciousness. The word 'hatch' is also pregnant with meaning: Hatching is something that can be both done to, or done by, an egg, thus troubling senses of agency. (Will the 'something' in Hamlet's soul hatch itself, or be hatched? Claudius' syntax leaves both possibilities open.) The figurative use of the 'hatching' of ideas and plans implies, according to the *OED*, 'a covert or clandestine process', as, for example, when Freud says in a letter that he 'no longer understand[s] the state of mind in which [he] hatched [*ausgebrütet*] the psychology' (and we will be returning to this letter at the end of this chapter), or in another when he complains that his 'Vienna brood had banded together in indignation or fear and were hatching out all sorts of plans'.[105] We will be reading the egg in Lispector's text, then, via all these kinds of hatchings.

Which came first?

The woman is apparently the source or cause of the text, the one that sees the egg, that speaks the body of the text, that says 'I'. She is the chicken that lays the egg/text. Take the following lines: 'The chicken's unknown ailment is the egg. – She doesn't know how to explain herself: "I know that the error is inside me," she calls her life an error, "I don't know what I feel anymore," etc.' (280). These are not the locutions one might typically associate with a chicken. It is as if the play of metaphor is breaking the surface of the text, poking its head out: this is more than a chicken that we are dealing with. Later the association between the chicken and the woman is clearly drawn:

> Inside herself the chicken doesn't recognize the egg, but neither does she recognize it outside herself. When the chicken sees the egg she thinks she's dealing with something impossible. And with her heart beating, with her heart beating so, she doesn't recognize it.
> Suddenly I look at the egg in the kitchen and all I see in it is food. I don't recognize it, and my heart beats. (281)

On the one hand, the immediate juxtaposition of the non-recognitions and the heartbeats of chicken and woman strongly suggest an identity between 'the chicken' and the 'I'. On the other hand, however, the transformation from 'egg' to 'food' inscribes a blatant non-identity: the relation is of the order of a simultaneous *is* and *is not*. Indeed, she admits, 'I started talking about the chicken and for a while now I have no longer been talking about the chicken' (282). The chicken is just a 'disguise' (278). But even if the writer is the source of the text, as the chicken is the source of the egg, she at the same time comes out of the text, is constituted by the text, as a chicken comes out of an egg – and so the writer/chicken owes her existence to the text/egg, even as she is its origin. Any simple logic of causation is subject to incessant play. The text/egg separates itself from the writer/chicken, living on, sur-viving, living a life of its own – 'The chicken exists so that the egg can traverse the ages' (278); the chicken is a mere 'mode of transport for the egg' (280) – yet it also creates the writer as such. The structure of the text, then, is one of chiasmatic invagination, where the writer, narrator, text and egg inhabit each other in inextricable ways. A question is posed: 'Is it freedom or am I being controlled?' (285). Is this the writer (Lispector), the voice of the text (the 'narrator'), the text itself, or the egg (which, as we have seen, seems to 'symbolize' the text)? Do any exist independently, individually ('Individually it does not exist' (276)), or is each abyssally divided and constituted by its others?

'As for which came first, it was the egg that found the chicken' (280). Though the egg comes out of the chicken, it is other, it seems to arrive fully formed from elsewhere, finding or founding the chicken as the producer of the egg. 'The chicken looks at the horizon. As if it were from the line of the horizon that an egg is coming' (280). This anticipates Clark's description of the way that artistic 'inspiration' is characterized

> as a chiasmatic structure in which the scene of composition is already a prolepsis of reception, a scene in which the writer recognizes in his or her emergent

material such apparent force that it seems to be coming from another and to be part of a work which is somehow both already-read and also yet to emerge. The work thus announces itself as a certain compulsion-to-be.[106]

The text emerges as if it has its own agency, by which the writer is directed, and to which they must be receptive. This is forcefully articulated in the last lines of Lispector's text:

> In the face of my possessive adoration it could retreat and never again return. But if it is forgotten. ... Then – free, delicate, with no message for me – perhaps one last time it will move from space over to this window that I have always left open. And at dawn it will descend into our building. Serene all the way to the kitchen. Illuminating it with my pallor. (286)

The last two sentences here, though separated by full stops, are grammatically incomplete and therefore read as clauses of the preceding one. And yet, if this is the case, the final line switches the subject of the sentence from the egg to the woman: at dawn the egg will descend into the building, serene all the way to the kitchen – but then the next verb, 'illuminating', has the woman as its subject and the egg as its object: 'Illuminating it with my pallor.' The egg has freedom, alterity, moves of its own accord, descends unasked into the kitchen, yet in the last moment it is the woman who illuminates it – though the force behind this illumination, thanks to the play of the verbal subjects, seems to come from the egg. This final movement thereby collapses the distinction between the egg/text and the chicken/writer – where both, again, give birth to, or hatch, each other.

Inaugural text

It is not fortuitous that the egg is an egg. As Cixous writes, 'an egg is enough to make the world come into being', it is a 'Cosmic kernel': 'Egg rhymes with fire, with child, with mother and in every language, as we know, with creation.'[107] 'From one egg to another one arrives at God', says Lispector's text (278). David Leeming notes in his study on *Creation Myths of the World* that the 'cosmic egg or something like it appears in all parts of the world'.[108] In many of the myths Leeming recounts, what hatches out of the egg is *difference*: male and female, sky and earth, light and dark, order and disorder, yin and yang.[109] To account for the ubiquity of the egg as a symbol of the inauguration of difference, he quotes Jungian psychoanalyst Marie Louise von Franz, who writes that 'we can easily recognize in [the egg] the motif of preconscious totality. It is psychic wholeness conceived as the thing that came before the rise of ego consciousness, or any kind of dividing consciousness.'[110] To put it in Freudian terms, the egg symbolizes the 'initial state', prior to the arising of tension, back towards which all organisms strive: 'the aim of all life is death,' says Freud (*BPP*, 38); 'Living leads to death,' says Lispector (279). Leeming concludes by saying that 'the egg is a symbol of nondifferentiation, differentiation between things being the essence of the creation of anything'.[111]

What the concept of 'differentiation' lacks, however, as Derrida points out, is a sense of 'temporalizing delay' or 'deferring' that his notion of 'differance' ties to the spatial sense of 'difference'.[112] If the cosmic egg is to inaugurate the world – if it is the beginning of time – it must also hold deferral and delay in its hatching. After 'arriv[ing] at God' via the egg, Lispector's text gives us the following: 'Is the egg basically a vessel? Could it have been the first vessel sculpted by the Etruscans? No. The egg originated in Macedonia. There it was calculated, fruit of the most arduous spontaneity. In the sands of Macedonia a man holding a stick drew it. And then erased it with his bare foot' (278). This passage negates the conception of a cosmic egg as a kind of 'vessel' out of which the world is born and gives instead its origin as a textual origin: it is drawn in the sand. The word 'inaugurate' here is apt, connecting as it does the word *avis*, 'bird' (that which comes from an egg), and *garrire*, 'to talk' (which is what texts do). The egg's 'origin', like the origin of life itself (or the origin of species, as we saw in my last chapter), is no origin, or origin as differance, a mark in the sand. Derrida writes,

> What we note as *differance* will thus be the movement of play that 'produces' (and not by something that is simply an activity) ... effects of difference. This does not mean that the differance which produces differences is before them in a simple and in itself unmodified and indifferent present. Differance is the nonfull, nonsimple 'origin'; it is the structured and differing origin of differences.[113]

Differance as 'origin' cannot be thought of on the basis of presence or the present ('Seeing an egg never remains in the present' (E, 276)): 'differance holds us in a relation with what exceeds ... the alternative of presence or absence'. This 'effacement belongs to the very structure of the trace': 'Like differance, the trace is never presented as such. In presenting itself it becomes effaced.'[114] The egg is drawn in the sand and then quickly erased: the mark (time, world, text, being) that it inaugurates has its effacement as its condition of possibility. The egg drawn in the sand is also the egg drawn in or by this text, and its presence is therefore erased or withdrawn time and again: 'an egg seen is an egg lost' (276); 'The egg is a suspended thing' (277); 'the egg is invisible' (279); 'the egg does not exist' (281); 'from this precise moment there was never an egg' (282); 'the egg is an evasion' (286). The necessary possibility of effacement threatens every mark, and its force is radically non-human. Claire Colebrook comments that, in the Anthropocene, 'there is a tracing or archival force that precedes any command of signifying systems, *and* that would operate in the absence of human life and intentionality', thereby exposing the non-human force at work even in traces made by humans: 'the conditions for the possibility of human meaning and inscription are also the conditions for meaning's destruction and non-survival'.[115] The world is *fort*.

Translation: Future hatching

Let's return again to the last lines of Lispector's text that I quoted previously: 'perhaps one last time it will move from space over to this window that I have always left open. And at dawn it will descend into our building. Serene all the way to the kitchen. Illuminating it with my pallor' (286). As I discussed, there is a sense of reciprocal relation, where the writer is figured as neither purely active nor passive in relation to the text, and any simple causal logic is thereby disrupted. There is also a strange multiplication of tenses (a potential future, 'perhaps it will'; an ongoing past, 'I have always'; a present that has not yet come to be, 'Illuminating it with my pallor'). We can contrast the receptiveness to alterity figured here by the open window (as in Woolf) to the more destructive relation that the woman has with the egg elsewhere in the text: 'I don't understand the egg. I only understand a broken egg'; 'I break its shell and shape' (282). The egg, writes Cixous, 'is a form that presents itself as having to be nonviolated' (103). To understand it – to read it, to translate it – is necessarily to alter it. An egg is a fragile thing.

Keeping those points in mind (openness to alterity, reciprocal relations, futurity and potential destruction), let us return to the idea of translation with which I opened this chapter. Reading Walter Benjamin's 'On Language as Such', Wills figures a kind of originary translation as the 'conceiving mechanism on the basis of which words come to be'.[116] If there is a beyond of language, it is (like the unconscious) radically inaccessible and must therefore be translated *into* language. Benjamin writes that 'it is necessary to found the concept of translation at the deepest level of linguistic theory, for it is much too far-reaching and powerful to be treated in any way as an afterthought'.[117] Wills continues, 'There where human language comes to be, there is translation as that very coming to be. Translation is thus the life of language.'[118] The 'life of language', its capacity for survival, is bound to its capacity for translation, for breaking its context, splitting its identity, becoming other. It transforms. And, as Derrida writes, this transformation is not just of the text being translated but should always also be 'the transformation of one language by another'.[119]

I described in my second chapter how reading and writing are necessarily co-implicated, and one way to understand this is to realize that they both operate via translation. Elissa Marder writes that every 'singular act of reading would … also necessarily be a singular act of writing the words of the other in translation'.[120] To read or to write is to translate – not only the text but also oneself – and to disturb the stable oppositions between active and passive, cause and effect. Further, we can understand translation as not only the translation between languages but also as the necessary relation to otherness through which we live. As Derrida writes in 'Des Tours': 'experience is translation'.[121]

Translation is the necessary and inevitable becoming-other of text. As Derrida says in *The Ear of the Other*, regarding the experience of hearing one's 'own' texts read by another, 'it is never the same text, never an echo, that comes back to you', and this happens 'even before someone cites or reads it to you': 'the text's identity has been lost, and it's no longer the same as soon as it takes off, as soon as it has begun, as soon as it's on the page. By the end of the sentence, it's no longer the same sentence that it was at the beginning.'[122] The text translates *itself*, between voice and ear, between page and eye, even when the 'writer' and the 'reader', the 'speaker' and the 'listener', apparently inhabit the same language or even the same body (and I suspend these terms to recognize that the identity of each is already divided just as the text divides itself). The sentence you are reading is never the same as the one I am writing, even when I read it back to myself ('because I'm not myself, you see', as Alice would say).[123] Cixous notes that 'a quantity of supplementary effects is produced by the fact that the text is made with language and that language always speaks several languages.'[124] Language always speaks several languages: it translates itself into foreignness as soon as it is. This is perhaps what Freud is getting at when he remarks in 'The Uncanny', that 'we ourselves speak a language that is foreign'.[125]

Derrida then goes on to liken the experience of writing – the way that texts you write always become other – to that of having children; they are 'talking beings who can always outtalk you':[126]

A child is not only that toward which or for which a father or mother remains; it is an other who starts talking and goes on talking by itself, without your help, who doesn't even answer you except in your fantasy. You think it's talking to you, that you are talking in it, but in fact it talks by itself. On this basis, one constructs paternity or maternity fantasies; one says that, after all, it's still one's own …. Finally, however … one knows that children don't belong to us but we console ourselves with the fantasy that they do. Like everyone, then, I have fantasies of children and of texts.[127]

The child or text has its own future, a future in which it lives on and 'talks by itself', troubling notions of ownership or propriety. In 'The Egg and the Chicken', the life of the writer is subordinate to the life of the text: 'The chicken exists so that the egg can traverse the ages. That's what a mother is for. – The egg is constantly persecuted for being too ahead of its time. – An egg, for now, will always be revolutionary' (278). The essential possibility of being read or translated is the text's relation to the future; it will always be 'ahead of its time', pregnant with potential meanings that come to be as it 'traverse[s] the ages'. 'An egg, for *now*, will always be revolutionary.' At each moment that the text meets a new 'now', it effects a revolution – in all the senses that I discussed with regards to Copernicus in my second chapter: first, a repetition, a rereading; second, an upheaval or disruption, its reiteration as differance; and third, an event in the mind, an experience that happens between text and reader, including all the incalculable conscious and unconscious effects that come into play, each time differently – as I. A. Richards says of reading, 'a new being is growing in the mind'.[128]

Hatch into thought

I promised earlier to return to the letter in which Freud tells Wilhelm Fliess that he 'no longer understand[s] the state of mind in which [he] hatched the psychology'.[129] You will have been wondering what this particular 'psychology' was that Freud hatched and then disavowed. It was a text from 1895 (later published as *Project for a Scientific Psychology*), which, as James Strachey writes in his introduction to the *Standard Edition*, was not well regarded by Freud: 'He dashed it off in two or three weeks, left it unfinished, and criticized it severely at the time of writing it. Later in life he seems to have forgotten it or at least never to have referred to it.'[130] Despite this, Strachey continues, 'the *Project*, or rather its invisible ghost, haunts the whole series of Freud's theoretical writings to the very end'.[131] Indeed, in the introduction to a text written by Freud twenty-five years later – *Beyond the Pleasure Principle* – Strachey notes that 'what is particularly remarkable is the closeness with which some of the earlier sections of the present work follow the *Project*'.[132] The relations between these two works are not limited to 'closeness' of theoretical content, however. There are three other ways in which these works speak to or through each other and via the elaboration of which I hope also to reiterate not only the several aspects of Freud's indebtedness to literature but also why this indebtedness is important today.

First relation: *fort/da composition*. As Derrida writes in 'To Speculate', and as we saw earlier, the 'athesis' of *Beyond* 'constructs-deconstructs itself according to an interminable detour (*Umweg*): that it describes "itself", writes and unwrites'.[133] Every 'step' that is taken by the text is made 'only to take it back in advance'.[134] The composition of the *Project* anticipates this *fort/da* structure quite precisely. Freud conceived the earlier text between April and November 1895 whilst in frequent correspondence with Fliess, and his feelings towards the nascent theory vacillate wildly from 'immense pleasure' at how it is coming along to a sense of embarrassment about it: 'It makes me quite uncomfortable to think that I am supposed to tell you about it' (131, 135). In September, after visiting Fliess in Berlin, Freud reports that his 'rested head is now making *child's play* of the difficulties previously encountered' (and I underline here another anticipation of *Beyond*), but still stresses uncertainty: 'How much of this progress will on closer inspection again dissolve into thin air [*in Schein zerfließt*, melt into appearance/ illusion] remains to be seen' (139–40/143). On the 8th of October, he is worried that his 'theoretical fantasies' will be put 'to shame'. He is 'alternately proud and overjoyed and ashamed and miserable', and 'apathetically tell[s] [him]self: it does not yet, perhaps never will, hang together' (141). On the 16th, he writes that for all the 'enticing hopes' there are corresponding 'disappointments' (145). On the 20th, he feels he has had a breakthrough – 'the barriers suddenly lifted, the veils dropped, and everything became transparent . . . . I can scarcely manage to contain my delight' (146) – only to retract it again eleven days later, when he writes that he has 'begun to have doubts' (148). On the 2nd of November, his 'confidence' has been again 'strengthened', so that he can enjoy 'a moment of satisfaction', although he adds that 'a lot of work still remains to be done on the succeeding acts of the tragedy' (149). (Enter the explicitly theatrical language that was to set the scene of *Beyond*.) On the 8th of November, he says he has, exasperated, put the manuscripts away ('I threw everything away [*warf ich alles weg*]', like an as yet unborn grandson whose favourite game will consist in throwing his toys away), determined not to return to them until the following year (150/154), and on the 29th, he writes the letter from which I quoted earlier: 'I no longer understand the state of mind in which I hatched the psychology; cannot conceive how I could have inflicted it on you' (152). After half a year of *fort* and *da*, he now implies that the withdrawal is final. On the 8th of December, however, commenting on some of Fliess's work, he writes, 'We cannot do without people who have the courage to think something new before they can demonstrate it' (155). His speculating, as we know, was not yet over.

Second relation: *limping*. Freud concludes *Beyond* by quoting Friedrich Rückert: 'What we cannot reach flying we must reach limping' (63). As Strachey's note to that page tells us, Freud also sent these lines to Fliess on the 20th October 1895 – the letter in which he proclaims that everything has fallen into place for the *Project*. As far as I can tell, these are the only instances of him quoting these lines. The words work to defend his speculative procedure, attesting to the *necessity* of its particular gait: we *must* limp when we cannot fly. Derrida remarks that 'the allusion to limping … has an oblique, lateral, winking *relation* to Freud's very procedure' – the *fort/da* of *Beyond*, which is, on the final page, 'immobilized over limping': it cannot go any further.[135] Freud's invocation of the same quotation in the two texts attests that their composition inspired similar vacillating feelings in him. The reference to limping also, however, sends us back, via the theatre, to a much earlier moment in *Beyond* – when another limping character comes on stage: Oedipus. The name literally means 'swollen-footed' (from the ancient Greek οἰδεῖν, 'to swell', and πούς, 'foot'), and Oedipus is therefore denominated as a limper even if he no longer actually limps.[136] Attempting to thwart the prophecy that said his own son would kill him, Laius pinned the baby's feet together and left him to die. Oedipus lived, but his feet were forever scarred: he is named after his feet, and his marked feet bear his name. Oedipus' name and feet mark him out as the son that Laius left for dead, a mark the significance of which will only come to consciousness when it is too late. In *The Interpretation of Dreams*, Freud summarizes the background plot of the play (the events that have occurred before the actual opening of the play, which are then revealed in hindsight – just like the drama of psychoanalysis) and then quotes the following lines: 'But he, where is he? Where shall now be read / The fading trace [*schwer erkennbar dunkle Spur*, difficult to recognize, dark trace] of this ancient guilt?'[137] The answer, of course, is in his foot-name, which marks him, even before he consciously realizes it, as Laius' son, the baby whose feet were pinned. (And we should remember that etymologically both the English 'trace' and the German *Spur* refer to footprints, to treads and tracks.[138]) Modern audiences, Freud tells us, 'shrink back from him with the whole force of the repression by which those wishes have since that time been held down within us',[139] and it is up to the work of psychoanalysis, then, to read the 'trace' of this 'ancient guilt': a limping not physical, but psychic, effected by the repression of these primal desires. Freud first proffers his idea of the universal Oedipus complex in 1897 – again in a letter to Fliess ('I have not told it to anyone else, because I can well imagine in advance the bewildered rejection' (277)) – two years after writing the *Project*. However, on the 15th October 1895 – a few days before he sends the quotation about limping – he reveals 'the great clinical secret' to Fliess (in which we can detect the germ of the 'infantile sexual life' which was to be characterized as the Oedipus complex (*BPP*, 18)): 'Obsessional neurosis is the consequence of a presexual *sexual pleasure*, which is later transformed into [self-] *reproach*. "Presexual" means actually before puberty, before the release of sexual substances; the relevant events become effective only as *memories*' (144). The references to limping, then, not only mark the mode of Freud's procedure but also perhaps mark the (swollen) footprint of the character which was to go on to play such a central role in his theory of the psyche. As Derrida asks in 'My Chances', 'even if these affinities are purely lexical and apparently fortuitous, should they be considered insignificant, accidental, or, for that very reason, symptoms?'[140] Every allusion, scene or context laid or determined by Freud will always be exceeded by the unconscious effects of the language(s) in which he writes.

Third relation: *writing*. In the composition of the *Project*, we see the importance of linguistic conception to Freud's work. After telling Fliess of his breakthrough, and just before quoting the lines about limping, he writes, 'If I had only waited two weeks longer before reporting to you, everything would have turned out so much clearer. Yet it was only in attempting to report it to you that the whole matter became obvious to me. So it could not have been done any other way' (146). *It could not have been done any other way*. It was done *in language*, in being communicated to Fliess. A couple of weeks earlier, he has complained of being 'alone with a head in which so much is germinating and, for the time being, thrashing around' (141). He needed to put it into words in order for it to hatch out. Likewise, he admits towards the end of *Beyond* that he has been 'obliged' to use 'figurative language': 'We could not otherwise describe the processes in question at all, and indeed we could not become aware of them' (60). As Derrida remarks in 'Force and Signification', to write is 'to be incapable of making meaning absolutely precede writing: it is thus to lower meaning while simultaneously elevating inscription'.[141]

These three relations underline, then, Freud's indebtedness to literature – not just as a source but also as a *poetic* (in the strong sense, poietic) art.

Psychoanalysis, as an interpretive or hermeneutic method, is self-evidently a reading practice. It is also, however, a writing practice: a practice that understands the power of writing, that cannot do without writing or being written, a practice that writes. In 'Force and Signification', Derrida suggests that the 'experience of *secondarity*' is 'tied to the strange redoubling by means of which constituted – written – meaning presents itself as prerequisitely and simultaneously *read*: … Meaning is neither before nor after the act.'[142] The text translates itself as soon as it is on the page, so that it might come back to you, irrevocably other ('I no longer understand the state of mind in which I hatched the psychology', as Freud says). Clark comments that the 'strange redoubling' Derrida evokes – the sense of external or foreign agency that stirs in writing – 'is itself but an effect of the irreducible secondarity of the sign – that it is no sooner written than read, diverging from what may have been intended': 'Self-reading', then, names 'a very fissure or hiatus in the structure of subjectivity, unassimilable to notions of the subject as reflexive consciousness or simple interiority'.[143] That is to say, *the act of writing* (and the self-reading which is indissociable from it) *gives to experience the revelations of psychoanalysis*: the 'hiatus in the structure of subjectivity' through which forces not identifiable with the 'self' or ego are at work. Writing is not the description of psychoanalysis but its very performance, the stage upon which it enacts its strange dis/appearing drama.

The third blow to human narcissism hatches out of writing – out of an otherness that comes from within, like a chicken out of an egg, or, indeed, an egg out of a chicken. Text gives life to thought, and vice versa. Given that, as this book has shown, text cannot be reduced to human language, what are we to make of the text of the Anthropocene? And what will it make of us? The Anthropocene marks a 'fissure or hiatus' in our collective subjectivity: it is an autobiography that calls into question the very humanity which it nevertheless geologically inscribes. If human identity is predicated on being separated or separable from 'nature' and 'the environment', the advent of the Anthropocene demonstrates beyond dispute – as the 'environment' closes in, and the necessary conditions for our own existence begin to waver – that the thought of any such separation is a mere fairy tale. Climate change is the fourth (and most potent) blow to human narcissism, that shows how far our notions of intentional agency and conscious control are mere fictions, and how far even the most significant (or world-shattering) of texts are inevitably subject to the workings of unconscious forces. It is a blow that cannot be ignored, a blow that demands that we live and act differently. The Anthropocene is reading – and writing – us.

Necessary narcissism

In 'A Difficulty in the Path of Psycho-Analysis' – before describing the three scientific blows to the 'naïve self-love of man' – Freud explains how he has come to the conception of a universal primary narcissism, when an individual's 'capacity for love' is turned inwards: the libido cathects the ego.[144] 'It is only later,' he tells us, 'that, being attached to the satisfaction of the major vital needs, the libido flows over from the ego on to external objects.' And so,

> the individual advances from narcissism to object-love. But we do not believe that the *whole* of the libido ever passes over from the ego to objects. A certain quantity of libido is always retained in the ego; even when object-love is highly developed, a certain amount of narcissism persists. The ego is a great reservoir from which the libido that is destined for objects flows out and into which it flows back from those objects. Object-libido was at first ego-libido and can be transformed back into ego-libido. For complete health it is essential that the libido should not lose this full mobility.[145]

The 'full mobility' necessary for psychic health entails, then, a capacity for *both* object-love and self-love, and, further, a capacity for retaining a certain amount of both at once. After the stage of primary narcissism, a non-pathological manifestation of either type of love is dependent on the possibility of the other: Object-libido develops out of the primary ego-libido – relation to otherness, that is to say, develops out of a prior self-relation – and secondary ego-libido depends upon object-libido or risks descent into paranoiac delusion and withdrawal from the world. Or to put it in less jargonistic terms, to love others you must know how to love yourself, but a healthy self-love is never *only* self-love. Indeed, as Freud writes in 'On Narcissism', self-love is not 'a perversion, but the libidinal complement to the egoism of the instinct of self-preservation, a measure of which may justifiably be attributed to every living creature'.[146] Narcissism is, that is to say, *for life*.

Following the paragraph I quoted above, Freud briefly mentions the forms of 'normal' narcissism exhibited by amoebas, young children and 'primitive man', before moving on to the three blows around which I have organized this book: 'After this introduction,' he writes, 'I propose to describe how the universal narcissism of men, their self-love, has up to the present suffered three severe blows from the researches of science.'[147] He makes no comment, that is to say, on the divorce between the two halves of the paper: the first half speaking of normal and necessary narcissism at an individual level, and the second half concerned with a pathological narcissism of the human species. One must assume that Man's 'inclination to regard himself as lord of the world', his breaking of 'the bond of community between him and the animal kingdom', his assumption of sovereignty 'within his own mind' (as Freud characterizes the expressions of narcissism struck by the three blows) do not constitute a healthy or a necessary form of self-love.[148] Indeed, these narcissistic tendencies of the human species, in their propensity to exclude the otherness of non-human agencies – which constitutes, as this book has shown, a disavowal or refusal of radical animism – have in fact proved to be hugely detrimental to the very species that was thereby to be aggrandized.

In *The Right to Narcissism*, Pleshette DeArmitt writes that 'one cannot simply deny or dispense with narcissism, one cannot occupy a position of non-narcissism, and to attempt to occupy such a position would even be perilous'.[149] Or, as Freud writes, 'a certain amount of narcissism persists' alongside object-libido and is 'essential' to psychic health. DeArmitt suggests, therefore, that 'a rethinking and reinscription of narcissism is not only possible but also vitally necessary in order to address the very problems of what is commonly associated with the term "narcissism" – solipsism, egoism, ipseity, in other words, a pathological self-return, a phantasmatic circularity that dreams of self-enclosure and unleashes a cruel violence on both the "other" and the "self"'.[150] She distinguishes, then, between a narcissism of 'pathological self-return' – which closes itself to alterity and therefore closes its *self* – and one that is instead 'based on a new understanding of self-relation in which to speak of and for oneself would … pass by way of and be indebted to the other'.[151] In the lecture in which he discusses the three blows, Freud refers to the universal 'self-love of men' also as 'human megalomania', and, indeed, as I noted in my first chapter, he characterizes each of its expressions in terms of a delusion of mastery.[152] This tendency works to unleash, in DeArmitt's words, 'a cruel violence on both the "other" and the "self"'. An anthropocentrism that seeks to master, control, dominate, exclude (i.e. a narcissism of 'pathological self-return') becomes inadvertently masochistic – as the notion that human beings are independent of and superior to other life forms and the planet not only justifies maltreatment and abuse of the non-human but also, blind to the radical interrelation and interdependence of human and non-human life, ultimately threatens the human itself.

In 'On Narcissism', Freud also discusses the secondary form of narcissism that sets up an 'ideal' ego, by which the actual ego is measured (and also, therefore, divided – in order that it can become its own object):

> This ideal ego is now the target of the self-love which was enjoyed in childhood by the actual ego. The subject's narcissism makes its appearance displaced on to this new ideal ego, which, like the infantile ego, finds itself possessed of every perfection that is of value. As always where the libido is concerned, man has here again shown himself incapable of giving up a satisfaction he had once enjoyed. He is not willing to forgo the narcissistic perfection of his childhood; and when, as he grows up, he is disturbed by the admonitions of others and by the awakening of his own critical judgement, so that he can no longer retain that perfection, he seeks to recover it in the new form of an ego ideal. What he projects before him as his ideal is the substitute for the lost narcissism of his childhood in which he was his own ideal.[153]

The formation of such an ideal 'heightens the demands of the ego', which can manifest itself in two ways: *either* it can 'prompt' – but not 'enforce' – the sublimation of instincts in the interest of attaining the ideal, *or* the unattainability of the ideal (as, for example, when it is too distant from reality) can result in repression and neurosis.[154] For example, one's idea of oneself as being concerned with the environment can prompt behavioural changes that accord with that ideal (such as choosing to fly less), or it can cause (conscious or unconscious) guilt about behaviours that one is unwilling or unable to change, such as eating meat. Freud also suggests that these notions are important 'for the understanding of group psychology': 'In addition to its individual side, this ideal has a social side; it is also the common ideal of a family, a class or a nation.'[155] The universal human narcissism of which Freud writes in 'A Difficulty' involves a fundamentally erroneous ideal, one repeatedly contradicted and undermined by the realities revealed by each of the three blows, and that therefore results in pathological repression. Freud recognizes this movement in terms of the psychological blow: 'No wonder, then,' he writes, 'that the ego does not look favourably upon psycho-analysis and obstinately refuses to believe in it.'[156] Isn't it also true, however, that 'Man', as I suggested in my first chapter, also refuses to 'believe' in the other two blows, insofar as he continues to maintain the 'ideal' which should have been deconstructed by them? While on one level humans know that the earth is not the centre of the universe and that they are descended from other animals, such knowledge is not taken into account – it has not transformed the way we live – and is therefore effectively repressed. Such repression enables, I suggest, what Claire Colebrook calls 'the perpetual, insistent and demonic return of anthropocentrism'.[157]

The three blows reveal that the ego-ideal of 'Man' is based on a deluded megalomania, a pernicious narcissism that ultimately injures the self it attempts to elevate. Climate change demands that we rethink that ideal – not to dispense with narcissism (which would anyway be impossible) but to reconfigure it to allow for a self-conception that admits the otherness essential not only to healthy development but also to any ethical relation to the non-human. We must imagine a new ego-ideal for humankind that recognizes and understands that our humanity is dependent upon and interrelated with other forms of life and non-living agents, including not just the plants, animals and fungi that we eat, but also things like atmospheric carbon and weather events. As Derrida writes, 'There is not narcissism and non-narcissism; there are narcissisms that are more or less comprehensive, generous, open, extended. What is called non-narcissism is but the economy of a much more welcoming, hospitable narcissism, one that is much more open to the experience of the other as other.'[158]

Dodds recognizes that 'despite the anxiety, guilt and terror that climate change forces us to face, this moment of crisis can also offer us an opportunity for a more open vision of ourselves, as subjects, as societies, and as a species among the interconnected life systems of the Earth'.[159] If we are to mobilize human narcissism towards a non-pathological manifestation, it will be necessary to orient human self-understanding around an 'ideal' which is closer to reality than the one that has shaped so much of our history. This would be an ideal that recognizes the non-central position of humankind within the universe, that recognizes the radical interrelation of all life and that recognizes that egological (and ecological) mastery is a fiction: a recognition, then, of what I have called radical animism. It would be an ideal that, in these recognitions, does not impoverish or destroy human self-regard but reconfigures it within the field of innumerable and heterogeneous alterities that make it possible – an ideal which enables, that is to say, a 'generous, open, extended' narcissism, one 'open to the experience of the other as other'.

Conclusion

During the years I have spent working on this book, the blow to human narcissism struck by climate change has continued to gather force. The material conditions necessary for human existence are under threat, posing a challenge that we cannot continue to ignore or repress. The climate crisis disrupts the literal (rather than merely philosophical or intellectual) ground upon which we stand and therefore demands to be reckoned with in a way that the Copernican, Darwinian and Freudian paradigm shifts did not. This is not to lessen the importance of these discoveries but merely to recognize the resilience of the pathological human narcissism that continues to function in spite of them. The advent of the Anthropocene has also, as I have shown, made the particular animistic force of each of the previous three blows reverberate with a new significance: the decentring and rescaling of the cosmological blow, the mindless agency and radical interrelation of the biological blow, the undoing of mastery of the psychological blow. While Sigmund Freud characterized animism as the belief in the 'omnipotence of thoughts', in the face of anthropogenic climate change, never has an *impotence* of human thought and intention made itself so strongly felt.[1] Indeed, to read climate change as animistic is not only to recognize the non-human agencies at work there, and it is not only to call into question the intentionality of human agency, but it is also to recognize animism as having a 'truth' – albeit a somewhat sinister one – that the past conceptions of it as a 'primitive' and 'mistaken' belief system insistently denied.

Animism refers to all that which will not submit to human mastery and control, to the forces that move before us, after us, within us and without us. Freud admitted that animism is 'the living basis of our speech, our beliefs and our philosophies' and that it is retained in 'in the field of art'.[2] The preceding pages have extended these definitions somewhat and have shown how animism might also be found in astronomy, autobiography, breath, capitalism, chance, chemical activity, climate change, the death drive, the earth, eggs, etymology, examples, fiction, haunting, inspiration, letters, limits, literature, materiality, the market, meaning, metaphor, movement, naming, narrative, natural selection, poetry, quantum physics, reading, reaction, revolutions, rhythm, roots, scale effects, sound, speed, spirit, text, theatre, traces, translation, the unconscious, viruses, weather, windows and writing.

The compiling of this list compels me to add 'the alphabet', which has here become an organizing force, and then I might find myself having to add 'supplementarity', that which, as Jacques Derrida writes, 'adds itself, … is a surplus, a plenitude enriching another plenitude', but the place of which 'is assigned in the structure by the mark of an emptiness'.[3] Indeed, if, as I have been saying, animism can be thought of as *radical* – that is, innovative, vital, fundamental – its proliferation can only be interminable. The radicalization of animism, as this book has shown, provides a way of thinking the non-human and non-living forces that conspire to animate and create the world in which we live.

I have used the three blows to human narcissism named by Freud to guide this book, but to suggest that they are definitive would be to miss the point. One might have started, for example, with quantum physics, with a sustained engagement with animistic mythologies, with autoimmunity, with dark matter, with synthetic biology or with AI. At the same time, however, I believe that each of the three paradigm shifts that I have thought through engenders a singular experience of animism. Likewise, the 'literary' texts I have read (although I suspend the term to remind you of the literary effects also at work in, for example, the texts of Freud and Darwin) were all chosen for the ways in which, for me, they animated with particular force the arguments I was making – showing a remarkable attunement to non-human forces and working to call into question assumptions about human agency and centrality. The ways that each work is transformed by, and works to transform, the new contexts within which it is read also demonstrates, I hope, how the radical animism of literature will never be put to rest.

Notes

Introduction: Reading for Life

1 Sarah Wood, *Without Mastery: Reading and Other Forces* (Edinburgh: EUP, 2014).
2 Adam Trexler, *Anthropocene Fictions: The Novel in a Time of Climate Change* (Charlottesville: University of Virginia Press, 2015), 10.
3 Tom Bristow, *The Anthropocene Lyric: an Affective Geography of Poetry, Person, Place* (Houndmills: Palgrave Macmillan, 2015); Sam Solnick, *Poetry and the Anthropocene: Ecology, Biology and Technology in Contemporary British and Irish Poetry* (London: Routledge, 2017), 4.
4 Nicholas Royle, 'Reading Joseph Conrad: Episodes from the Coast', *Mosaic* 47, no. 1 (2014): 43, emphasis in original.
5 Sigmund Freud, 'Fixation to Traumas – The Unconscious', *SE* XVI, 284–5.

1 Radical Animism: Climate Change and Other Transformations

1 William Shakespeare, *Macbeth*, ed. Sandra Clark and Pamela Mason (London: Arden Shakespeare, 2015), 3.4.108–10.
2 Franz Kafka, *The Metamorphosis and Other Stories*, trans. Joyce Crick (Oxford: OUP, 2009), 29. Translation modified from 'bedspread' to 'bed cover [*Bettdecke*]'; Kafka, *Die Verwandlung* (Frankfurt am Main: Fischer, 1982), 7. Further references are given parenthetically. When I am also quoting from the German text, the page number for the latter is given following a slash.
3 Martin Heidegger, *The Fundamental Concepts of Metaphysics: World, Finitude, Solitude*, trans. William McNeill and Nicholas Walker (Bloomington: Indiana University Press, 1995), 5–6.
4 Antonio Stoppani, quoted in Paul J. Crutzen, 'Geology of Mankind', *Nature* 415 (2002): 23.
5 Crutzen, 'Geology of Mankind', 23.
6 T. J. Demos, *Against the Anthropocene: Visual Culture and Environment Today* (Berlin: Sternberg Press, 2017), 21.
7 Adam Trexler, *Anthropocene Fictions: The Novel in a Time of Climate Change* (Charlottesville: University of Virginia Press, 2015), 4.

8   Bruno Latour, *Facing Gaia: Eight Lectures on the New Climatic Regime*, trans. Catherine Porter (Cambridge: Polity Press, 2017), 9, 8.
9   Jeremy Davies, *The Birth of the Anthropocene* (Oakland: University of California Press, 2016), 47, 68.
10 Sarah Wood, *Without Mastery: Reading and Other Forces* (Edinburgh: EUP, 2014), 9.
11 Davies, *Birth of the Anthropocene*, 83.
12 Timothy Clark, *Ecocriticism on the Edge: The Anthropocene as a Threshold Concept* (London: Bloomsbury, 2015), 15.
13 Bronislaw Szerszynski, 'The End of the End of Nature: The Anthropocene and the Fate of the Human', *Oxford Literary Review* 34, no. 2 (2012): 181.
14 Wood, *Without Mastery*, 8.
15 Jane Bennett, *Vibrant Matter: A Political Ecology of Things* (Durham, NC: Duke University Press, 2010), 20.
16 Timothy Clark, 'Some Climate Change Ironies: Deconstruction, Environmental Politics and the Closure of Ecocriticism', *Oxford Literary Review* 32, no. 1 (2010): 134.
17 David Wallace-Wells, *The Uninhabitable Earth: A Story of the Future* (London: Allen Lane, an imprint of Penguin Books, 2019), 129, 138.
18 Davies discusses the Global Boundary Stratotype Section and Point markers (or 'golden spikes') being considered as stratigraphic markers for the start of the new epoch in *Birth of the Anthropocene*, 85–111.
19 Clark, *Ecocriticism on the Edge*, xi.
20 David Wills, *Inanimation: Theories of Inorganic Life* (Minneapolis: University of Minnesota Press, 2016), 52.
21 Ibid.
22 Nicholas Royle, *Veering* (Edinburgh: EUP, 2011), 86 n.6.
23 The IPCC website states that the organization 'is celebrating its 30th anniversary in 2018'. 'IPCC 30th Anniversary'. Available online: https://www.ipcc.ch/reports/ipcc-30th-anniversary/ (accessed 24 April 2019). One might wonder if such a landmark is any cause for 'celebration' given the ever-receding goalposts over which it presides. This is not to denounce the scientists that produce the IPCC reports – no doubt they feel the gravity of the situation more than any of us. Instead, it is to wonder at the madness of a system in which governments can state their commitment to cutting carbon with one hand (the IPCC) while working to deregulate fracking with the other.
24 Jacques Derrida, *The Animal That Therefore I Am*, ed. Marie-Louise Mallet, trans. David Wills (New York: Fordham University Press, 2008), 32.
25 Wills, *Inanimation*, 44.
26 Joyce Crick, 'Note on the Translation', in Kafka, *The Metamorphosis and Other Stories*, xxxviii.

27 Ibid., xxxviii–xxxix.
28 Timothy Clark, 'Editorial', *Oxford Literary Review* 34, no. 2 (2012): vi.
29 Jacques Derrida, 'The *Retrait* of Metaphor', trans. Peggy Kamuf, in *Psyche: Inventions of the Other*, vol. I, ed. Kamuf and Elizabeth Rottenberg (Stanford: SUP, 2007), 49.
30 Ibid., 50.
31 Jacques Derrida, 'White Mythology: Metaphor in the Text of Philosophy', in *Margins of Philosophy*, trans. Alan Bass (Chicago: University of Chicago Press, 1982), 213.
32 'Imagine that I am walking like him, to his rhythm,' Derrida writes as he embodies Freud, 'Telepathy', trans. Nicholas Royle, in *Psyche*, 243. Or, as Peggy Kamuf puts it in her introduction to 'Che cos'e la poesia?', Derrida 'always' 'works to abolish the distance between what he is writing *about* … and what his writing is *doing*', *A Derrida Reader: Between the Blinds*, ed. Kamuf (London: Harvester, 1991), 221. Sarah Wood comments on this 'familiar difficulty approaching Derrida in a Derrida text. Where is he? What does he really think? Which voice is his? He is not simply there, or he is there in a diffuse, irregular, aneconomic way. His commentary does not distinguish itself finally from what it is reading', *Derrida's Writing and Difference: A Reader's Guide* (London: Continuum, 2009), 104.
33 Jacques Derrida, 'Edmond Jabès and the Question of the Book', in *Writing and Difference*, trans. Alan Bass (London: Routledge, 2001), 88–9.
34 Wood, *Derrida's Writing and Difference*, 69, 70–1.
35 Wills, *Inanimation*, 112.
36 Paul Celan, from *Atemwende* (Frankfurt am Main: Suhrkamp, 1967), 93. The poem is printed in its entirety (in both German and English) in Jacques Derrida, *Sovereignties in Question: the Poetics of Paul Celan*, ed. Thomas Dutoit and Outi Pasanen (New York: Fordham University Press, 2005), 141.
37 Jacques Derrida, *The Beast and the Sovereign*, vol. II, trans. Geoff Bennington, ed. Michel Lisse, Marie-Louise Mallet and Ginette Michaud (Chicago: University of Chicago Press, 2011), 258, 105.
38 Ibid., 266.
39 Jacques Derrida, 'Autoimmunity: Real and Symbolic Suicides –', trans. Pascale-Anne Brault and Michael Naas, in *Philosophy in a Time of Terror*, ed. Giovanna Borradori (Chicago: University of Chicago Press, 2003), 127–8.
40 Translation modified from 'beast like that' to 'such an animal [*einem solchen Tier*]'.
41 See Elizabeth Kolbert, *The Sixth Extinction: An Unnatural History* (London: Bloomsbury, 2014). I will return to the anthropogenic nature of this extinction event in the next chapter.
42 Michael Wood, *Literature and the Taste of Knowledge* (Cambridge: CUP, 2005), 77.
43 Sigmund Freud, 'Fixation to Traumas – The Unconscious', *SE* XVI, 284–5; *GW* XI, 295.

44 Sigmund Freud, 'A Difficulty in the Path of Psycho-Analysis', *SE* XVII, 140–3; *GW* XII, 7–10.
45 Simon Glendinning, 'The End of the World Designed with Men in Mind', *Journal of Historical Sociology* 26, no. 3 (2013): 297.
46 Freud, 'Fixation to Traumas', *SE* XVI, 284.
47 Jacques Derrida, 'Psychoanalysis Searches the States of Its Soul: The Impossible Beyond of a Sovereign Cruelty', trans. Peggy Kamuf, in *Without Alibi* (Stanford: SUP, 2002), 238–80.
48 Jacques Derrida, *Specters of Marx: The State of the Debt, the Work of Mourning, and the New International*, trans. Peggy Kamuf (London: Routledge, 1994), 121, 122.
49 Ibid., 122.
50 Glendinning, 'The End of the World', 310–11.
51 Ibid., 312.
52 Derrida, *Specters of Marx*, 74.
53 Ibid., 106.
54 Clark, *Ecocriticism on the Edge*, 3.
55 Naomi Klein, *This Changes Everything: Capitalism vs the Climate* (London: Penguin, 2014), 310.
56 Rob Nixon, *Slow Violence and the Environmentalism of the Poor* (Cambridge, MA: Harvard University Press, 2011), 9.
57 Jacques Derrida, 'Eating Well', trans. Peter Connor and Avital Ronell, in *Points … Interviews 1974–1994*, ed. Elisabeth Weber (Stanford: SUP, 1995), 278.
58 The indirect putting to death of those that have found themselves or will find themselves in the ever-growing sacrifice zones, of those that will starve or drown or be poisoned, and the direct putting to death of those who are killed (but somehow not 'murdered') in the name of profit: in the wars waged for overt or covert financial gain (like the 'interventions' of the United States and the United Kingdom in the Middle East around the turn of the century), or those killed for choosing to dissent against the fossil fuel industry – for instance, in the Niger Delta, in December 1998, fifteen thousand troops were mobilized by the government against those protesting against the fossil fuel corporations, and perhaps around two hundred people were killed for staging non-violent demonstrations (see Klein, *This Changes Everything*, 307–8).
59 David Wallace-Wells, *The Uninhabitable Earth: A Story of the Future* (London: Allen Lane, an imprint of Penguin Books, 2019), 28.
60 Klein, *This Changes Everything*, 329, 429.
61 Clark, 'Some Climate Change Ironies', 133.
62 Klein, *This Changes Everything*, 314.
63 Karl Marx, *Capital*, vol. III, trans. David Fernbach (London: Penguin, 1981), 949.
64 Karl Marx, *Capital*, vol. I, trans. Ben Fowkes (London: Penguin, 1976), 638.

65 For a discussion of how this came about, see Yuval Noah Harari, *Sapiens: A Brief History of Humankind* (New York: HarperCollins, 2015), 28–31.
66 Wallace-Wells comments on our 'generations-long deference to market forces as something like an infallible, or at least an unbeatable, overseer', *The Uninhabitable Earth*, 159.
67 Ibid., 162.
68 Ibid., 165.
69 Ibid., 166.
70 Jacques Derrida, *Glas*, trans. John P. Leavey and Richard Rand (Lincoln: University of Nebraska Press, 1990), 27.
71 Ibid.
72 Charles Darwin, *On the Origin of Species: By Means of Natural Selection*, vol. II (New York: PF Collier, 1909), 526, 525.
73 Wills, *Inanimation*, xii.
74 Ibid., 58.
75 Nick Lane, *The Vital Question: Why Is Life the Way It Is?* (London: Profile, 2015), 82, emphasis added.
76 Derrida, *The Animal That Therefore I Am*, 31.
77 E. B. Tylor, *Primitive Culture: Researches into the Development of Mythology, Philosophy, Religion, Art, and Custom*, vol. I (London: John Murray, 1871), 402.
78 Caroline Rooney, *African Literature, Animism and Politics* (London: Routledge, 2000), 8.
79 Ibid., 18.
80 Latour, *Facing Gaia*, 70.
81 Derrida, *Glas*, 27.
82 Tom Cohen, 'The Geomorphic Fold: Anapocalyptics, Changing Climes and "Late" Deconstruction', *Oxford Literary Review* 32, no. 1 (2010): 74.
83 I have compiled this list, which makes no claim to completion, from the following three sources: L. D. Arnett, 'The Soul: A Study of Past and Present Beliefs', *American Journal of Psychology* 15, no. 2 (1904): 127–8; Jay Griffiths, *Wild: An Elemental Journey* (London: Penguin, 2008), 275–6; Tylor, *Primitive Culture*, 389–90.
84 Elizabeth A. Povinelli, *Geontologies: A Requiem to Late Liberalism* (Durham, NC: Duke University Press, 2016), 42.
85 Lester S. King, 'Stahl and Hoffmann: A Study in Eighteenth Century Animism', *Journal of the History of Medicine* 19, no. 2 (1964): 123, 122.
86 Tylor, *Primitive Culture*, 412.
87 Eduardo Viveiros de Castro, personal communication to Donna Haraway, quoted in Haraway, 'Cosmopolitical Critters', in *Cosmopolitan Animals*, ed. Kaori Nagai et al. (Basingstoke: Palgrave Macmillan, 2015), xi.
88 E. B. Tylor, 'The Religion of Savages', *Fortnightly Review* 6 (1866), 73, 84.

89 Tylor, *Primitive Culture*, 385.
90 Tylor, 'The Religion of Savages', 84–5.
91 Tylor, *Primitive Culture*, 422, 431.
92 Tylor, 'The Religion of Savages', 86.
93 Martin D. Stringer, 'Rethinking Animism: Thoughts from the Infancy of Our Discipline', *Journal of the Royal Anthropological Institute* 5, no. 4 (1999): 542.
94 Stringer writes that he finds *Primitive Culture* to be 'a very sensitive, sophisticated, intellectually complex text written by a scholar whose ideas seemed to bear very little relation to [the] popular conception of his writing', ibid., 541.
95 Klein, *This Changes Everything*, 11.
96 Harari, *Sapiens*, 32, 37.
97 Ibid., 30.
98 Povinelli, *Geontologies*, 20.
99 See Wallace-Wells, *The Uninhabitable Earth*, 44.
100 Tylor, *Primitive Culture*, 450, 453.
101 Ibid., 452.
102 Ibid., 402.
103 Robin Horton, *Patterns of Thought in Africa and the West: Essays on Magic, Religion and Science* (Cambridge: CUP, 1997), 106–7.
104 James Frazer, *The Golden Bough: A Study in Magic and Religion* (London: Macmillan, 1922), 933. Further references are given parenthetically.
105 Rooney, *African Literature*, 69.
106 Wallace-Wells writes that 'the European Academies' Science Advisory Council found that existing negative-emissions technologies have "limited realistic potential" to even slow the increase in concentration of carbon in the atmosphere – let alone meaningfully reduce that concentration,' whilst '*Nature* dismissed all scenarios built on CCS as "magical thinking"', *The Uninhabitable Earth*, 45.
107 Ibid., 76.
108 Johann Wolfgang von Goethe, *Der Zauberlehrling*, ed. Heidrun Boddin (Munich: Middelhauve, 1999), no page numbers. Translation my own.
109 Bill McKibben, *Eaarth: Making a Life on a Tough New Planet* (New York: Henry Holt, 2010), 39–40.
110 Ibid.
111 Sigmund Freud, 'Animism, Magic and the Omnipotence of Thoughts', *SE* XIII, 76.
112 Ibid., 90.
113 Ibid., 97.
114 Ibid., 99.
115 In 'Jokes and their Relation to the Unconscious', *SE* VIII, 72; 'Delusions and Dreams in Jensen's *Gradiva*', *SE* IX, 8; 'From the History of an Infantile Neurosis',

SE XVII, 12; 'Psycho-Analysis and Telepathy', *SE* XVIII, 178; and 'Dreams and Occultism', *SE* XXII, 31.

116 Ernest Jones, *Sigmund Freud: Life and Works*, vol. III (London: Hogarth Press, 1957), 402.

117 Ibid., 414, 409, 408; Derrida writes that Freud was 'for a long time dancing the hesitation-waltz' around the idea of telepathy (Derrida, 'Telepathy', in *Psyche*, 238).

118 Freud, 'Animism', *SE* XIII, 77.

119 Freud, *GW* IX, 96.

120 Eduardo Viveiros de Castro, 'The Relative Native', trans. Julia Sauma and Martin Holbraad, *HAU: Journal of Ethnographic Theory* 3, no. 3 (2013): 490.

121 Freud, 'Animism', *SE* XIII, 77, emphasis added.

122 Derrida, 'Edmond Jabès and the Question of the Book', in *Writing and Difference*, 89.

123 Freud, 'Animism', *SE* XIII, 90.

124 Sigmund Freud, 'The Uncanny', *SE* XVII, 247–8.

125 Timothy Morton, *Ecology without Nature: Rethinking Environmental Aesthetics* (Cambridge, MA: Harvard University Press, 2007).

126 Bruno Latour and Timothy M. Lenton, 'Extending the Domain of Freedom, or Why Gaia Is So Hard to Understand', *Critical Inquiry* 45, no. 3 (2019): 670.

127 Bennett, *Vibrant Matter*, ix, viii.

128 Ibid., xvii–xviii.

129 Ibid., x.

130 The work of, e.g., David Abram, Tim Ingold, Bruno Latour, Caroline Rooney, Michel Serres.

131 Alf Hornborg, 'Animism, Fetishism, and Objectivism as Strategies for Knowing (or Not Knowing) the World', *Ethnos: Journal of Anthropology* 71, no. 1 (2006): 28.

132 Tim Ingold, 'Rethinking the Animate, Re-Animating Thought', *Ethnos: Journal of Anthropology* 71, no. 1 (2006): 10.

133 Cohen, 'The Geomorphic Fold', 76.

2 Surviving the Anthropocene: Revolutionary Rhythms

1 Lewis Carroll, *Alice's Adventures in Wonderland* (London: Macmillan, 1869), 11–12.

2 Sigmund Freud, 'A Difficulty in the Path of Psycho-Analysis', *SE* XVII, 140; *GW* XII, 7. Translation modified from 'token' to 'guarantee [*Gewähr*]', and from 'part' to 'role [*Rolle*]'.

3 Sigmund Freud, 'Fixation to Traumas – The Unconscious', *SE* XVI, 284–5. While 'something similar had already been asserted by Alexandrian science', the shift

from a geocentric to a heliocentric conception of the universe is, as Freud notes, 'associated in our minds with the name of Copernicus' (285).
4. Sigmund Freud, 'A Difficulty', *SE* XVII, 139–40.
5. Timothy Ferris, *Coming of Age in the Milky Way* (New York: HarperCollins, 2003), 34.
6. Jacques Derrida, 'White Mythology: Metaphor in the Text of Philosophy', *Margins of Philosophy*, trans. Alan Bass (Chicago: University of Chicago Press, 1982), 224.
7. Jacques Derrida, 'I Have a Taste for the Secret', in Derrida and Maurizio Ferraris, *A Taste for the Secret*, trans. Giacomo Donis (Cambridge: Polity Press, 2001), 9.
8. The three senses in the following paragraph can be traced back to the twelfth century (I); to *c.*1400 (II); and to the twelfth century (III). See 'revolution, n.', *OED*: etymology and definition II.7.a.
9. As Ferris notes, the heliocentric cosmology of Aristarchus 'predated that of Copernicus by some seventeen hundred years', but, unfortunately for science, it was 'all but forgotten'; Ferris, *Coming of Age*, 35, 38.
10. Jean Laplanche, 'The Unfinished Copernican Revolution', trans. Luke Thurston, in *Essays on Otherness*, ed. John Fletcher (London: Routledge, 1999), 55.
11. Laplanche suggests that the 'fate of the word "revolution" is linked in a curious manner to the name of Copernicus', and that 'only the properly astronomical or geometrical meaning of the term existed in his time'. This is not quite true: the revolutionary sense of 'revolution' – the sense of a great change or upheaval – was used, according to the *OED*, as early as 1400, and Copernicus' text was written in the 1530s, before being published in 1543. See Laplanche, 'The Unfinished Copernican Revolution', 53; and recorded uses of senses II.7.a. and b. of 'revolution, n.', *OED*.
12. Hubert Krivine, *The Earth: From Myths to Knowledge* (London: Verso, 2015), 125.
13. Ibid., emphasis added.
14. Laplanche, 'The Unfinished Copernican Revolution', 57.
15. Sigmund Freud, 'Beyond the Pleasure Principle', *SE* XVIII, 41.
16. The word comes from the name for the Arabic numbering system, *Alchoarismus*, a Latinization of the surname of mathematician Abū Jaʿfar Muhammad b. Mūsā. Etymologies of 'algorithm' and 'algorism', *OED*.
17. One of the compound words listed for 'rhythm', *OED*.
18. Kirsty Martin, *Modernism and the Rhythms of Sympathy: Vernon Lee, Virginia Woolf, D.H. Lawrence* (Oxford: OUP, 2013), 27–8.
19. David Wills, *Inanimation: Theories of Inorganic Life* (Minneapolis: University of Minnesota Press, 2016), 89.
20. Ibid., xii.
21. Virginia Woolf, letter to Vita Sackville-West, 7 January 1926, in *Letters of Virginia Woolf*, vol. III, ed. Nigel Nicholson and Joanne Trautmann (London: Hogarth Press: 1975–80), 227.

22 Virginia Woolf, 'A Letter to a Young Poet', in *The Virginia Woolf Reader*, ed. Mitchell A. Leaska (London: Harcourt, 1984), 271.
23 Virginia Woolf, 'Street Music', in *The Essays of Virginia Woolf*, vol. I. ed. Andrew McNeillie (London: Hogarth Press, 1986), 29–30.
24 Diana Swanson also recognizes a 'Copernican shift' in Woolf's writing, suggesting that the 'reframing and defamiliarizing of the human world in her later novels' can be traced to 'her experimental stories and sketches of 1917–1921' (such as 'The Mark on the Wall' and 'Kew Gardens') in 'Woolf's Copernican Shift: Nonhuman Nature in Virginia Woolf's Short Fiction', *Woolf Studies Annual* 18 (2012): 71.
25 Virginia Woolf, *A Room of One's Own and Three Guineas* (Oxford: OUP, 1998), 149.
26 Jemma Deer, 'Quenched: Five Fires for Thinking Extinction', *Oxford Literary Review* 41, no. 1 (July 2019): 13.
27 Virginia Woolf, *The Diary of Virginia Woolf*, vol. III, ed. Anne Olivier Bell and Andrew McNeillie (London: Hogarth Press, 1980), 76.
28 Virginia Woolf, *To the Lighthouse* (1927) (London: Penguin, 2000), 91, 140, 194. Further references are given parenthetically.
29 'The six characters were supposed to be one,' Woolf writes in a letter to G. L. Dickinson, 27 October 1931, in *Letters*, vol. IV, 397.
30 Woolf, *Diary*, vol. III, 203.
31 Virginia Woolf, *The Waves* (1931) (Harmondsworth: Penguin, 1973), 31, 69. Further references are given parenthetically.
32 There are just two human characters that appear towards the end of the section: the two cleaning women, Mrs McNab and Mrs Bast, who, rather problematically, given the classist implications, seem to have more in common with the non-human forces in the house than with the Ramsays. Mrs McNab is described as 'witless', 'lurch[ing]' and 'leer[ing]'; Mrs Bast as 'creak[ing]' (142, 151).
33 Woolf, letter to Vita Sackville-West, 7 January 1926, in *Letters*, vol. III, 227.
34 Leslie Stephen, *History of English Thought in the 18th Century*, vol. I (Cambridge: CUP, 1876, 2012), 48.
35 David Farrell Krell, *Derrida and Our Animal Others: Derrida's Final Seminar, 'The Beast and the Sovereign'* (Bloomington: Indiana University Press, 2013), 114.
36 Erich Auerbach, 'The Brown Stocking', *Mimesis: The Representation of Reality in Western Literature*, trans. Willard Trask (Princeton: PUP, 2013), 534.
37 Laura Marcus, *Virginia Woolf* (Devon: Northcote House, 2004), 88, 98–9.
38 Ibid., 99.
39 There are at least twenty instances in which Mrs Ramsay is described as looking out of or sitting/standing at a window. See *To the Lighthouse*, pages: 13, 20, 22, 38, 39, 43, 53, 55, 58, 88, 89, 97, 114, 119, 120, 126, 134 (twice), 191, 214.
40 Françoise Defromont, 'Mirrors and Fragments', trans. Rachel Bowlby, in *Virginia Woolf*, ed. Bowlby (London: Routledge, 1992), 64.

41 All of the text of the interludes is printed in italics.
42 He suggests that 'every word or phrase … is a portal. And the novel would be a place of portals, a portal of the name, and every word and phrase another portal.' Nicholas Royle, 'Jacques Derrida and the Future of the Novel', *Derrida Now: Current Perspectives in Derrida Studies*, ed. John W. P. Phillips (Cambridge: Polity Press, 2016), 204.
43 James Jeans, *The Mysterious Universe* (Cambridge: CUP, 1930), 3.
44 Gustavo Mercado, *The Filmmaker's Eye: Learning (and Breaking) the Rules of Cinematic Composition* (Boston: Focal Press/Elsevier, 2011), 149.
45 Rhett Herman, 'How Fast Is the Earth Moving?', *Scientific American*. Available online: https://www.scientificamerican.com/article/how-fast-is-the-earth-mov/ (accessed 31 March 2019).
46 Timothy Clark, *Ecocriticism on the Edge: The Anthropocene as a Threshold Concept* (London: Bloomsbury, 2015), 13.
47 Ibid., 38, 30.
48 Susan Stewart, *On Longing: Narratives of the Miniature, the Gigantic, the Souvenir, the Collection* (Durham, NC: Duke University Press, 1993), 55.
49 Clark, *Ecocriticism on the Edge*, 72.
50 As, for example, in the passage discussed by Auerbach that describes the formation and falling of a tear in darkness that occurs without any explanation or anchoring (*To the Lighthouse*, 33), *Mimesis*, 532.
51 Caroline Rooney, *African Literature, Animism and Politics* (London: Routledge, 2000), 25, 164.
52 I am referring to the famous 'double-slit experiment', in which light is shown to behave alternatively as a particle or as a wave, depending on whether it is observed or not.
53 Brian Cox and Jeff Forshaw, *The Quantum Universe* (Boston, MA: Da Capo Press, 2011), 16, emphasis added.
54 Jim Al-Khalili and Johnjoe Mcfadden, *Life on the Edge: The Coming of Age of Quantum Biology* (London: Bantam, 2014), 23.
55 Ibid.
56 Ibid., 297 fig. 10.1, 296.
57 Tim Ingold, 'Rethinking the Animate, Re-Animating Thought', *Ethnos: Journal of Anthropology* 71, no. 1 (2006): 19.
58 Ibid., 10.
59 Jeans, *The Mysterious Universe*, 77.
60 Gillian Beer, *Virginia Woolf: The Common Ground* (Edinburgh: EUP, 1996), 113.
61 Jeans, *The Mysterious Universe*, 79.
62 Frédérique Aït-Touati, *Fictions of the Cosmos: Science and Literature in the Seventeenth Century*, trans. Susan Emanuel (Chicago: University of Chicago Press, 2011), 19.

63 Woolf, *A Room of One's Own and Three Guineas*, 143.
64 Woolf, *Diary*, vol. III, 337.
65 Beer, *The Common Ground*, 121.
66 Martin, *Modernism*, 115.
67 Karen Barad, 'Quantum Entanglements and Hauntological Relations of Inheritance: Dis/continuities, SpaceTime Enfoldings, and Justice-to-Come', *Derrida Today* 3, no. 2 (2010): 260.
68 J. Hillis Miller, 'Anachronistic Reading', *Derrida Today* 3, no. 1 (2010): 76.
69 Jacques Derrida, 'Signature Event Context', trans. Samuel Weber and Jeffrey Mehlman, *Limited Inc* (Evanston, IL: Northwestern University Press, 1988), 9.
70 Jacques Derrida, 'Freud and the Scene of Writing', in *Writing and Difference*, trans. Alan Bass (London: Routledge, 2001), 284.
71 Derrida, 'Signature Event Context', 10, 9.
72 Ibid., 9–10. For an explanation of Derrida's notion of 'differance', see Jemma Deer, 'Deconstruction', *Oxford Research Encyclopedia of Literature* (Oxford: OUP, 2020).
73 Rooney, *African Literature*, 133.
74 David Wills, 'Post/Card/Match/Book/"Envois"/Derrida', *SubStance* 13, no. 2 (1984): 34.
75 Jacques Derrida, 'Force and Signification', in *Writing and Difference*, 12.
76 Rooney, *African Literature*, 92.
77 Leo Bersani, *Thoughts and Things* (Chicago: University of Chicago Press, 2015), 89.
78 Ibid., 89.
79 Ibid., 83.
80 Ibid., 94–5.
81 This passage brings to mind a moment in Hélène Cixous's *Three Steps on the Ladder of Writing*, trans. Sarah Cornell and Susan Sellers (New York: Columbia University Press, 1993), 151:

> There is passage through the animal state, then through the vegetal state, and so we move away from humankind; from the vegetal we descend into the earth, by the stem, by the root, until we reach what doesn't concern us, although it exists and inscribes itself, which is of the mineral order, although it doesn't hold together since we are aiming toward disassembly, toward decomposition.

82 Bersani, *Thoughts and Things*, 80.
83 Woolf, letter to Vita Sackville-West, 3 December 1939, in *Letters*, vol. VI, 373.
84 Jeans, *The Mysterious Universe*, 144.
85 Gillian Beer, *Darwin's Plots: Evolutionary Narrative in Darwin, George Eliot and Nineteenth Century Fiction* (Cambridge: CUP, 1983, 2000), 12.
86 See 'will-o'-the-wisp' and '*ignis fatuus*', *OED*. That such fire is cause by the 'spontaneous combustion of an inflammable gas … derived from decaying organic matter' serves to redouble Woolf's metaphor.

87   Beer, *The Common Ground*, 133.
88   Similarly, in *Night and Day* (1920) (New York: Harvest, 1948), there is a mention of Sir Thomas Browne's *Urn Burial*, and the vessels are later paired with another symbol of death: 'urns and skulls', 75, 456.
89   Epigenetics names the changes in organisms caused by modification of gene expression rather than alteration of the genetic code itself.
90   In *The Waves* too, trailing has to do with language. Bernard's phrases are said to 'trail away' (14), words 'trail drearily' for Louis (81), and Susan jumps after 'words that trailed … escaping' (164).
91   Jacques Derrida, *The Beast and the Sovereign*, vol. II, trans. Geoff Bennington, ed. Michel Lisse, Marie-Louise Mallet and Ginette Michaud (Chicago: University of Chicago Press, 2009), 130–1.
92   Susan Dick, 'Literary Realism in *Mrs Dalloway*, *To the Lighthouse*, *Orlando* and *The Waves*', in *The Cambridge Companion to Virginia Woolf*, ed. Sue Roe and Susan Sellers (Cambridge: CUP, 2000), 67.
93   Jacques Derrida, 'Living On', trans. James Hulbert, *Deconstruction and Criticism*, ed. Harold Bloom (London: Continuum, 1979, 2004), 79.
94   Ibid., 82.
95   Marcus, *Virginia Woolf*, 138.
96   Derrida, 'Living On', 83.
97   Ibid., 82–3.
98   Michel Serres, '*Feux et Signaux de Brume*: Virginia Woolf's Lighthouse', trans. Judith Adler, *SubStance* 37, no. 2 (2008): 123, 128. Serres also calls Woolf an 'animist'.
99   Beer, *The Common Ground*, 118.
100 Elizabeth Kolbert, *The Sixth Extinction: An Unnatural History* (London: Bloomsbury, 2014), 268.
101 Ibid., 267–8.
102 Ibid., 17.
103 I have explored the relation between speed and extinction further in 'Quenched: Five Fires for Thinking Extinction', 1–17.
104 Claire Colebrook, *Death of the Post Human: Essays on Extinction*, vol. I (Ann Arbor, MI: Open Humanities Press, 2014), 40.
105 Jacques Derrida, 'No Apocalypse, Not Now: Full Speed Ahead, Seven Missiles, Seven Missives', trans. Catherine Porter and Philip Lewis, *Psyche: Inventions of the Other*, vol. I, ed. Peggy Kamuf and Elizabeth Rottenberg (Stanford: SUP, 2007), 393–4.
106 Hans M. Kristensen and Robert S. Norris, 'Status of World Nuclear Forces', *Federation of American Scientists*. Available online: https://fas.org/issues/nuclear-weapons/status-world-nuclear-forces/ (accessed 7 April 2019).

107 Derrida, 'No Apocalypse, Not Now', 387.
108 Rob Nixon, *Slow Violence and the Environmentalism of the Poor* (Cambridge, MA: Harvard University Press, 2011), 2.
109 Tom Cohen, 'Anecographics: Climate Change and "Late" Deconstruction', in *Impasses of the Post-Global: Theory in the Era of Climate Change*, ed. Henry Sussman (Ann Arbor, MI: Open Humanities Press, 2012), 43.
110 Timothy Morton, 'Poisoned Ground: Art and Philosophy in the Time of Hyperobjects', *Symploke* 21, nos. 1–2 (2013): 37, 44.
111 Ibid., 40.
112 Jacques Derrida, 'Telepathy', trans. Nicholas Royle, in *Psyche*, 259.
113 Owen Gaffney and Will Steffen, 'The Anthropocene Equation', *Anthropocene Review* 4, no. 1 (2017): 3.
114 Kolbert, *The Sixth Extinction*, 123–4.
115 David A. Collings, *Stolen Future, Broken Present: The Human Significance of Climate Change* (Ann Arbor, MI: Open Humanities Press, 2014), 15.
116 Ibid., 129, 134.
117 Nicholas Royle, *Jacques Derrida* (London: Routledge, 2003), 21–3.
118 David Wallace-Wells, *The Uninhabitable Earth: A Story of the Future* (London: Allen Lane, an imprint of Penguin Books, 2019), 199.
119 Bruno Latour and Timothy M. Lenton, 'Extending the Domain of Freedom, or Why Gaia Is So Hard to Understand', *Critical Inquiry* 45, no. 3 (2019): 661.
120 Martin Heidegger, *The Fundamental Concepts of Metaphysics: World, Finitude, Solitude*, trans. William McNeill and Nicholas Walker (Bloomington: Indiana University Press, 1995), 176. Further references are given parenthetically.
121 Derrida, *The Beast and the Sovereign*, 6.
122 See, in particular, 196–7.
123 Derrida, *The Beast and the Sovereign*, 197.
124 Sarah Wood, *Without Mastery: Reading and Other Forces* (Edinburgh: EUP, 2014), 8.

3 Animals at the End of the World: The Evolution of Life and Language

1 Charles Darwin, *On the Origin of Species: By Means of Natural Selection* (London: John Murray, 1859), 484. This is from the first edition. Later quotations are from another edition, as referenced.
2 Helen Macdonald, *H is for Hawk* (London: Jonathan Cape, 2014), 5.
3 In what follows, I have chosen to use the uncommon plural 'deers' (used 'occasionally', according to the *OED*; here is such an occasion) to oppose the

violence of the invariant plural I commented on above. If you, dear reader, happen to find it jarring, so much the better.

4 All biblical references are to the King James Version, and the Hebrew references are taken from the interlinear English–Hebrew translation. Available online: http://biblehub.com/interlinear/genesis/1.htm (accessed 8 April 2019).

5 David Farrell Krell, *Derrida and Our Animal Others: Derrida's Final Seminar, 'The Beast and the Sovereign'* (Bloomington: Indiana University Press, 2013), 160.

6 Nick Lane, *The Vital Question: Why Is Life the Way It Is?* (London: Profile, 2015), 80–1.

7 As Hélène Cixous writes: 'We must all deal with the unconscious effects of our proper name. We find this aspect of language's intervention in our destiny on the flesh of our imagination.' Cixous, *Three Steps on the Ladder of Writing*, trans. Sarah Cornell and Susan Sellers (New York: Columbia University Press, 1993), 145.

8 Jacques Derrida, *Of Grammatology*, trans. Gayatri Chakravorty Spivak (Baltimore: Johns Hopkins University Press, 1976), 217.

9 Charles Darwin, *On the Origin of Species: By Means of Natural Selection*, vol. II (New York: PF Collier, 1909), 526, 525.

10 Ibid., 95.

11 Ibid., 97.

12 Human minds have played a part in the development of various domesticated species, but these conscious effects are negligible on the long scale of the evolution of life on earth. Further, the origins of what we call 'domestication' would not have been entirely intentional, as I will go on to discuss.

13 Gillian Beer remarks on the 'dysteleological' character of evolutionary theory in *Darwin's Plots: Evolutionary Narrative in Darwin, George Eliot and Nineteenth Century Fiction* (Cambridge: CUP, 1983, 2000), xviii.

14 Michael Pollan, *The Botany of Desire: A Plant's Eye View of the World* (New York: Random House, 2001), xiv.

15 Ibid., xiv.

16 Ibid., xx.

17 Ibid.

18 Ibid., xv.

19 Yuval Noah Harari, *Sapiens: A Brief History of Humankind* (New York: Harper Collins, 2015), 81.

20 Ibid.

21 Jane Bennett, *Vibrant Matter: A Political Ecology of Things* (Durham, NC: Duke University Press, 2010), 34.

22 Charles Darwin, *The Descent of Man*, vol. I (New York: Appleton, 1872), 53, 58–9, 57.

23 Daniel Dennett, *From Bacteria to Bach and Back: The Evolution of Minds* (New York: Norton, 2017), 182.
24 Gillian Beer, *Open Fields: Science in Cultural Encounter* (Oxford: OUP, 1996), 95.
25 Lane, *The Vital Question*, 35.
26 Darwin, *Descent of Man*, 51–2.
27 Ibid., 34.
28 Jacques Derrida, *The Animal That Therefore I Am*, ed. Marie-Louise Mallet, trans. David Wills (New York: Fordham University Press, 2008), 40–1. Further references are given parenthetically, with the abbreviation *A* where appropriate.
29 Giorgio Agamben, *The Open: Man and Animal* (Stanford: SUP, 2004), 26.
30 Walter Benjamin, 'On Language as Such and on the Language of Man' (1916), trans. Edmund Jephcott, in *Selected Writings*, vol. I, ed. Marcus Bullock and Michael W. Jennings (Cambridge, MA: Belknap Press of Harvard University Press, 2002), 62, 64, emphasis added.
31 Thomas A. Sebeok, 'Communication', in *A Sign Is Just a Sign* (Bloomington: Indiana University Press, 1991), 22, quoted in Timo Maran, 'Biosemiotic Criticism', in *The Oxford Handbook of Ecocriticism*, ed. Greg Garrard (New York: Oxford University Press, 2014), 261.
32 As Jesper Hoffmeyer writes, 'It's questionable, in fact, if one can at all understand advanced biochemistry and molecular biology without thinking in semiotic terms', *Biosemiotics: An Examination into the Signs of Life and the Life of Signs* (Scranton, PA: University of Scranton Press, 2008), 15. Hoffmeyer's book gives emphasis to the internal biosemiotics, or endosemiotics, of organisms.
33 Thomas A. Sebeok, *An Introduction to Semiotics* (Toronto: University of Toronto Press, 2001), 13.
34 Jacques Derrida, 'Envois', in *The Post Card: From Socrates to Freud and Beyond*, trans. Alan Bass (Chicago: University of Chicago Press, 1987), 66.
35 Benjamin, 'On Language as Such', 72, 71.
36 Ibid., second emphasis added.
37 This fact is perhaps what necessitates the prohibition of God's 'name': the ineffability of YHWH is an assurance against the name doing without the bearer. Only God knows how to pronounce his own name, and the 'I am that I am [*ehyeh ăšer ehyeh*, which becomes, elliptically, *yhwh*]' (Exod. 3.14) at its root does its best to collapse the distance between being and name. No one can say YHWH. I can, however, write and read it without any trouble – which suggests that 'effability' cannot, finally, be prevented, even by God.
38 Jacques Derrida, *The Beast and the Sovereign*, vol. II, trans. Geoff Bennington, ed. Michel Lisse, Marie-Louise Mallet and Ginette Michaud (Chicago: University of Chicago Press, 2009, 2011), 266.

39 Sarah Wood, *Without Mastery: Reading and Other Forces* (Edinburgh: EUP, 2014), 30.
40 Jacques Derrida, 'Violence and Metaphysics', in *Writing and Difference*, trans. Alan Bass (London: Routledge, 2001), 112. Ellipses in original.
41 Jacques Derrida, 'Edmond Jabès and the Question of the Book', in *Writing and Difference*, 89.
42 Jacques Derrida, 'White Mythology: Metaphor in the Text of Philosophy', in *Margins of Philosophy*, trans. Alan Bass (Chicago: University of Chicago Press, 1982), 213.
43 Ibid., 248.
44 Derrida, 'A Silkworm of One's Own', in Hélène Cixous and Derrida, *Veils*, trans. Geoffrey Bennington (Stanford: SUP, 2001), 89.
45 Wood, *Without Mastery*, 25.
46 Jacques Derrida, 'This Strange Institution Called Literature', trans. Geoffrey Bennington and Rachel Bowlby, in *Acts of Literature*, ed. Derek Attridge (London: Routledge, 1992), 36–8.
47 E.g. Thomas Nagel's essay 'What Is It Like to Be a Bat?' does not tell us what it is like to be a bat. Rather, it tells us why such knowledge is impossible. Thomas Nagel, 'What Is It Like to Be a Bat?', *Philosophical Review* 83, no. 4 (1974): 439.
48 Macdonald, *H is for Hawk*, 82. Further references are given parenthetically.
49 Derrida, 'White Mythology', in *Margins of Philosophy*, 241.
50 Nicholas Royle, *Quilt* (Brighton: Myriad, 2010), 52. Further references are given parenthetically.
51 Derrida, *The Beast and the Sovereign*, 8–9.
52 Ibid., 265.
53 Ibid., 266, 265.
54 Ibid., 268.
55 Wood, *Without Mastery*, 32.
56 Jacques Derrida, 'As If It Were Possible, "Within Such Limits"…', trans. Benjamin Elwood and Elizabeth Rottenberg, in *Negotiations: Interventions and Interviews, 1971–2001*, ed. Elizabeth Rottenberg (Stanford: SUP, 2002), 353, 354.
57 Michael Naas, *The End of the World and Other Teachable Moments: Jacques Derrida's Final Seminar* (New York: Fordham University Press, 2015), 47.
58 Derrida, *The Beast and the Sovereign*, 9, 266.
59 Beer, *Darwin's Plots*, 12.
60 Kari Weil, *Thinking Animals: Why Animal Studies Now?* (New York: Columbia University Press, 2012), 17.
61 Samuel Weber, *The Legend of Freud* (Stanford: SUP, 2000), 28, 29.
62 Elizabeth Grosz, 'Darwin and Ontology', *Public* 26 (2002): 41.
63 Darwin, *Origin of Species*, vol. II, 527–8.

64 Ibid., 528.
65 Beer, *Darwin's Plots*, xix.
66 Ibid., xxiii–xxiv.
67 Jeremy Davies, *The Birth of the Anthropocene* (Oakland: University of California Press, 2016), 139–40.
68 Jordan Gaines Lewis, 'Smells Ring Bells: How Smell Triggers Memories and Emotions', *Psychology Today*, January 2015. Available online: https://www.psychologytoday.com/blog/brain-babble/201501/smells-ring-bells-how-smell-triggers-memories-and-emotions (accessed 19 April 2019).
69 Karl Marx, *Capital*, vol. I, trans. Ben Fowkes (London: Penguin, 1976), 176, 169. Translation modified. The English translation has 'magic and necromancy' for '*Zauber and Spuk*'.
70 Ibid., 165.
71 Keston Sutherland, *Stupefaction: A Radical Anatomy of Phantoms* (Calcutta: Seagull Books, 2011), 52.
72 Marx, *Capital*, vol. I, 163.
73 Ibid.
74 Ibid., 164.
75 Sutherland, *Stupefaction*, 43.
76 Translation my own.
77 Sutherland, *Stupefaction*, 41.
78 Ibid., 43.
79 Ibid., 49, 47–8.
80 'UK Cow Numbers', *AHDB* (Agriculture and Horticulture Development Board) website (March 2019). Available online: http://dairy.ahdb.org.uk/market-information/farming-data/cow-numbers/uk-cow-numbers/ (accessed 19 April 2019).
81 Ruth Bollongino, Joachim Burger, Adam Powell, Marjan Mashkour, Jean-Denis Vigne and Mark G. Thomas, 'Modern Taurine Cattle Descended from Small Number of Near-Eastern Founders', *Molecular Biology and Evolution* 29, no. 9 (2012): 2101.
82 Julia Kollewe, 'Bank of England to keep animal fat in banknotes despite complaints', *The Guardian* (11 August 2017). Available online: https://www.theguardian.com/business/2017/aug/10/bank-of-england-to-keep-animal-fat-in-banknotes-despite-complaints (accessed 19 April 2019).
83 Harari, *Sapiens*, 379.
84 For an ironic yet plausible vision of such a future see Simon Amstell's mockumentary *Carnage* (London: BBC, 2017).
85 See George Monbiot, 'How We Ended Up Paying Farmers to Flood Our Homes', *The Guardian* (18 February 2014). Available online: http://www.theguardian.com/

commentisfree/2014/feb/17/farmers-uk-flood-maize-soil-protection (accessed 19 April 2019).
86. Simon Fairlie, 'Can Britain Feed Itself?', *The Land* 4 (Winter 2007/8): 19, 20.
87. 'Regulating for People, the Environment and Growth: 2017 Summary', *Environment Agency*, October 2018. Available online: https://assets.publishing.service.gov.uk/government/uploads/system/uploads/attachment_data/file/748416/Regulating_for_people_the_environment_and_growth_2017_summary.pdf (accessed 19 April 2019).
88. According to a recent meta-analysis, a global switch to a plant-based diet would be the fourth most effective reduction in greenhouse gases, coming in above, e.g., switching to solar, nuclear and offshore wind power. See Paul Hawken, *Drawdown: The Most Comprehensive Plan Ever Proposed to Reverse Global Warming* (New York: Penguin Books, 2017), 222.
89. 'EU Farming Support Package Allocations Announced', *Gov.uk*. Available online: https://www.gov.uk/government/news/eu-farming-support-package-allocations-announced (accessed 19 April 2019).
90. Jacques Derrida, 'Eating Well', trans. Peter Connor and Avital Ronell, in *Points… Interviews 1974–1994*, ed. Elisabeth Weber, trans. Peggy Kamuf et al. (Stanford: SUP, 1995), 280.
91. David Wood, 'The Eleventh Plague: Thinking Ecologically after Derrida', in *Eco-Deconstruction: Derrida and Environmental Philosophy*, ed. Matthias Fritsch, Philippe Lynes and David Wood (New York: Fordham University Press, 2018), 36.
92. Charles Dodgson gave a version called *Alice's Adventures under Ground* to Alice Liddell as a Christmas gift. See Peter Hunt, 'Introduction', in Lewis Carroll, *Alice's Adventures in Wonderland and Through the Looking Glass*, ed. Peter Hunt (Oxford: OUP, 2009), xxv–xxvi. The strangeness of separating the two words (i.e. 'under Ground' instead of 'underground', the latter compound having been in use since the seventeenth century) has the effect of emphasizing the 'Ground' which it undermines – a fact that, given Dodgson was a logician, is worthy of note.
93. Lewis Carroll, *Alice's Adventures in Wonderland and Through the Looking Glass*, ed. Peter Hunt (Oxford: OUP, 2009), 11. Further references are given parenthetically.
94. Its meat was mainly too tough to eat, but its stomach, however, was the 'best-tasting' part and 'so large that 2 men can make a delicious meal'. Journal of Heyndrick Dirrecksen Jolinck (20 September 1600). Quoted in Jolyon C. Parish, *The Dodo and the Solitaire: A Natural History* (Bloomington: Indiana University Press, 2013), 14.
95. Robert Douglas-Fairhurst, *The Story of Alice* (Harvard: HUP, 2015), 422.
96. Derrida, 'Eating Well', 258.
97. Ibid., 261–2.
98. Ibid., 278.

99 Ibid.
100 Ibid., 279.
101 Robert Alter, *The Hebrew Bible: A Translation with Commentary*, vol. I (New York: Norton, 2019), 17 n. 15.
102 Ibid., 15 n. 1. Alter writes, 'In the kind of pun in which the ancient Hebrew writers delighted, *arum*, "cunning," plays against *arumim*, "naked," of the previous verse.'
103 Paul Celan, *Atemwende* (Frankfurt am Main: Suhrkamp, 1967), 93. The poem is printed in its entirety (in German and English) in Jacques Derrida, 'Rams: Uninterrupted Dialogue – Between Two Infinities, the Poem', trans. Thomas Dutoit and Philippe Romanski, in *Sovereignties in Question: the Poetics of Paul Celan*, ed. Thomas Dutoit and Outi Pasanen (New York: Fordham University Press, 2005), 141.
104 Derrida, 'Rams', 161–2.
105 Ibid., 159.
106 Sarah Wood, 'A Huge Thing', *Oxford Literary Review* 35, no. 1 (2013): 82.
107 Derrida, 'Rams', 140.

4 Hatching: Psychoanalysis and the Textual Unconscious

1 Sigmund Freud, letter to Wilhelm Fliess, 29 November 1895, in *The Complete Letters of Sigmund Freud to Wilhelm Fliess: 1887–1904*, trans. Jeffrey M. Masson (Cambridge, MA: Harvard University Press, 1985), 152.
2 Sigmund Freud, 'The Ego and the Id', *SE* XIX, 13.
3 Ibid., 19, emphasis in original.
4 Jacques Derrida, 'Differance', in *Speech and Phenomena and Other Essays on Husserl's Theory of Signs*, trans. David Allison (Evanston, IL: Northwestern University Press, 1973), 151–2.
5 Ibid., 152.
6 Sigmund Freud, 'The Unconscious', *SE* XIV, 169.
7 Decisions are made up to ten seconds before they enter conscious awareness. See Chun Siong Soon, Marcel Brass, Hans-Jochen Heinze and John-Dylan Haynes, 'Unconscious Determinants of Free Decisions in the Human Brain', *Nature Neuroscience* 11, no. 5 (2008): 543–5.
8 Derrida, 'Differance', in *Speech and Phenomena*, 152.
9 Sigmund Freud, 'A Difficulty in the Path of Psycho-Analysis', *SE* XVII, 141.
10 Ibid., 139.
11 Sigmund Freud, 'Fixation to Traumas – The Unconscious', *SE* XVI, 285. He uses the same phrase when he discusses the blows in 'A Difficulty', *SE* XVII, 143.
12 Sigmund Freud, 'Fixation to Traumas', *SE* XVI, 284–5.

13 The image of the house might be apt for another reason too. Yuval Noah Harari speculates that the agricultural revolution – which saw humans leave behind a nomadic lifestyle in favour of fixed houses from which they could tend their crops – had an impact that 'was psychological as much as architectural': 'attachment to "my house" and separation from the neighbours became the psychological hallmark of a much more self-centred creature.' Was the physical house the precursor to the Freudian house of the mind? Did the feeling of mastery that early humans experienced in their own homes enable the species to presume mastery over the rest of the world? Yuval Noah Harari, *Sapiens: A Brief History of Humankind* (New York: HarperCollins, 2015), 98–9.
14 William T. Vollmann, *Carbon Ideologies*, vol. I (New York: Viking, 2018), 3.
15 Eli Zaretsky, *Political Freud: A History* (New York: Columbia University Press, 2015), 28.
16 Lawrence R. Samuel, '"Order Out of Chaos": Freud, Fascism, and the Golden Age of American Advertising', in *The Oxford Handbook of Propaganda Studies*, ed. Jonathan Auerbach and Russ Castronovo (Oxford: OUP, 2013), 261–77.
17 For a documentary exploration of Bernays's role in transforming consumerism in America, see Adam Curtis, *The Century of the Self* (London: BBC Four, 2002).
18 Edward L. Bernays, 'Manipulating Public Opinion: The Why and The How', *American Journal of Sociology* 33, no. 6 (1928): 958–71; Bernays, *The Engineering of Consent* (Norman: University of Oklahoma Press, 1955).
19 Samuel, '"Order Out of Chaos"', 264–70.
20 Ibid., 268.
21 Ibid., 266, 262.
22 Joseph Dodds, *Psychoanalysis and Ecology at the Edge of Chaos: Complexity Theory, Deleuze/Guattari and Psychoanalysis for a Climate in Crisis* (London: Routledge, 2011), 7.
23 George Marshall, *Don't Even Think About It: Why Our Brains Are Wired to Ignore Climate Change* (London: Bloomsbury, 2014); Kari Marie Norgaard, *Living in Denial: Climate Change, Emotions, and Everyday Life* (Cambridge, MA: MIT Press, 2011); Sally Weintrobe, *Engaging with Climate Change: Psychoanalytic and Interdisciplinary Perspectives* (London: Routledge, 2013).
24 Marshall, *Don't Even Think About It*, 105.
25 Sigmund Freud, 'Beyond the Pleasure Principle', *SE* XVIII, 24, 7. Further references are given parenthetically, with the abbreviation *BPP* where appropriate. When I am also quoting from the German (*GW* XIII), the page number for the latter is given following a slash.
26 Sigmund Freud, 'Anxiety and Instinctual Life', *SE* XXII, 95.
27 Jacques Derrida, 'The Supplement of Copula: Philosophy before Linguistics', in *Margins of Philosophy*, trans. Alan Bass (Chicago: University of Chicago Press, 1982), 180.

28 Sigmund Freud, 'The Interpretation of Dreams', *SE* IV, 278.
29 Sigmund Freud, 'The Aetiology of Hysteria', *SE* III, 192.
30 Freud, 'The Interpretation of Dreams', *SE* IV, 277.
31 Jacques Derrida, 'Force and Signification', in *Writing and Difference*, trans. Alan Bass (London: Routledge, 2001), 31.
32 Jacques Derrida, 'Des Tours de Babel', trans. Joseph F. Graham, in *Psyche: Inventions of the Other*, vol. I, ed. Peggy Kamuf and Elizabeth Rottenberg (Stanford: SUP, 2007), 202, 197.
33 Ibid., 223, emphasis added.
34 See Jacques Derrida, 'To Speculate – On Freud' (1980), in *The Post Card: From Socrates to Freud and Beyond*, trans. Alan Bass (Chicago: University of Chicago Press, 1987), in particular 284, 354–5, and throughout.
35 Ibid., 214.
36 Hélène Cixous, *Reading with Clarice Lispector*, trans. Verena Andermatt Conley (Minneapolis: University of Minnesota Press, 1990), 105.
37 Sigmund Freud, 'Animism, Magic and the Omnipotence of Thoughts', *SE* XIII, 88.
38 Ibid., 77, 90.
39 Jacques Derrida, *H. C. for Life, That Is to Say…*, trans. Laurent Milesi and Stefan Herbrechter (Stanford: SUP, 2006), 111; 111–12.
40 Sigmund Freud, letter to Wilhelm Fliess, 21 September 1897, in *Complete Letters of Sigmund Freud to Wilhelm Fliess*, 264.
41 Sigmund Freud, 'Psychical (or Mental) Treatment', *SE* VII, 283; *GW* V, 289.
42 Ibid., 284/291.
43 Ibid., 283/289.
44 What follows has been modified from an article originally published in the *Oxford Literary Review*. Jemma Deer, 'More Strange Return: What Freud Owes Literature', *Oxford Literary Review* 38, no. 2 (2016): 221–39.
45 William Shakespeare, *Hamlet*, ed. G. R. Hibbard (Oxford: OUP, 1987), 4.7.53-58.
46 Sarah Kofman, *Freud and Fiction*, trans. Sarah Wykes (Cambridge: Polity Press, 1974, 1991), 7.
47 Derrida, 'My Chances/*Mes Chances*: A Rendezvous with Some Epicurean Stereophonies', trans. Irene Harvey and Avital Ronell, in *Psyche*, 361.
48 Ann Wordsworth, 'Chance in Other Words', *Oxford Literary Review* 12, no. 1&2 (1990): 228.
49 Ibid.
50 Translation modified. The Strachey translation uses 'staging' again here to indicate the theatrical analogy – 'staging the disappearance and return of the objects within his reach' (15) – but the German reads as follows: '*dasselbe Verschwinden und Wiederkommen mit den ihm erreichbaren Gegenständen selbst* in Szene setzte', *GW* XIII, 13.

51 Derrida, 'To Speculate – On Freud', in *The Post Card*, 262.
52 Ibid., 261, 269.
53 Ibid., 268.
54 David Wills, *Inanimation: Theories of Inorganic Life* (Minneapolis: University of Minnesota Press, 2016), 72, 73.
55 Ibid., 9.
56 Samuel Weber, 'Sidestepping: "Freud after Derrida"', *Mosaic* 44, no. 3 (2011): 5.
57 Caroline Rooney, *African Literature, Animism and Politics* (London: Routledge, 2000), 137.
58 Ibid., 140.
59 Ibid., 141.
60 Sigmund Freud, 'Animism', *SE* XIII, 75, 91.
61 Derrida, *H. C. for Life*, 113.
62 Peter Brooks, 'Freud's Masterplot', *Yale French Studies* 55/56 (1977): 299, 283.
63 Ibid., 285.
64 Derrida discusses Freud's disappointment that it does not occur to Ernst to play at train in 'To Speculate – On Freud', in *The Post Card*, 314–16.
65 William Shakespeare, *Hamlet: The Texts of 1603 and 1623*, ed. Ann Thompson and Neil Taylor (London: Arden Shakespeare, 2006), 5.2.312–13 and the note to line 313 (p. 358).
66 William Shakespeare, *Hamlet*, ed. Ann Thompson and Neil Taylor (London: Arden Shakespeare, 2006), 1.5.165–6. This edition gives 'your philosophy', but I have followed the Folio edition, which gives the more general 'our'. For Freud's use of the phrase, see note 114 of Chapter 1.
67 Freud, 'The Interpretation of Dreams', *SE* IV, 263.
68 Sigmund Freud, letter to Fliess, 15 October 1897, in *Complete Letters of Sigmund Freud to Wilhelm Fliess*, 272.
69 Freud, 'The Interpretation of Dreams', *SE* IV, 264.
70 Ibid.
71 This is not the only psychoanalytic reading, but rather, as I will go on to explain, specifically suited to confirming Freud's own theories. Jean-Michel Rabaté, in his survey of psychoanalytic readings of the play, notes how Ella Sharpe offers an opposing view:

> Her 1929 paper on Hamlet reverses the usual pattern: whereas most commentators insist on the indecision of the hero, she foregrounds his haste and precipitation. Sharpe's provocative thesis is that to describe *Hamlet* as the tragedy of procrastination is misleading. It makes more sense to characterize it as the "tragedy of impatience," by which she means that, in spite of the protracted denouement of the last act, the main symptom exhibited by the play's eponymous hero is melancholia caused by a failed mourning.

See Rabaté, *The Cambridge Introduction to Literature and Psychoanalysis* (Cambridge: CUP, 2014), 31.
72 Freud, 'The Interpretation of Dreams', *SE* IV, 265.
73 Ibid.
74 Maurice Charney, *Hamlet's Fictions* (Oxon: Routledge, 1988), 48.
75 Shakespeare, *Hamlet* (2006), 3.1.78–9. Further references given parenthetically.
76 Ernest Jones, 'The Œdipus-Complex as an Explanation of Hamlet's Mystery: A Study in Motive', *American Journal of Psychology* 21, no. 1 (1910): 86.
77 Rooney, *African Literature*, 142.
78 Freud, 'The Ego and the Id', *SE* XIX, 46.
79 William Shakespeare, *Twelfth Night*, ed. Keir Elam (London: Arden Shakespeare, 2008), 3.3.15–16; Shakespeare, *The Merry Wives of Windsor*, ed. Giorgio Melchiori (London: Arden Shakespeare, 2000), 4.6.28.
80 While this sense of 'coil' as concentric rings of rope has no recorded usage in the *OED* prior to 1611 as a verb (v.3), and 1627 as a noun (n.3), the etymology of the former recognizes that 'as nautical words, they were no doubt in spoken use much earlier'. That given, it is fair to assume that Shakespeare would have been aware of these senses too.
81 André Green, *The Tragic Effect: The Oedipus Complex in Tragedy*, trans. Alan Sheridan (Cambridge: CUP, 1979), 1.
82 It perhaps goes without saying that the fact that I can reinscribe Freud's words for my own purpose here – as he so often did with Shakespeare's – attests to Derrida's recognition that 'inscription has as its essential objective, and indeed takes this fatal risk, the emancipation of meaning', 'Force and Signification', in *Writing and Difference*, 13.
83 Etymology of '*Beispiel*, n.', Friedrich Kluge, *Etymological Dictionary of the German Language*, translated by John Francis Davis (London: George Bell, 1891), 25.
84 Freud, 'Psychical (or Mental) Treatment', *SE* VII, 283.
85 Rooney, *African Literature*, 70–1.
86 Kofman, *Freud and Fiction*, 3, 4.
87 Sigmund Freud, 'An Autobiographical Study', *SE* XX, 63; See Kofman, *Freud and Fiction*, 39, 64, 71, 100, 129, 157.
88 Kofman, *Freud and Fiction*, 7.
89 Ibid., 28–9.
90 Sigmund Freud, 'Psychopathic Characters on the Stage', *SE* VII, 310. Similarly, in 'An Autobiographical Study', he remarks that before the psychoanalytic interpretation '*Hamlet* … had been admired for three hundred years without its meaning being discovered or its author's motives guessed', *SE* XX, 63.
91 Avital Ronell, 'Goethezeit', in *Taking Chances: Derrida, Psychoanalysis, and Literature*, ed. Joseph H. Smith and William Kerrigan (Baltimore: Johns Hopkins University Press, 1984), 147.

92 Jacques Derrida, *The Ear of the Other: Otobiography, Transference, Translation*, trans. Peggy Kamuf, ed. Christie V. McDonald (New York: Schocken Books, 1985), 70.
93 Derrida, 'My Chances', in *Psyche*, 360.
94 Nicholas Royle, *Veering* (Edinburgh: EUP, 2011), 75.
95 Sarah Wood, *Without Mastery: Reading and Other Forces* (Edinburgh: EUP, 2014), 82.
96 Timothy Clark, *The Theory of Inspiration: Composition as a Crisis of Subjectivity in Romantic and Post-Romantic Writing* (Manchester: MUP, 1997), 15.
97 Ibid., 23–4.
98 Ibid., 3.
99 Clarice Lispector, 'The Egg and the Chicken' (1964), in *Complete Stories*, trans. Katrina Dodson (London: Penguin, 2015), 276; Lispector, 'O ovo e a galinha', in *A Legião Estrangeira*, ed. Coleção Nosso Tempo (São Paulo: Editora Atica, 1983), 49. Further quotations given parenthetically, with the abbreviation E where appropriate. When I am also quoting from the Portuguese text, the page number for the latter is given following a slash.
100 Cixous, *Reading with Clarice Lispector*, 101, 111.
101 Clark, *Theory of Inspiration*, 275.
102 Derrida, 'Force and Signification', in *Writing and Difference*, 12.
103 Hélène Cixous, 'Clarice Lispector: The Approach', in *Coming to Writing and Other Essays*, trans. Sarah Cornell, Deborah Jenson, Ann Liddle and Susan Sellars, ed. Jenson (Cambridge, MA: Harvard University Press, 1991), 70–1.
104 There is also a strange recurrence of egg-imagery running through the play: Polonius telling Laertes to steer clear of 'new-hatched, unfledged' fellows (1.3.64); Hamlet noting how Fortinbras will expose 'what is mortal and unsure / To all that fortune, death and danger dare / Even for an eggshell' (4.4.50–2); and Horatio likening Osric to a 'lapwing' that 'runs away with the shell on his head' (5.2.165–6). Eggs, in these instances, seem to have to do with certain rash or impulsive behaviours.
105 Sigmund Freud, letter to Fliess, 29 November 1895, in *Complete Letters of Sigmund Freud to Wilhelm Fliess*, 152; and letter to Jung, 04 October 1909, in *The Freud/Jung Letters*, trans. Ralph Manheim and R. F. C. Hull (Princeton: PUP, 1974), 248. The German can be found in Freud, *Briefe an Wilhelm Fliess, 1887–1904*, ed. Jeffrey Moussaieff Masson and Michael Schröter (Frankfurt am Main: Fischer, 1986), 158. Interestingly, Jung picked up the same metaphor when he wrote to Freud some fifteen months later (18 January 1911) about his own nascent transgressions against the latter; he says, 'It is a risky business for an egg to try to be cleverer than the hen. Still, what is in the egg must eventually summon the courage to creep out. So you see what fantasies I must resort to in order to protect

myself against your criticism' (*The Freud/Jung Letters*, 385). Freud's 'eggs', it seems, were wont to hatch into creatures that turned against or away from him.
106 Clark, *Theory of Inspiration*, 29–30.
107 Hélène Cixous, *Manna: For the Mandelstams for the Mandelas*, trans. Catherine A. F. MacGillivray (Minneapolis: University of Minnesota Press, 1993), 103, 104, 103.
108 David Adams Leeming, *Creation Myths of the World: An Encyclopedia*, vol. I (Santa Barbara, CA: ABC-Clio, 2010), 12.
109 Ibid., 13, 313.
110 Marie Louise von Franz, *Creation Myths* (Boston: Shambala, 1995), 229, quoted in Leeming, *Creation Myths of the World*, 314.
111 Leeming, *Creation Myths of the World*, 314.
112 Derrida, 'Differance', in *Speech and Phenomena*, 143.
113 Ibid., 141.
114 Ibid., 151, 156, 154.
115 Claire Colebrook, 'Archiviolithic: The Anthropocene and the Hetero-Archive', *Derrida Today* 7, no. 1 (2014): 34–5.
116 Wills, *Inanimation*, 156, 158.
117 Walter Benjamin, 'On Language as Such and on the Language of Man' (1916), trans. Edmund Jephcott, in *Selected Writings*, vol. I, ed. Marcus Bullock and Michael W. Jennings (Cambridge, MA: Belknap Press of Harvard University Press, 2002), 69.
118 Wills, *Inanimation*, 158.
119 Derrida, 'Differance', in *Speech and Phenomena*, 144.
120 Elissa Marder, *The Mother in the Age of Mechanical Reproduction: Psychoanalysis, Photography, Deconstruction* (New York: Fordham University Press, 2012), 44.
121 Derrida, 'Des Tours de Babel', in *Psyche*, 223.
122 Derrida, *The Ear of the Other*, 158.
123 Lewis Carroll, *Alice's Adventures in Wonderland and Through the Looking Glass* (Oxford: OUP, 2009), 41.
124 Cixous, *Reading with Clarice Lispector*, 101.
125 Sigmund Freud, 'The Uncanny', *SE* XVII, 221.
126 Derrida, *The Ear of the Other*, 158.
127 Ibid., 157.
128 I. A. Richards, 'The Interactions of Words', in *The Language of Poetry*, ed. Allen Tate (New York: Russell and Russell, 1960), 76.
129 Freud, letter to Fliess, 29 November 1895, in *Complete Letters of Sigmund Freud to Wilhelm Fliess*, 152. Further references are given parenthetically. When I am also quoting from the German edition (*Briefe an Wilhelm Fliess*), the page number for the latter is given following a slash.

130 James Strachey, 'Editor's Introduction' to *Project for a Scientific Psychology*, *SE* I, 290.
131 Ibid.
132 James Strachey, 'Editor's Introduction' to *Beyond*, *SE* XVIII, 6.
133 Derrida, 'To Speculate – On Freud', in *The Post Card*, 269.
134 Ibid., 336.
135 Ibid., 406.
136 We can assume that Freud would have been more aware of this etymology than most, given his medical training and the relative frequency with which he wrote about 'oedema' (swelling); see e.g. *SE* I, 168, 177.
137 Freud, 'The Interpretation of Dreams', *SE* IV, 261; *GW* II–III, 268. Translation modified from 'record' to 'trace [*Spur*]'.
138 Etymology of 'trace, v.1', *OED*; and of *Spur*, Kluge, *Etymological Dictionary of the German Language*, 344.
139 Freud, 'The Interpretation of Dreams', *SE* IV, 263.
140 Derrida, 'My Chances', in *Psyche*, 353.
141 Derrida, 'Force and Signification', in *Writing and Difference*, 11.
142 Ibid., 12.
143 Clark, *Theory of Inspiration*, 18–19.
144 Freud, 'A Difficulty', *SE* XVII, 139.
145 Ibid.
146 Sigmund Freud, 'On Narcissism', *SE* XIV, 73–4.
147 Freud, 'A Difficulty', *SE* XVII, 139.
148 Ibid., 140, 141.
149 Pleshette DeArmitt, *The Right to Narcissism: A Case for an Im-possible Self-Love* (New York: Fordham University Press, 2014), 2.
150 Ibid., 3.
151 Ibid., 140.
152 Freud, 'Fixation to Traumas', *SE* XVI, 285.
153 Freud, 'On Narcissism', *SE* XIV, 94.
154 Ibid., 95.
155 Ibid., 101.
156 Freud, 'A Difficulty', *SE* XVII, 143.
157 Claire Colebrook, 'Not Symbiosis, Not Now: Why Anthropogenic Change Is Not Really Human', *Oxford Literary Review* 34, no. 2 (2012): 202.
158 Jacques Derrida, 'There is No *One* Narcissism', trans. Peggy Kamuf, in *Points … Interviews 1974–1994*, ed. Elisabeth Weber, trans. Peggy Kamuf et al. (Stanford: SUP, 1995), 199.
159 Dodds, *Psychoanalysis and Ecology at the Edge of Chaos*, 200–1.

Conclusion

1 Sigmund Freud, 'Animism, Magic and the Omnipotence of Thoughts', *SE* XIII, 85.
2 Ibid., 77, 90.
3 Jacques Derrida, *Of Grammatology*, trans. Gayatri Chakravorty Spivak (Baltimore: Johns Hopkins University Press, 1976), 144–5.

Bibliography

Agamben, Giorgio. *The Open: Man and Animal*. Stanford: SUP, 2004.
Aït-Touati, Frédérique. *Fictions of the Cosmos: Science and Literature in the Seventeenth Century*. Translated by Susan Emanuel. Chicago: University of Chicago Press, 2011.
Al-Khalili, Jim, and Johnjoe Mcfadden. *Life on the Edge: The Coming of Age of Quantum Biology*. London: Bantam, 2014.
Alter, Robert. *The Hebrew Bible: A Translation with Commentary*. Vol. I. New York: Norton, 2019.
Amstell, Simon, dir. *Carnage*. London: BBC, 2017.
Arnett, L. D. 'The Soul: A Study of Past and Present Beliefs'. *American Journal of Psychology* 15, no. 2 (1904): 347–82.
Auerbach, Erich. *Mimesis: The Representation of Reality in Western Literature*. Translated by Willard Trask. Princeton: PUP, 2013.
Barad, Karen. 'Quantum Entanglements and Hauntological Relations of Inheritance: Dis/continuities, SpaceTime Enfoldings, and Justice-to-Come'. *Derrida Today* 3, no. 2 (2010): 240–68.
Beer, Gillian. *Darwin's Plots: Evolutionary Narrative in Darwin, George Eliot and Nineteenth Century Fiction*. Cambridge: CUP, 1983, 2000.
Beer, Gillian. *Open Fields: Science in Cultural Encounter*. Oxford: OUP, 1996.
Beer, Gillian. *Virginia Woolf: The Common Ground*. Edinburgh: EUP, 1996.
Benjamin, Walter. 'On Language as Such and on the Language of Man'. Translated by Edmund Jephcott. In *Selected Writings*. Vol. I, edited by Marcus Bullock and Michael W. Jennings, 62–74. Cambridge, MA: Belknap Press of Harvard University Press, 2002.
Bennett, Jane. *Vibrant Matter: A Political Ecology of Things*. Durham, NC: Duke University Press, 2010.
Bernays, Edward L. *The Engineering of Consent*. Norman: University of Oklahoma Press, 1955.
Bernays, Edward L. 'Manipulating Public Opinion: The Why and The How'. *American Journal of Sociology* 33, no. 6 (1928): 958–71.
Bersani, Leo. *Thoughts and Things*. Chicago: University of Chicago Press, 2015.
Bollongino, Ruth, Joachim Burger, Adam Powell, Marjan Mashkour, Jean-Denis Vigne and Mark G. Thomas. 'Modern Taurine Cattle Descended from Small Number of Near-Eastern Founders'. *Molecular Biology and Evolution* 29, no. 9 (2012): 2101–4.
Bristow, Tom. *The Anthropocene Lyric: An Affective Geography of Poetry, Person, Place*. Houndmills: Palgrave Macmillan, 2015.

Brooks, Peter. 'Freud's Masterplot'. *Yale French Studies* 55/56 (1977): 280–300.
Carroll, Lewis. *Alice's Adventures in Wonderland*. London: Macmillan, 1869.
Carroll, Lewis. *Alice's Adventures in Wonderland and Through the Looking Glass*. Edited by Peter Hunt. Oxford: OUP, 2009.
Celan, Paul. *Atemwende*. Frankfurt am Main: Suhrkamp, 1967.
Charney, Maurice. *Hamlet's Fictions*. Oxon: Routledge, 1988.
Cixous, Hélène. *Coming to Writing and Other Essays*. Translated by Sarah Cornell, Deborah Jenson, Ann Liddle and Susan Sellars. Edited by Deborah Jenson. Cambridge, MA: Harvard University Press, 1991.
Cixous, Hélène. *Manna: For the Mandelstams for the Mandelas*. Translated by Catherine A. F. MacGillivray. Minneapolis: University of Minnesota Press, 1993.
Cixous, Hélène. *Reading with Clarice Lispector*. Translated by Verena Andermatt Conley. Minneapolis: University of Minnesota Press, 1990.
Cixous, Hélène. *Three Steps on the Ladder of Writing*. Translated by Sarah Cornell and Susan Sellers. New York: Columbia University Press, 1993.
Clark, Timothy. *Ecocriticism on the Edge: The Anthropocene as a Threshold Concept*. London: Bloomsbury, 2015.
Clark, Timothy. 'Editorial'. *Oxford Literary Review* 34, no. 2 (2012): v–vi.
Clark, Timothy. 'Some Climate Change Ironies: Deconstruction, Environmental Politics and the Closure of Ecocriticism'. *Oxford Literary Review* 32, no. 1 (2010): 131–49.
Clark, Timothy. *The Theory of Inspiration: Composition as a Crisis of Subjectivity in Romantic and Post-Romantic Writing*. Manchester: MUP, 1997.
Cohen, Tom. 'Anecographics: Climate Change and "Late" Deconstruction'. In *Impasses of the Post-Global: Theory in the Era of Climate Change*, edited by Henry Sussman, 34–57. Ann Arbor, MI: Open Humanities Press, 2012.
Cohen, Tom. 'The Geomorphic Fold: Anapocalyptics, Changing Climes and "Late" Deconstruction'. *Oxford Literary Review* 32, no. 1 (2010): 71–89.
Colebrook, Claire. 'Archiviolithic: The Anthropocene and the Hetero-Archive'. *Derrida Today* 7, no. 1 (2014): 21–43.
Colebrook, Claire. *Death of the Post Human: Essays on Extinction*. Vol. I. Ann Arbor, MI: Open Humanities Press, 2014.
Colebrook, Claire. 'Not Symbiosis, Not Now: Why Anthropogenic Change Is Not Really Human'. *Oxford Literary Review* 34, no. 2 (2012): 185–209.
Collings, David A. *Stolen Future, Broken Present: The Human Significance of Climate Change*. Ann Arbor, MI: Open Humanities Press, 2014.
Cox, Brian, and Jeff Forshaw. *The Quantum Universe*. Boston, MA: Da Capo Press, 2011.
Crick, Joyce. 'Note on the Translation'. In Franz Kafka. *The Metamorphosis and Other Stories*. Translated by Joyce Crick, xi–xxxiii. Oxford: OUP, 2009.
Crutzen, Paul J. 'Geology of Mankind'. *Nature* 415 (2002): 23.
Curtis, Adam. *The Century of the Self*. London: BBC Four, 2002.
Darwin, Charles. *The Descent of Man*. Vol. I. New York: Appleton, 1872.

Darwin, Charles. *On the Origin of Species: By Means of Natural Selection*. London: John Murray, 1859.

Darwin, Charles. *On the Origin of Species: By Means of Natural Selection*. Vol. II. New York: PF Collier, 1909.

Davies, Jeremy. *The Birth of the Anthropocene*. Oakland: University of California Press, 2016.

DeArmitt, Pleshette. *The Right to Narcissism: A Case for an Im-possible Self-Love*. New York: Fordham University Press, 2014.

de Castro, Eduardo Viveiros. 'The Relative Native'. Translated by Julia Sauma and Martin Holbraad. *HAU: Journal of Ethnographic Theory* 3, no. 3 (2013): 473–502.

Deer, Jemma. 'Deconstruction'. *Oxford Research Encyclopedia of Literature*. Oxford: OUP, 2020.

Deer, Jemma. 'More Strange Return: What Freud Owes Literature'. *Oxford Literary Review* 38, no. 2 (2016): 221–39.

Deer, Jemma. 'Quenched: Five Fires for Thinking Extinction'. *Oxford Literary Review* 41, no. 1 (2019): 1–17.

Defromont, Françoise. 'Mirrors and Fragments'. Translated by Rachel Bowlby. In *Virginia Woolf*, edited by Bowlby, 62–76. London: Routledge, 1992.

Demos, T. J. *Against the Anthropocene: Visual Culture and Environment Today*. Berlin: Sternberg Press, 2017.

Dennett, Daniel. *From Bacteria to Bach and Back: The Evolution of Minds*. New York: Norton, 2017.

Derrida, Jacques. *The Animal That Therefore I Am*. Edited by Marie-Louise Mallet. Translated by David Wills. New York: Fordham University Press, 2008.

Derrida, Jacques. 'As If It Were Possible, "Within Such Limits"…'. Translated by Benjamin Elwood and Elizabeth Rottenberg. In *Negotiations: Interventions and Interviews, 1971–2001*, edited by Elizabeth Rottenberg. Stanford: SUP, 2002.

Derrida, Jacques. 'Autoimmunity: Real and Symbolic Suicides –'. Translated by Pascale-Anne Brault and Michael Naas. In *Philosophy in a Time of Terror*, edited by Giovanna Borradori, 84–136. Chicago: University of Chicago Press, 2003.

Derrida, Jacques. *The Beast and the Sovereign*. Vol. II. Translated by Geoff Bennington. Edited by Michel Lisse, Marie-Louise Mallet and Ginette Michaud. Chicago: University of Chicago Press, 2011.

Derrida, Jacques. *The Ear of the Other: Otobiography, Transference, Translation*. Translated by Peggy Kamuf. Edited by Christie V. McDonald. New York: Schocken Books, 1985.

Derrida, Jacques. 'Eating Well'. Translated by Peter Connor and Avital Ronell. In *Points… Interviews 1974–1994*, edited by Elisabeth Weber, 255–87. Stanford: SUP, 1995.

Derrida, Jacques. *Glas*. Translated by John P. Leavey and Richard Rand. Lincoln: University of Nebraska Press, 1990.

Derrida, Jacques. *H. C. for Life, That Is to Say ...*. Translated by Laurent Milesi and Stefan Herbrechter. Stanford: SUP, 2006.
Derrida, Jacques. 'I Have a Taste for the Secret'. In Jacques Derrida and Maurizio Ferraris. *A Taste for the Secret*. Translated by Giacomo Donis, 3–92. Cambridge: Polity Press, 2001.
Derrida, Jacques. 'Living On'. Translated by James Hulbert. In *Deconstruction and Criticism*, edited by Harold Bloom, 75–176. London: Continuum, 1979, 2004.
Derrida, Jacques. *Margins of Philosophy*. Translated by Alan Bass. Chicago: University of Chicago Press, 1982.
Derrida, Jacques. *Of Grammatology*. Translated by Gayatri Chakravorty Spivak. Baltimore: Johns Hopkins University Press, 1976.
Derrida, Jacques. *The Post Card: From Socrates to Freud and Beyond*. Translated by Alan Bass. Chicago: University of Chicago Press, 1987.
Derrida, Jacques. *Psyche: Inventions of the Other*. Vol. I. Edited by Peggy Kamuf and Elizabeth Rottenberg. Stanford: SUP, 2007.
Derrida, Jacques. 'Psychoanalysis Searches the States of Its Soul: The Impossible Beyond of a Sovereign Cruelty'. Translated by Peggy Kamuf, 238–80. In *Without Alibi*. Stanford: SUP, 2002.
Derrida, Jacques. 'Rams: Uninterrupted Dialogue – Between Two Infinities, the Poem'. Translated by Thomas Dutoit and Philippe Romanski. Translation revised by Thomas Dutoit and Outi Pasanen. In *Sovereignties in Question: the Poetics of Paul Celan*, edited by Thomas Dutoit and Outi Pasanen, 135–63. New York: Fordham University Press, 2005.
Derrida, Jacques. 'Signature Event Context'. Translated by Samuel Weber and Jeffrey Mehlman. In *Limited Inc.*, 1–23. Evanston, IL: Northwestern University Press, 1988.
Derrida, Jacques. 'A Silkworm of One's Own'. In Hélène Cixous and Jacques Derrida. *Veils*. Translated by Geoffrey Bennington, 17–92. Stanford: SUP, 2001.
Derrida, Jacques. *Specters of Marx: The State of the Debt, the Work of Mourning, and the New International*. Translated by Peggy Kamuf. London: Routledge, 1994.
Derrida, Jacques. *Speech and Phenomena and Other Essays on Husserl's Theory of Signs*. Translated by David Allison. Evanston, IL: Northwestern University Press, 1973.
Derrida, Jacques. 'There Is No One Narcissism'. Translated by Peggy Kamuf. In *Points... Interviews 1974–1994*, edited by Elisabeth Weber, 196–215. Stanford: SUP, 1995.
Derrida, Jacques. 'This Strange Institution Called Literature'. Translated by Geoffrey Bennington and Rachel Bowlby. In *Acts of Literature*, edited by Derek Attridge, 33–75. London: Routledge, 1992.
Derrida, Jacques. *Writing and Difference*. Translated by Alan Bass. London: Routledge, 2001.
Dick, Susan. 'Literary Realism in *Mrs Dalloway*, *To the Lighthouse*, *Orlando* and *The Waves*'. In *The Cambridge Companion to Virginia Woolf*, edited by Sue Roe and Susan Sellers, 50–71. Cambridge: CUP, 2000.

Dodds, Joseph. *Psychoanalysis and Ecology at the Edge of Chaos: Complexity Theory, Deleuze/Guattari and Psychoanalysis for a Climate in Crisis*. London: Routledge, 2011.
Douglas-Fairhurst, Robert. *The Story of Alice*. Harvard: HUP, 2015.
Fairlie, Simon. 'Can Britain Feed Itself?'. *The Land* 4 (2007–8): 18–26.
Ferris, Timothy. *Coming of Age in the Milky Way*. New York: HarperCollins, 2003.
Frazer, James. *The Golden Bough: A Study in Magic and Religion*. London: Macmillan, 1922.
Freud, Sigmund. *Briefe an Wilhelm Fliess, 1887–1904*. Edited by Jeffrey M. Masson and Michael Schröter. Frankfurt am Main: Fischer, 1986.
Freud, Sigmund. *The Complete Letters of Sigmund Freud to Wilhelm Fliess: 1887–1904*. Translated by Jeffrey M. Masson. Cambridge, MA: Harvard University Press, 1985.
Freud, Sigmund. *The Freud/Jung Letters*. Translated by Ralph Manheim and R. F. C. Hull. Princeton: PUP, 1974.
Freud, Sigmund. *Gesammelte Werke*. Vols I–XVIII. London: Imago, 1940–52.
Freud, Sigmund. *The Standard Edition of the Complete Psychological Works of Sigmund Freud*. Vols I–XXIV. Translated and edited by James Strachey, Alix Strachey and Alan Tyson. London: Hogarth Press, 1953–74.
Gaffney, Owen, and Will Steffen. 'The Anthropocene Equation'. *Anthropocene Review* 4, no.1 (2017): 53–61.
Glendinning, Simon. 'The End of the World Designed with Men in Mind'. *Journal of Historical Sociology* 26, no. 3 (2013): 291–317.
Goethe, Johann Wolfgang von. *Der Zauberlehrling*. Edited by Heidrun Boddin. Munich: Middelhauve, 1999.
Green, André. *The Tragic Effect: The Oedipus Complex in Tragedy*. Translated by Alan Sheridan. Cambridge: CUP, 1979.
Griffiths, Jay. *Wild: An Elemental Journey*. London: Penguin, 2008.
Grosz, Elizabeth. 'Darwin and Ontology'. *Public* 26 (2002): 38–48.
Harari, Yuval Noah. *Sapiens: A Brief History of Humankind*. New York: Harper Collins, 2015.
Haraway, Donna. 'Cosmopolitical Critters'. In *Cosmopolitan Animals*, edited by Kaori Nagai, Karen Jones, Donna Landry, Monica Mattfield, Caroline Rooney and Charlotte Seigh, vii–xiv. Basingstoke: Palgrave Macmillan, 2015.
Hawken, Paul. *Drawdown: The Most Comprehensive Plan Ever Proposed to Reverse Global Warming*. New York: Penguin Books, 2017.
Heidegger, Martin. *The Fundamental Concepts of Metaphysics: World, Finitude, Solitude*. Translated by William McNeill and Nicholas Walker. Bloomington: Indiana University Press, 1995.
Herman, Rhett. 'How Fast Is the Earth Moving?' *Scientific American*. Accessed 31 March 2019. https://www.scientificamerican.com/article/how-fast-is-the-earth-mov/.
Hoffmeyer, Jesper. *Biosemiotics: An Examination into the Signs of Life and the Life of Signs*. Scranton, PA: University of Scranton Press, 2008.

Hornborg, Alf. 'Animism, Fetishism, and Objectivism as Strategies for Knowing (or Not Knowing) the World'. *Ethnos: Journal of Anthropology* 71, no. 1 (2006): 21–32.

Horton, Robin. *Patterns of Thought in Africa and the West: Essays on Magic, Religion and Science.* Cambridge: CUP, 1997.

Hunt, Peter. 'Introduction'. In Lewis Carroll. *Alice's Adventures in Wonderland and Through the Looking Glass*, edited by Peter Hunt, vi–xlii. Oxford: OUP, 2009.

Ingold, Tim. 'Rethinking the Animate, Re-Animating Thought'. *Ethnos: Journal of Anthropology* 71, no. 1 (2006): 9–20.

Jeans, James. *The Mysterious Universe.* Cambridge: CUP, 1930.

Jones, Ernest. 'The Œdipus-Complex as an Explanation of Hamlet's Mystery: A Study in Motive'. *American Journal of Psychology* 21, no. 1 (1910): 72–113.

Jones, Ernest. *Sigmund Freud: Life and Works.* Vol. III. London: Hogarth Press, 1957.

Kafka, Franz. *The Metamorphosis and Other Stories.* Translated by Joyce Crick. Oxford: OUP, 2009.

Kafka, Franz. *Die Verwandlung.* Frankfurt am Main: Fischer, 1982.

Kamuf, Peggy, ed. *A Derrida Reader: Between the Blinds.* London: Harvester, 1991.

King, Lester S. 'Stahl and Hoffmann: A Study in Eighteenth Century Animism'. *Journal of the History of Medicine* 19, no. 2 (1964): 118–30.

Klein, Naomi. *This Changes Everything: Capitalism vs the Climate.* London: Penguin, 2014.

Kluge, Friedrich. *Etymological Dictionary of the German Language.* Translated by John Francis Davis. London: George Bell, 1891.

Kofman, Sarah. *Freud and Fiction.* Translated by Sarah Wykes. Cambridge: Polity Press, 1974, 1991.

Kolbert, Elizabeth. *The Sixth Extinction: An Unnatural History.* London: Bloomsbury, 2014.

Kollewe, Julia. 'Bank of England to keep animal fat in banknotes despite complaints'. *The Guardian*, 11 August 2017. Accessed 19 April. https://www.theguardian.com/business/2017/aug/10/bank-of-england-to-keep-animal-fat-in-banknotes-despite-complaints.

Krell, David Farrell. *Derrida and Our Animal Others: Derrida's Final Seminar, 'The Beast and the Sovereign'.* Bloomington: Indiana University Press, 2013.

Kristensen, Hans M., and Robert S. Norris. 'Status of World Nuclear Forces'. *Federation of American Scientists.* Accessed 7 April 2019. https://fas.org/issues/nuclear-weapons/status-world-nuclear-forces/.

Krivine, Hubert. *The Earth: From Myths to Knowledge.* London: Verso, 2015.

Lane, Nick. *The Vital Question: Why Is Life the Way It Is?* London: Profile, 2015.

Laplanche, Jean. 'The Unfinished Copernican Revolution'. Translated by Luke Thurston. In *Essays on Otherness*, edited by John Fletcher, 53–85. London: Routledge, 1999.

Latour, Bruno. *Facing Gaia: Eight Lectures on the New Climatic Regime.* Translated by Catherine Porter. Cambridge: Polity Press, 2017.

Latour, Bruno, and Timothy M. Lenton. 'Extending the Domain of Freedom, or Why Gaia Is So Hard to Understand'. *Critical Inquiry* 45, no. 3 (2019): 659–80.

Leeming, David Adams. *Creation Myths of the World: An Encyclopedia*. Vol. I. Santa Barbara, CA: ABC-Clio, 2010.

Lewis, Jordan Gaines. 'Smells Ring Bells: How Smell Triggers Memories and Emotions'. *Psychology Today*, 12 January 2015. https://www.psychologytoday.com/blog/brain-babble/201501/smells-ring-bells-how-smell-triggers-memories-and-emotions.

Lispector, Clarice. *A Legião Estrangeira*. Edited by Coleção Nosso Tempo. São Paulo: Editora Atica, 1983.

Lispector, Clarice. *Complete Stories*. Translated by Katrina Dodson. London: Penguin, 2015.

Macdonald, Helen. *H is for Hawk*. London: Jonathan Cape, 2014.

Maran, Timo. 'Biosemiotic Criticism'. In *The Oxford Handbook of Ecocriticism*, edited by Greg Garrard, 260–75. New York: Oxford University Press, 2014.

Marcus, Laura. *Virginia Woolf*. Devon: Northcote House, 2004.

Marder, Elissa. *The Mother in the Age of Mechanical Reproduction: Psychoanalysis, Photography, Deconstruction*. New York: Fordham University Press, 2012.

Marshall, George. *Don't Even Think About It: Why Our Brains Are Wired to Ignore Climate Change*. London: Bloomsbury, 2014.

Martin, Kirsty. *Modernism and the Rhythms of Sympathy: Vernon Lee, Virginia Woolf, D.H. Lawrence*. Oxford: OUP, 2013.

Marx, Karl. *Capital*. Vol. I. Translated by Ben Fowkes. London: Penguin, 1976.

Marx, Karl. *Capital*. Vol. III. Translated by David Fernbach. London: Penguin, 1981.

McKibben, Bill. *Eaarth: Making a Life on a Tough New Planet*. New York: Henry Holt, 2010.

Mercado, Gustavo. *The Filmmaker's Eye: Learning (and Breaking) the Rules of Cinematic Composition*. Boston: Focal Press/Elsevier, 2011.

Miller, J. Hillis. 'Anachronistic Reading'. *Derrida Today* 3, no. 1 (2010): 75–91.

Monbiot, George. 'How We Ended Up Paying Farmers to Flood Our Homes'. *The Guardian*, 18 February 2014. Accessed 19 April 2019. http://www.theguardian.com/commentisfree/2014/feb/17/farmers-uk-flood-maize-soil-protection.

Morton, Timothy. *Ecology without Nature: Rethinking Environmental Aesthetics*. Cambridge, MA: Harvard University Press, 2007.

Morton, Timothy. 'Poisoned Ground: Art and Philosophy in the Time of Hyperobjects'. *Symploke* 21, no. 1 (2013): 37–50.

Naas, Michael. *The End of the World and Other Teachable Moments: Jacques Derrida's Final Seminar*. New York: Fordham University Press, 2015.

Nagel, Thomas. 'What Is It Like to Be a Bat?'. *Philosophical Review* 83, no. 4 (1974): 435–50.

Nixon, Rob. *Slow Violence and the Environmentalism of the Poor*. Cambridge, MA: Harvard University Press, 2011.

Norgaard, Kari Marie. *Living in Denial: Climate Change, Emotions, and Everyday Life*. Cambridge, MA: MIT Press, 2011.

Parish, Jolyon C. *The Dodo and the Solitaire: A Natural History*. Bloomington: Indian University Press, 2013.

Pollan, Michael. *The Botany of Desire: A Plant's Eye View of the World*. New York: Random House, 2001.

Povinelli, Elizabeth A. *Geontologies: A Requiem to Late Liberalism*. Durham, NC: Duke University Press, 2016.

Rabaté, Jean-Michel. *The Cambridge Introduction to Literature and Psychoanalysis*. Cambridge: CUP, 2014.

Richards, I. A. 'The Interactions of Words'. In *The Language of Poetry*, edited by Allen Tate, 65–87. New York: Russell and Russell, 1960.

Ronell, Avital. 'Goethezeit'. In *Taking Chances: Derrida, Psychoanalysis, and Literature*, edited by Joseph H. Smith and William Kerrigan, 146–82. Baltimore: Johns Hopkins University Press, 1984.

Rooney, Caroline. *African Literature, Animism and Politics*. London: Routledge, 2000.

Royle, Nicholas. *Jacques Derrida*. Londo: Routledge, 2003.

Royle, Nicholas. 'Jacques Derrida and the Future of the Novel'. In *Derrida Now: Current Perspectives in Derrida Studies*, edited by John W. P. Phillips, 184–212. Cambridge: Polity Press, 2016.

Royle, Nicholas. *Quilt*. Brighton: Myriad, 2010.

Royle, Nicholas. 'Reading Joseph Conrad: Episodes from the Coast'. *Mosaic* 47, no. 1 (2014): 41–67.

Royle, Nicholas. *Veering*. Edinburgh: EUP, 2011.

Samuel, Lawrence R. ' "Order Out of Chaos": Freud, Fascism, and the Golden Age of American Advertising'. In *The Oxford Handbook of Propaganda Studies*, edited by Jonathan Auerbach and Russ Castronovo, 261–77. Oxford: OUP, 2013.

Sebeok, Thomas A. *A Sign Is Just a Sign*. Bloomington: Indiana University Press, 1991.

Sebeok, Thomas A. *An Introduction to Semiotics*. Toronto: University of Toronto Press, 2001.

Serres, Michel. '*Feux et Signaux de Brume*: Virginia Woolf's Lighthouse'. Translated by Judith Adler. *SubStance* 37, no. 2 (2008): 110–31.

Shakespeare, William. *Hamlet*. Edited by G. R. Hibbard. Oxford: OUP, 1987.

Shakespeare, William. *Hamlet*. Edited by Ann Thompson and Neil Taylor. London: Arden Shakespeare, 2006.

Shakespeare, William. *Hamlet: The Texts of 1603 and 1623*. Edited by Ann Thompson and Neil Taylor. London: Arden Shakespeare, 2006.

Shakespeare, William. *Macbeth*. Edited by Sandra Clark and Pamela Mason. London: Arden Shakespeare, 2015.

Shakespeare, William. *The Merry Wives of Windsor*. Edited by Giorgio Melchiori. London: Arden Shakespeare, 2000.

Shakespeare, William. *Twelfth Night*. Edited by Keir Elam. London: Arden Shakespeare, 2008.

Solnick, Sam. *Poetry and the Anthropocene: Ecology, Biology and Technology in Contemporary British and Irish Poetry*. London: Routledge, 2017.

Soon, Chun Siong, Marcel Brass, Hans-Jochen Heinze and John-Dylan Haynes. 'Unconscious Determinants of Free Decisions in the Human Brain'. *Nature Neuroscience* 11, no. 5 (2008): 543–5.

Stephen, Leslie. *History of English Thought in the 18th Century*. Vol. I. Cambridge: CUP, 1876, 2012.

Stewart, Susan. *On Longing: Narratives of the Miniature, the Gigantic, the Souvenir, the Collection*. Durham, NC: Duke University Press, 1993.

Stringer, Martin D. 'Rethinking Animism: Thoughts from the Infancy of Our Discipline'. *Journal of the Royal Anthropological Institute* 5, no. 4 (1999): 541–56.

Sutherland, Keston. *Stupefaction: A Radical Anatomy of Phantoms*. Calcutta: Seagull Books, 2011.

Swanson, Diana. 'Woolf's Copernican Shift: Nonhuman Nature in Virginia Woolf's Short Fiction'. *Woolf Studies Annual* 18 (2012): 53–74.

Szerszynski, Bronislaw. 'The End of the End of Nature: The Anthropocene and the Fate of the Human'. *Oxford Literary Review* 34, no. 2 (2012): 165–84.

Trexler, Adam. *Anthropocene Fictions: The Novel in a Time of Climate Change*. Charlottesville: University of Virginia Press, 2015.

Tylor, E. B. *Primitive Culture: Researches into the Development of Mythology, Philosophy, Religion, Art, and Custom*. Vol. I. London: John Murray, 1871.

Tylor, E. B. 'The Religion of Savages'. *Fortnightly Review* 6 (1866): 71–86.

Vollmann, William T. *Carbon Ideologies*. Vol. I. New York: Viking, 2018.

von Franz, Marie Louise. *Creation Myths*. Boston: Shambala, 1995.

Wallace-Wells, David. *The Uninhabitable Earth: A Story of the Future*. London: Allen Lane, an imprint of Penguin Books, 2019.

Weber, Samuel. *The Legend of Freud*. Stanford: SUP, 2000.

Weber, Samuel. 'Sidestepping: "Freud after Derrida"'. *Mosaic* 44, no. 3 (2011): 1–14.

Weil, Kari. *Thinking Animals: Why Animal Studies Now?* New York: Columbia University Press, 2012.

Weintrobe, Sally. *Engaging with Climate Change: Psychoanalytic and Interdisciplinary Perspectives*. London: Routledge, 2013.

Wills, David. *Inanimation: Theories of Inorganic Life*. Minneapolis: University of Minnesota Press, 2016.

Wills, David. 'Post/Card/Match/Book/"Envois"/Derrida'. *SubStance* 13, no. 2 (1984): 19–38.

Wood, David. 'The Eleventh Plague: Thinking Ecologically after Derrida'. In *Eco-Deconstruction: Derrida and Environmental Philosophy*, edited by Matthias Fritsch, Philippe Lynes and David Wood, 24–49. New York: Fordham University Press, 2018.

Wood, Michael. *Literature and the Taste of Knowledge*. Cambridge: CUP, 2005.

Wood, Sarah. *Derrida's Writing and Difference: A Reader's Guide*. London: Continuum, 2009.
Wood, Sarah. 'A Huge Thing'. *Oxford Literary Review* 35, no. 1 (2013): 79–88.
Wood, Sarah. *Without Mastery: Reading and Other Forces*. Edinburgh: EUP, 2014.
Woolf, Virginia. *The Diary of Virginia Woolf*. Vols I–V. Edited by Anne Olivier Bell and Andrew McNeillie. London: Hogarth Press, 1977–84.
Woolf, Virginia. *The Essays of Virginia Woolf*. Vols I–IV. Edited by Andrew McNeillie. London: Hogarth Press, 1986–94.
Woolf, Virginia. *The Letters of Virginia Woolf*. Vols I–VI. Edited by Nigel Nicholson and Joanne Trautmann. London: Hogarth Press, 1975–80.
Woolf, Virginia. *Night and Day*. New York: Harvest, 1948.
Woolf, Virginia. *A Room of One's Own and Three Guineas*. Oxford: OUP, 1998.
Woolf, Virginia. *To the Lighthouse*. London: Penguin, 2000.
Woolf, Virginia. *The Virginia Woolf Reader*. Edited by Mitchell A. Leaska. London: Harcourt, 1984.
Woolf, Virginia. *The Waves*. Harmondsworth: Penguin, 1973.
Wordsworth, Ann. 'Chance in Other Words'. *Oxford Literary Review* 12, no. 1 (1990): 227–37.
Zaretsky, Eli. *Political Freud: A History*. New York: Columbia Univeristy Press, 2015.

Online Resources

'EU Farming Support Package Allocations Announced'. Gov.uk. Accessed 19 April 2019. https://www.gov.uk/government/news/eu-farming-support-package-allocations-announced.
Interlinear English–Hebrew Bible. http://biblehub.com/interlinear/genesis/1.htm.
'IPCC 30th Anniversary'. Accessed 24 April 2019. https://www.ipcc.ch/reports/ipcc-30th-anniversary/.
Oxford English Dictionary Online. https://www.oed.com/.
'Regulating for People, the Environment and Growth: 2017 Summary'. *Environment Agency*, October 2018. Accessed 19 April 2019. https://assets.publishing.service.gov.uk/government/uploads/system/uploads/attachment_data/file/748416/Regulating_for_people_the_environment_and_growth_2017_summary.pdf.
'UK Cow Numbers'. *Agriculture and Horticulture Development Board*. Accessed 19 April 2019. http://dairy.ahdb.org.uk/market-information/farming-data/cow-numbers/uk-cow-numbers/.

Index

agency
  definition of 12–13
  human 10–14, 17, 53, 90, 104–5, 144, 185
  non-human 8, 12–13, 27, 48, 50–2, 103–5
  non-living 21, 27, 34, 48, 50–1, 103, 172
agriculture 10, 104–5, 129–31, 206 n.13.
  See also meat and dairy industry
anima 7, 38–9, 62, 101, 150
animism. *See also* animism, definitions of
  disavowal of 36, 39, 41, 49–51, 182
  of capitalism 34, 41–2, 105, 127. *See also* capitalism
  of climate 10, 13, 27, 31, 37, 50, 52–3 93–4, 185
  of evolution 103–4
  of language 9, 21, 38, 40, 48, 53, 63, 75–6, 109, 111, 150, 166–7, 174
  of literature or art 1, 2, 40, 48, 53, 86, 149–50, 186
  modern forms of 34, 41–4, 47–9, 73–4, 127, 148, 185–6
  of psychoanalysis 150–1, 155–7, 164
  of reading 53, 76, 78, 86, 176. *See also* reading
  of Woolf 60–3, 198 n.98. *See also* Woolf
animism, definitions of
  contemporary 40, 50, 52–3
  radical animism 1, 7, 13, 38–40, 48, 50, 53, 184–6
  traditional 36, 39–40, 46–9
Anthropocene
  as cognitive disruption 11–15, 18, 24–5, 31, 69–70, 93–4, 124, 141, 180, 185
  as material event 8, 10–11, 30
  as reading 2, 13–15, 31, 180
anthropocentrism 26–8, 37, 55, 64, 118–19, 182–3. *See also* narcissism
autobiography 14–15, 102, 106, 180

Beer, Gillian 74, 76, 83–4, 89, 106, 119, 124, 200 n.13
Benjamin, Walter 108–10, 174–5
Bennett, Jane, 12–13, 51, 105
Bersani, Leo 79, 81
Bible 106, 109–10
  Exodus 201 n.37
  Genesis 83, 101, 106, 109–10, 123, 138–40
  Proverbs 140
biodiversity loss. *See* extinction
biosemiotics 108
blows to human narcissism
  of climate change. *See climate change*
  Copernican blow 25–7, 55–6, 182–3, 185
  Darwinian blow 25–7, 34–5, 37, 102–3, 182–3, 185
  Freudian blow 25–7, 144–5, 180, 182–3, 185
  Marxian blow 27–8
breath 39, 86, 101

capitalism 15, 24, 27–34, 41–2, 105, 127–9, 145–6. *See also* animism of capitalism *and* fetishism (of commodities)
Carroll, Lewis 132–6, 138–9, 175, 204 n.92
Celan, Paul 21, 141
chiasmatic invagination 88–9, 171
Cixous, Hélène 149, 169–70, 172, 174–5, 197 n.81, 200 n.7
Clark, Timothy
  Ecocriticism on the Edge 12–14, 30, 70–1
  'Editorial' 18
  'Some Climate Change Ironies' 13, 33
  The Theory of Inspiration 167–9, 171–2, 180
climate change. *See also* animism of climate

as blow to human narcissism 9, 27, 30–1, 37, 94, 180, 184–5
as cognitive disruption 9, 11, 13–14, 25, 31–3, 35, 44, 50, 71, 92–3
vs Cold War 89–93
and psychoanalysis 144–7, 184
Cohen, Tom 37, 52–3, 91–2
Colebrook, Claire 90, 174, 183
commodity fetishism 127, 131
consumerism 24, 31, 34, 126–8, 145–6, 206 n.17. *See also* eating animals *and* commodity fetishism
Copernican revolution 25, 55–8, 60, 64, 74–5, 92, 94
Copernicus 55, 58, 194 n.11

dairy industry. *See* meat and dairy industry
Darwin, Charles 25, 35, 80–1, 102, 136
Descent of Man 105–6
Origin of Species 35, 103, 123,
Darwinian revolution 27, 34–5, 37, 103–4, 106, 122–4. *See also* evolution
Davies, Jeremy 11, 12, 124–5
deanimation 36–7
de Castro, Eduardo Viveiros 40, 48, 50
Derrida Jacques
The Animal That Therefore I Am 16–17, 35, 100, 107–8, 110, 112–13, 119, 131–2, 138, 140
'Autoimmunity: Real and Symbolic Suicides –' 23
The Beast and the Sovereign 21–2, 86, 94–6, 110, 116–18
'Des Tours de Babel' 148, 175
'Différance' 143–4, 173, 175
The Ear of the Other 165–6, 175–6
'Eating Well' 32, 131, 137–8
'Edmond Jabès and the Question of the Book' 20, 48, 111
'Envois' 109
'Force and Signification' 148, 169, 179–80, 209 n.82
'Freud and the Scene of Writing' 77
Glas 34–5
Of Grammatology 102, 186
H. C. for Life 149–50, 157
'I Have a Taste for the Secret' 57
'Living On' 88–9
'My Chances' 151, 166, 179
'No Apocalypse, Not Now' 90–1
'Psychoanalysis Searches the States of Its Soul' 27, 151
'Rams' 141
'The Retrait of Metaphor' 19
'Signature Event Context' 77–8
'A Silkworm of One's Own' 112
Specters of Marx 27–30
'To Speculate – On Freud' 148, 153–4, 158, 177–8
'This Strange Institution Called Literature' 112
'The Supplement of Copula' 147
'Telepathy' 92, 189 n.33, 193 n.117
'There is No One Narcissism' 184
'Violence and Metaphysics' 111
'As If It Were Possible' 117
'White Mythology' 19, 57, 112, 115
Dodds, Joseph 146, 184
dolly-zoom 56, 69

eating animals 128–34, 137–9, 183, 203 n.84, 204 n.94. *See also* meat and dairy industry
economy. *See* capitalism
egg, as symbol 170, 172–3, 210 n.104, 210–11 n.105
entropy 82–5, 89
ethics 21–2, 24–5, 111, 137–8, 184
evolution. *See also* animism of evolution
biological 27, 35, 81, 83, 90, 103–6, 119, 122–4. *See also* Darwinian revolution
of thought 41–4, 46, 105–6
extinction
of humans 14, 27, 37, 61, 86, 89–90, 102
of other life 10, 24–5, 32, 83, 89–90, 97, 101, 136, 141
of the universe 82–3

fetishism. *See* commodity fetishism
fiction
of perception 56, 63–4, 73, 117–18, 150, 180
of science 58, 74–5
in writing 64, 113, 117, 147
fossil fuels 15, 32–3, 190 n.58
Frazer, James 43–6

Freud, Sigmund. *See also* psychoanalytic revolution
　'The Aetiology of Hysteria' 147
　'Animism, Magic and the Omnipotence of Thoughts' 46–8, 149, 157, 185
　'Anxiety and Instinctual Life' 147
　'An Autobiographical Study' 165, 209 n.87
　'Beyond the Pleasure Principle' 59, 147–8, 151–6, 158, 160–4, 166, 173, 177–9
　Complete Letters 143, 150, 159, 170, 176–9
　'A Difficulty in the Path of Psycho-Analysis' 26, 55–6, 144, 181–3
　'The Ego and the Id' 143, 161
　'Fixation to Traumas – The Unconscious' 3, 25, 27, 55, 144, 182
　'The Interpretation of Dreams' 147–8, 159–60, 178–9
　'On Narcissism' 181–3
　Project for a Scientific Psychology 176–8
　'Psychical (or Mental) Treatment' 150–1, 164
　'Psychopathic Characters on the Stage' 165
　'The Uncanny' 46, 49, 175
　'The Unconscious' 144

Gaia 51
Genesis *See* Bible
Glendinning, Simon 26, 28–9

Harari, Yuval Noah 42, 104–5, 130, 206 n.13
Heidegger 9, 94–7, 119
human rights 24–5, 30. *See also* ethics

inanimate 35, 40, 60, 94–5, 127, 155–6
Ingold, Tim 50, 52–3, 74
Intergovernmental Panel on Climate Change (IPCC) 15, 188 n.23

Jeans, James 68, 74–5, 82
Jones, Ernest 47, 49, 161
Jung, Carl 210–11 n.105

Kafka, Franz 8–9, 15–18, 20–4
Klein, Naomi 32–3, 41
Kolbert, Elizabeth 89–90, 93

Kofman, Sarah 164–5
Krell, David 64, 101

Lane, Nick 35, 101–2, 106
language. *See* animism of language
Latour, Bruno 11, 36, 50–1, 94
Lispector, Clarice 168–74, 176

Macdonald, Helen 99, 112–15, 120, 125, 127
man, concept of 25–6, 28, 35, 106, 108–10, 131
Marcus, Laura 65, 88
Martin, Kirsty 59, 76
Marx, Karl 33–4, 127–8
Marxism 27–9, 31, 33–4, 127–8. *See also* materialism
mastery 12, 25–6, 144–5, 153, 182, 184–5, 206 n.13
materialism 36, 39, 40, 51, 79. *See also* Marxism
meat and dairy industry 32, 129–32, 134, 136 *See also* eating animals
metaphor 18–21, 111–12, 114–15, 147
Morton, Timothy 50, 92

narcissism 2, 106, 149, 181–5. *See also* anthropocentrism *and* blows to human narcissism
new materialism 51
Nixon, Rob 32, 91
nuclear war 90–3

Oedipus 159–60, 163, 165, 178–9

performative language 117, 121, 149–50, 164. *See also* animism of language
Pollan, Michael 104, 119
Povinelli, Elizabeth 39, 42, 50
psyche. *See* anima
psychoanalytic revolution 25–6, 144–5. *See also* animism of psychoanalysis

quantum physics 72–4, 76

radical 37–8
reading. *See also* animism of reading *and* text

non-verbal 12–14, 31, 57, 85
  as transformative 2, 14, 20, 74, 77–8, 112, 143, 169, 175
responsibility 8, 10, 16–17, 21–4, 137–8, 141
rhythm 59–61, 63, 75
Rooney, Caroline 36, 44, 73, 78, 156–7, 161, 164
roots 37–8, 80–1, 102
Royle, Nicholas
  Jacques Derrida 93
  'Jacques Derrida and the Future of the Novel' 67
  Quilt 113, 115–16, 120–3, 125–6
  'Reading Joseph Conrad' 2
  Veering 15, 166

sacrifice zones 32–3, 190 n.58
scale effects 55–6, 68–71, 84, 92–3, 129
science, as a form of knowledge 26, 36, 43–4, 52, 64, 74
Shakespeare, William
  Hamlet 151, 158–62, 165–6, 170, 210 n.104
  Macbeth 7
  The Merry Wives of Windsor 162
  Twelfth Night 162
spirit. *See* anima
Stahl, Georg Ernst 39
subjectivity 64, 137–8, 167–8, 180
Sutherland, Keston 127–8

text, non-verbal 2, 11–14, 77, 85, 89, 106, 124, 170–1, 174, 180. *See also* reading *and* writing
textual unconscious 149, 166–7, 180

translation 110–11, 144, 147–8, 174–6
Trexler, Adam 2, 11, 30
Tylor, E. B. 36, 39–43

uncanny 10, 31, 49, 145, 175
unconscious 25, 56, 143–50, 162, 166–7. *See also* textual unconscious

vitalism 39, 51

Wallace-Wells, David 13, 32, 34, 45, 94, 191 n.66
Weber, Samuel 121, 156
Wills, David 14, 17, 21, 35, 59–60, 78, 155–6, 174–5
Wood, Sarah
  Derrida's Writing and Difference 20, 189 n.32
  'A Huge Thing' 141
  Without Mastery 2, 11–12, 97, 110, 112, 117, 167
Woolf, Virginia. *See also* animism of Woolf
  Diaries 61, 75
  'A Letter to a Young Poet' 60
  Letters 60–1, 63, 82
  To the Lighthouse 61–8, 70–2, 75, 81–2, 84–6, 94, 96–8
  'A Room of One's Own' 60, 75
  The Waves 61–2, 64, 66–9, 71, 74–6, 80–1, 83–5, 87–9, 198 n.90
writing. *See also* reading *and* text
  non-verbal 1–2, 11–13, 76, 86, 89, 180
  as transformative 53, 77–8, 97, 166–8, 179–80

www.ingramcontent.com/pod-product-compliance
Lightning Source LLC
Chambersburg PA
CBHW072230290426
44111CB00012B/2037